for Jean Swenson
with best wishes
for your senior
writers' publication
Asha Craine

THE MAN
WHO EATS SNAKES
and
Other Tales

THE MAN
WHO EATS SNAKES
and
Other Tales

Reminiscences of the Twentieth Century

"The next thing most like living one's life over again seems to be a recollection of that life, and to make that recollection as durable as possible by putting it down in writing."

BENJAMIN FRANKLIN

General Editor
HELEN HILL

Associate Editors
DONALD AXON
JAY CARP
MARJORIE READE

LEARNING IN RETIREMENT COLLECTIVE

Learning in Retirement
Turner Geriatric Center
University of Michigan
Ann Arbor, Michigan

ISBN 1-885761-0H-X

Cover Design by Robert V. Hammonds
Page Design and Composition by Sans Serif, Inc., Saline, MI
Manufactured in Canada

For our children and grandchildren
and for our friends
for whom these tales will evoke memories of their own.

Contents

CONTENTS

CONTENTS

Editor's Note

The reminiscences collected here have been written by a diverse group of people who have met for the past seven years under my leadership and the sponsorship of Learning in Retirement at the University of Michigan's Turner Resource Center. People have come into the group at different times. Three have been with us since the beginning. Some, having written all they wanted to about their lives, have now left. Not every one who has been in the group is represented here.

There have been no assignments. Everyone has been free to choose any experience to write about. Except during the summer and the winter holiday season we have met weekly, most often at the Turner Center, but sometimes at each other's homes. At each meeting we have read our pieces aloud and the group has responded with encouragement, suggestions, and constructive criticism. In sharing our memories we have laughed and wept together and have come to know each other well—an unexpected dividend for all of us.

Writers for this anthology have chosen what they considered their best or what they were willing to share with a larger audience. We then spent several months circulating all the pieces so that every one had a chance to make editorial suggestions. After each of us had made revisions there followed more rereadings by the editorial committee, once again reading aloud and listening for places that an author might clarify or polish before subjecting the piece to public scrutiny. The editors have been careful not to change an author's voice even when having a personal preference for different phrasing.

Our shared enthusiasm for working with words and the camaraderie of our weekly meetings have led to firm friendships among us. This collection is a testament to those friendships.

HELEN M. HILL,
General Editor

Acknowledgements

For help in funding the publication of this book the LIR Collective is indebted to Ruth Campbell and the Turner Resource Center; to the Kiwanis Club of Ann Arbor; and to the Learning in Retirement Division of the Turner Resource Center. We are also indebted to Karen Sernett of the LIR staff for her advice and help.

We owe special thanks to Professors Ellwood Derr and John Nystuen whom we consulted about *Der Czarevitch*; to Robert Hammonds for designing the cover of the book; to Don Axon for the simplified map of The Netherlands; to Shirley Axon and Eloise Snyder for invaluable help with proofreading; and to all the editors for the many hours they have spent in putting this collection together.

DONALD AXON

I left Missouri in 1940 when I was eighteen and have been back only half a dozen times, but still see myself as Missourian after a dozen years of wandering and 47 in Michigan. Having been told long ago that Missouri is a good place to be from, I have concluded that it was a good place to start. Life and public schools there prepared me well for William and Mary, MIT and Harvard, the army, marriage, thirty years at Ford, and for enjoying retirement.

In Missouri, I learned about social class distinctions from reading, not experience. I loved words. I read Mark Twain, Stevenson, Kipling, Dumas, De Maupassant and The Saturday Evening Post. *I read the Bible cover to cover while engrossed in Norse and Greek mythology and, especially in the Old Testament, saw more parallels than contradictions. A good French teacher equipped me to learn to read Romance languages easily and started me on years of French, and later Spanish, literature. My parents knew and quoted Shakespeare, Burns, Wordsworth, Browning, Kipling, Longfellow, Holmes, Poe and Robert Service among others. When I ran into those poets in high school and college they were old friends.*

Reading widely taught me to recognize good writing but not to write well. In 1952, discussing a report I had written, the president of the small oil company I worked for in Tulsa said, "You talk well enough, Axon. Why don't you write like that?"

Stung, I worked over my writing style. In William Strunk's The Elements of Style *and in Rudolph Flesch's* Art of Readable Writing *I found useful rules for improving prose. I took them into my 30—year career at the Ford Motor Company where, in editing reports, I excised passive verbs, insisting that they were generally used to avoid responsibility.*

Chores

All three of us had chores. We all set the table, made our beds and did dishes. Anne Louise was three years older than I and Tom a year younger. Her assignments reflected her greater maturity. She did house cleaning that required close attention like dusting. She helped in meal preparation as we did not. As her social and extracurricular activities increased Tom and I did more dishes. We boys ran the carpet sweeper and did rough mopping in the basement and garage. He and I mowed the lawn and weeded the garden.

In doing dishes we alternated between washing and drying. You would think the person drying would have to finish last. He has to wipe water off and put dishes away, and he can't dry them until they've been washed. In fact, Tom always finished first. Whoever washed had to scrape and clean up cooking pans, swabbing them off with the dish cloth so as not to dirty the towel. Tom washed methodically, mechanically and quickly, finishing the cooking utensils a little before I put the last dish away. When I washed, tumblers became glass bottomed boats exploring sudsy depths for sunken ships and silverware. Silverware had to come out of the dish pan in the same order as it appeared on the dining table: forks, then knives, then spoons. Get all the forks before starting on knives. Sometimes a fork hid under a knife. It irritated Tom, but it meant that he had dried the previous dish before I released another. The last dish he dried came from the dish water while I still had pans to go.

Yard work was a problem, too. Tom was serious about baseball and got up early on summer mornings to do his weeding or trimming before breakfast. I slept until breakfast and then had to weed before I went anywhere. Mother balanced our assignments meticulously, but working in the hot Missouri sun after Tom left to play ball irked me.

Jefferson City extended west a mile beyond us, but fields on which horses and cows grazed were a hundred yards north from the back end of our yard. When we were very small our parents had a Jersey cow. They got rid of her when Daddy's work kept him in St Louis most of most weeks. Mother had never done milking. When we were old enough to feed chickens and gather eggs, however, the folks bought a few chicks every year and we looked after them. By the time we were in high school I was often asked to kill a chicken for supper. If I killed it, Tom usually had to pluck it. I did not like killing, but I hated trying to get feathers off with boiling water.

Aunt Bella, up on her farm in northwest Missouri, wrung chickens' necks. Daddy sometimes did. Ordinarily, however, he laid the chicken's head on a short log and cut it off with a swift blow of the axe. I tried neck wringing, but could not jerk hard enough. When I put the chicken down to die, it jumped up and ran crazily around the yard with its head cocked sharply to one side. I was better at chopping, but the axe Daddy swung so easily and accurately was big for me. If the chicken drew its head in suddenly, I either missed it altogether or made an unsightly mess of its head.

One day I had an inspiration. On a family trip in the Ozarks Daddy had showed us how to use his Army Colt .45. I sometimes took it out to admire, to disassemble and to reassemble. When pressed hard, a knurled button under the barrel near the muzzle released a catch that held the barrel to the hand grip. In an early exploration I sat on a chair and clasped the grip between my thighs with the barrel pointed up. I pressed the button, unsure what was supposed to happen next. My thumb slipped off and the powerful recoil spring shot the button into the middle of my forehead. I thought I had shot myself. Nothing hurt much, but maybe that was what dying was like. I waited. There was no blood. I could still see, and among things I saw on the floor were the spring and the knurled button.

By the time of my inspiration I felt relatively comfortable with the gun. Daddy and Tom and I had built a flat-roofed chicken house behind the garage and fenced it in. I planned to lie on its roof, toss shelled corn on the ground, aim carefully and blow a chicken's head off. The chicken run was well away from the street, so a single explosion should pass unnoticed. We had fifteen almost fully grown white chickens. We needed one for supper. I put a cartridge in my pocket, laid the pistol on the flat roof of the chicken house six feet above the ground, and climbed up. I tossed out a handful of corn and put in the cartridge while waiting for chickens to assemble. They did. I lay with both elbows in front of me on the roof. I selected a pullet which had separated enough from the others so that I would not shoot two at once. I fired. The noise was louder than I had remembered. I slipped the gun under me and looked around. No one was hurrying toward me or shouting.

The chickens, however, were rushing around cackling wildly. A cloud of white feathers was beginning to settle where they had been. I looked for one without a head, but even close study showed none like that. I could not even tell which had been hit. Frustrated, I set out to find the wounded bird. It was the fourth one I caught. Holding it in my hands I saw that flesh under the fluffy breast feathers was deeply gouged, although the heavy bleeding was still being absorbed by feathers. No one would get much white meat from that bird. It might be mortally wounded, but I still had to cut its head off.

So much for inspiration. I never shot another chicken.

Another chore was hanging clothes. When Daddy was in town on Monday, he helped with the laundry. Mother and he worked in the basement laundry room, which opened onto our driveway at the back of the house. Beneath the single bare bulb hanging from the rafters, they ran the electric washing machine and its powered wringer. The washing machine had a tendency to walk around the concrete floor as it went through its wash and rinse cycles. Daddy kept it from wandering too far. Tom and I carried out loaded laundry baskets and hung clothes and sheets on lines we had strung for the day over the driveway and back yard.

Our next door neighbors to the east were the Rodemans. Like many people in Jefferson City, they were German. Mr. Rodeman was the unquestioned head of the house. His wife, Mary Cleofa, would answer a question with, "I'll have to ask Mr Rodeman." He owned and operated a successful feed mill and never did yard or house work.

Their oldest boy, John, was six when he wandered over one day to ask Tom or me to play catch with him. We sometimes did. Tom said we couldn't. We had to hang clothes.

We put John out of our minds, but he hung around, nose to the screen door, and stared into the poorly lit room where Daddy and Mother were putting sheets through the washing machine and the wringer. He was shocked to see my father there.

Mother said, "Elmer, start that next batch through the wringer."

John, horrified out of his silence, screamed, "Tell her you don't have to, Mr Axon."

Murky

From 1934 until 1938, I spent part of each June and July at Camp Maries, a Boy Scout camp 30 miles from Jefferson City, Missouri. I was 12 the first summer and a second class scout. My last summer I was an Eagle Scout and a counselor.

My brother Tom went to camp only once—my second year there. He was playing Little League and American Legion baseball, and a mastoid operation which had made him deaf in the left ear also kept him from swimming. Camp or no camp was a fork in the road for us. He excelled in baseball, softball and basketball and concentrated on whatever was in season. I played them casually but enjoyed hiking, swimming and climbing more. Camp Maries sat on a flat above the Maries River, a tributary of the Osage. To swim and canoe we walked down steep rocky paths to the river through cedar and scrub oak. Flowing through farmlands in central Missouri, the river was always murky. You never saw anything when you opened your eyes under water. We called it muddy, however, only when hard rains made the varying densities of mud visible, when every eddy was a coiling rope of brown soil. We swam between a small dock at the shore and a raft half way across the 100 foot wide river. The bottom was partly gravel, partly muck, with occasional boulders. At the beginning of every summer, counselors came early to set up the tents on wood decks, put in the dock and raft and shove boulders in the river bottom toward the other shore to improve swimming.

Moving boulders was particularly important a few steps up river from the raft. There a big steel ring hung out over the river on a long rope from a high sycamore branch. Starting on the steep bank, we would swing out, lifting our feet at the low point in the arc and wait for the pause before the return. From twelve feet above the river, we could drop, we could dive, or most demanding and most fun, we could somersault into the water. At that point it was generally about eight feet deep, but the invisible bottom was mostly boulders, some two feet higher than the rest.

Once in my third year at camp I swung out on the ring and dived. As my trajectory underwater curved upward when I pulled out of the dive, something rasped my breastbone. When I climbed out of the water and up the tree roots we used as a ladder, a friend said, "What did you do?" Blood from a three inch scrape mixed with the brown water was trickling down my chest and belly.

"I hit something—a big rock, I guess. We better move it. I was lucky. If my head had been a little forward, my forehead would have hit. I'll go check."

Reacting with bravado to the staring eyes, I swung out on the ring again, dropping feet first this time. Once in, I surface dived to the bottom, groped and found a sharp edged rock projecting above others nearby. Back to the air again, I shouted that I had found the monster I had hit and called for help to move it. Jimmy Parsons came in. Together we dived and groped for holds. Then, in a series of submersions limited by how long we could hold our breath, we moved the big stone away to an area we did not drop into. We never did see it. At the dispensary, tall, gangly Joe Summers, a vacationing premed student, who was also my counselor, swabbed me with Mercurochrome and put on a big gauze bandage.

I had been swimming since I was three. With no anxieties about the water, I rapidly picked up the swimming, boating and lifesaving skills that were parts of camp life, earning successive American Red

Cross patches for Mother to sew on my swimming trunks as well as various merit badges. In my third year, before I was a counselor, I became lifeguard and instructor. But not a good instructor. Most of the boys had swum in the Jefferson City municipal pool or in junior high, but some few had not. Some came from small nearby towns and had neither easy access to a swimming pool nor parents who were swimmers. I showed them what to do and expected them to try. Some did not, at least right away. In our buddy system swimmers paired off and buddies had to stay together. Even with a friend only inches away, some kids could not put their faces under water to learn to exhale, and the idea of lifting their feet off the bottom and dog paddling made their teeth chatter. I tried to be patient, but their problems seemed unreal. I had been cured of my reluctance to dive from the side of a swimming pool when a friend of Mother's said, "Donald, if you don't come up, I'll buy you an ice cream cone." There was no ridicule in my own teaching but not much sympathy either. Everyone learned eventually, but other instructors brought frightened kids along faster than I did.

A game I particularly liked was canoe jousting. I knew all about Lancelot du Lac and now I had a lance—a bamboo pole with padding like a boxing glove on one end. In jousting, a paddler sat at the stern of the canvas covered wood canoe and a lancer stood on the gunwales at the bow. Starting two canoe lengths apart, a paddler maneuvered towards the other canoe trying to gain both position and momentum to help his lancer knock the other combatant off his perch and into the water. There were more ways to do it wrong than to do it right. You might swing, miss and throw yourself into the water. You might fall in while ducking the other lance. You might simply not push or swing hard enough. Meantime the other guy was poking at you. The rules said aim for chest and stomach, but in the excitement the padded end might hit anything from an eye to an ankle. It was glorious though, when it went right, when your paddler brought you quickly into striking position and distance, while you half crouched with both hands and your right arm grasping the lance firmly, and the pad hit him squarely in the ribs and dumped him into the water even before your canoe hit his.

We did that for only part of one summer. There were too many ways to bang your head or arm or leg on the canoe as you fell. One lancer stepped off the gunwale and through the woven osier seat. His foot twisted and caught as he fell and he could not lift his head out of the water. The other team jumped in and held his face up while his partner turned his canoe over, working the foot loose. He was not much hurt, but we were all scared.

One merit badge I needed to become an Eagle Scout was Pioneering. Among the requirements for it were to "Lash spars properly together for scaffolding" and to "Build a bridge or derrick capable of supporting two hundred pounds." I decided to lash trees and branches into a bridge at a place where, in wet weather, a little creek made a stretch of the trail to the swimming dock a treacherous mixture of shaley rock and mud.

I measured what it would take and sketched a fifteen foot long structure, having already identified a forty foot sycamore on the other side of the river which could provide longitudinal base timbers, side rails and supports. I would split red cedar for foot boards. I showed the drawing to my counselor, Joe Summers. When he asked where I would get the wood, I said, "I'll cut it. There's plenty around."

He approved my plan and said the camp handyman would give me nails and lend me a hammer and a folding rule. When I reminded him that the structure was supposed to be lashed together and asked if nails were allowed, Summers said, "I'll allow them if I'm supposed to walk on that bridge."

Early next day I took my scout hatchet and walked across the reinforced wood floor of the old steel bridge near camp. I liked to climb it and to walk across its top. On quiet evenings, I sometimes sat up there and read while the light lasted. The sycamore I had selected was a short walk from the bridge. It stood in the flood plain near a picnic ground owned by a neighboring farmer who sometimes rented it out for group picnics. My target tree was not on the picnic ground, but it was close. I set to work to take it down with my hatchet. That was hard. It was eight inches through. I chopped and chopped, girdling the trunk like a beaver at about my shoulder height so that I did not have to stoop or reach too high. After two half days of work—I had other things I had to do with the rest of the time—it fell where I could chop off branches that would interfere most with getting it across the river. Tired of chopping, I decided to float the trunk to the building site as one piece and to borrow a saw on the other side from the handyman. I had no plan for getting that heavy log into position to saw—the bank on the camp side was much steeper than where the tree had grown—and I was not sure the Pioneering merit badge allowed sawing.

It was just as well I had not spent much time working out that part of the scheme. To my horror, when I rolled the trunk into the water, it disappeared except for projecting leaves on the ends of three branches. It sank. Until then I thought all wood floated. In 1937 fresh cut sycamore with the sap still in it did not. Moving a floating log with branches would have been work. Taking the sunken giant—its mass seemed to grow as I stood there even though I could not see it—taking it across a deep river without boat or rope was out of the question. I thought for an hour before I accepted the necessity of starting over, using different trees from the camp side of the river.

I reported the situation to Joe Summers that evening and said that in spite of the delay I could still finish the bridge before the awards campfire and get my merit badge. His reaction caught me off guard.

"What sycamore? The only sycamore on the camp side of the river is that big one with the drop ring for swimming. I know you didn't cut that down."

"Well, no. It's on the other side."

He walked me down to the river and I pointed across to the tall stump.

"Donald, do you see what you've done? You've gone on somebody else's property and chopped down one of his trees. He'll have the law on us. He'll have the law on you. I've got to tell Mr Glickman."

Mr Glickman was camp superintendent and head of the Boy Scouts in Jefferson City. Joe told him, then came to my tent and sent me to the mess hall where Glickman had his office.

Glickman, a heavy set man in his late forties with dark hair and eyes, sat behind his desk, lit by one bulb from the camp's rudimentary electrical system. He said, "You made Star Scout and Life Scout. All I thought you needed for Eagle was to convince me you'd identified enough birds for me to OK you for bird study merit badge."

Glickman was an amateur ornithologist. and the only examiner for the bird study badge. He was sure domestic cats were wiping out local song birds. When he tested me later on bird identifications, he wrapped up the interview by saying,

"You're a little shaky on one or two of those, but you know enough to pass. Before I sign your record, though, you have to promise me that any time you see a cat when you're out in the woods with your .22, you'll shoot it. If enough people do that, the birds will be around longer."

That was not part of the written requirements. I had a .22 rifle, but knew I would never shoot a cat. Still, after he waited out my long pause, I said, "OK."

The evening of the tree fiasco he went on, "Now you've cut down a tree on a neighbor's property. Is that 'helping other people'? Is that 'keeping yourself morally straight'?"

"No, sir."

"Well, Donald, let's try to get both of us out of trouble. You go down right now, *tonight,* and smear that stump lightly with mud. Make it look like it was cut before last spring's flood. Don't overdo it. Just wipe on a light layer that will dry fast, no clumps and no chunks. As for the tree itself, no matter how heavy that trunk is or how much branches drag, you move it into deep water and down stream. Do it alone. Don't bring any buddies in on this. If any one's going to get arrested I want it to be you. But if you do it by tomorrow night, we'll get back to thinking about Eagle Scout."

I did like he said. With my hands I scooped mud from the river bank and tried, in deepening twilight, to age and weather the stump to look as if it had been submerged in at least one season of high water. Then, in full darkness, I stripped off my clothes. I stepped into the river, felt my way around branches to the smaller end of the tree and began jerking. Nothing happened. I was panicky, but I made myself calm down. The log was only a little heavier than water, it was just big. It wasn't going to do anything quickly. When I just lifted persistently, instead of jerking, my end gradually rose off the bottom. Then when I held the top up and pulled along the surface, the trunk began to move and kept moving as long as I kept tension on. I had to grope carefully with my forward foot along the bottom so as not to step heavily on sharp rocks or broken branches, and it took a while to learn to feel with my foot while keeping the steady pull on the log. I had dreaded the cold water, but the work kept me warm. In half an hour the log lay near a gravel bank well down stream with a few projecting branches making small wakes in the slow current. Finally I could worry about mosquitoes and the chance that a car on the road might pick me up in its headlights.

I found my clothes, wiped off water and mud with my shirt. I tossed into the river the branches I had cut off before dropping the tree into the river. They disappeared quickly in the dark current. Then I walked back across the dark bridge to camp and my tent. I told Joe Summers what Glickman had said and what I had done. He said, "Cross your fingers."

Next day I substituted red cedar for sycamore in my bridge bill of material. Cedar is straight, strong, light, easy to work and grew plentifully on the Camp Maries bank. I had always planned to have split cedar floorboards. It took six trees to bridge the twelve foot gap comfortably.

My buddies and the counselors complimented me on the finished job. That waterfront trail was now negotiable even in a bad rain. Previously we had detoured in wet weather so as not to risk slipping into the river there.

I never knew whether the owner of the picnic ground noticed my incursion. Neither Glickman nor Summers ever mentioned it; but after they denounced my indifference to property rights I never felt good about the sycamore—or completely satisfied with how they were keeping me "morally straight." It seemed a little murky to me.

My handiwork lasted for at least a few years. Looking at it, I thought of my father's World War I Corps of Engineers story which ended with a master sergeant reporting to Captain Axon at dawn on November 11, 1918, that the pontoon bridge the company had worked on all night was "All done, Captain. She ain't much for looks, but she's hell for strong."

Swing, Bounce, Shove

On June 1, 1943, a final exam in fluid dynamics ended my junior year at MIT. During the War, classes ran all year. What would have been the fall term began July 8. All my fraternity brothers had gone home. My parents were in Edmonton, where my father kept track of Alaska Highway contractors for the United States Fidelity and Guaranty Company, which had written their performance bonds. My brother was in the army, coaching basketball at Swarthmore. My sister, a physicist at the Naval Ordnance Laboratory in Washington, shared a house in Georgetown with five other women. She could not invite me to stay.

After going from class to class, from exam to exam for two and a half academic years, here at last was a month without pressure, without due dates. Taking only $25 in cash I decided to bum around for a month where no one knew me. With an old laundry bag tied on my handle bar, I bicycled north out of Brookline, Mass. In the bag were two books, a change of underwear and socks, a second pair of jeans, a work shirt, comb, toothbrush and paste. There was food for noon and that evening: bread, a canteen of water, peanut butter, a banana. I started late on a Wednesday morning and stuck to paved secondary roads even though gas rationing kept traffic down. With the long June day I was into New Hampshire when fatigue and fading daylight made me pick, as a place to sleep, an unfenced grove of sumac just beyond the ditch.

With my bike out of sight from the road, I ate a peanut butter sandwich and the banana and lay down. The night was mild, but not the mosquitoes. Comfortable in the deep grass with the laundry bag and a grass hummock for a pillow, I fell asleep—briefly. Mosquitoes bit my face and hands. I buttoned and turned up my collar and pulled the laundry bag over my head, tightening the drawstring around my neck. The mosquitoes concentrated on my hands. Taking off my improvised hood I fished out my extra socks and put them on like mittens. I jerked the laundry bag over my head again and slept until sunlight and occasional car noises penetrated the laundry bag.

Early next morning I pedaled into Manchester. In a café which sold newspapers I had ham and eggs and coffee and read help wanted ads in the *Union Leader*. There were lots of them. Studley Box and Lumber in Rochester wanted lumber handlers, "no experience required." That sounded like me. With no map or knowledge of New Hampshire, I asked at the first gas station which way Rochester was and how far. The attendant said "Forty miles. Take US 101 there and 202. Not too hilly."

A truck driver paying for gas, said, "I'm not going to Rochester, but I'll take you most of the way. Put your bike in the truck."

Simple. From where he let me off I had bicycled the ten miles into Rochester by 10 a.m. It was a mill town on the Cocheco River flats, five miles from the Maine border. Most houses were modest, one story, but all had porches, some on two sides. Prominent churches included the Congregational—Trinitarian—on Main Street. Woolworth's, Rexall Drugs, a restaurant, a haberdashery and a service station were also on Main, which ran north and south. The grid of paved streets was square with the world, unusual for a New England village. There were homes at both ends of Main, but most were on other streets, the grandest in the northwest. Sidewalks were set well back. Big elms stood in front yards and between sidewalks and the streets. The lumber yard and box factory, beside the railroad track and the river two blocks east of Main, formed the eastern edge of town. There was a textile mill just up the river.

Mr. Brown, office and personnel manager at Studley, had me fill in an application: name, Social Security number, address. Address? I didn't have one. He said, "We'll get it when you do. I'll take you on as a lumber handler—six days a week, 87½ cents an hour. You can start this afternoon and work Friday and Saturday. Pay lags a week. You'll get this week's a week from Saturday and so on.

"Mrs. Dolan on Concord has a room to rent, and Mrs. Nelson, on Main close to Mrs. Dolan's, runs a boarding house. Here's their addresses. Punch in after lunch if you get settled."

I did. Mrs. Dolan's room two doors off Main cost seven dollars a week in advance. Her eyebrows rose when she saw I was traveling with only the laundry bag I left in the room. Mrs Nelson's boarding house was half a block away—on the corner across Main. Breakfast, lunch and supper were a dollar a day, payable a week in advance. Breakfast was at seven, lunch at noon, supper at 5:45. It was nearly twelve when I knocked on her door. She was busy and distracted but said I could start with lunch that day. I was down to $10, which had to last ten days. Even Saturday week I would get less than $20, but after that with $42 a week and only $14 for room and board, I could take the train back to Boston.

Mrs. Nelson looked me over and said, "You'll eat at that table. Everyone waits on the porch until I open the door."

As we talked eleven men gathered, chatted with each other and stared at me, nodding and saying hello but no more. When she opened the door, they poured in to assigned places. I saw why she put me where she did. Men at my table ate fast, reaching for bread, chicken, vegetables and potatoes and pitchers of lemonade, passing dishes only when asked. The other table, however, ate faster. Men bolted their meals and began leaving before I was firmly in my chair and reaching for chicken. Mrs. Nelson knew I could not handle that competition.

Studley sawed boards from pine trees cut within a few miles and made boxes and fruit crates. Business was good. Boards and boxes oozed resin. The atmosphere was turpentine. They shipped wood pallets and freshly sawed lumber. I had two assignments. I loaded box cars and sawed scraps into fuel for the steam engine. Overhead shafts from that engine with pulleys and belts drove enormous saws and transfer conveyors. I sawed up side pieces with bark still on and short ends on two unguarded 24-inch circular blades only 18 inches apart. Balancing ankle deep in sawdust, I pushed three to six foot scraps through the blades. It scared me. My footing was unsteady. I had to balance heavy chunks and push them steadily through the blades, allowing for abrupt changes in weight and balance when one end fell off before the other. Knots and sticky resin triggered jerks, twists and jumps. My elbows stuck out beyond both blades as I leaned to push the wood through. For years I dreamed occasionally of those saws, of a heavy plank jerking me off balance and both arms off above the elbows.

Most of my work was loading boxcars with 18-foot two-by-eights and two-by-twelves. Working with another man, it was easy. We each took one end of a board lying on a pallet where the fork lift driver set it fifteen feet from the waiting boxcar and swung the board through the open door into the car. When we had a few in, one of us climbed up and stacked. A loaded car had piles eight feet high at both ends and, finally, four feet high in the space between.

Sometimes, however, because the factory was shorthanded, I worked alone. Then I grabbed a board in its middle, rotated slowly with the board resting heavily on the front of my thighs, waddled to the car door and fed it in. Other handlers wore denim aprons, and I knew why on the third day when boards rubbed holes in both pant legs half way from knee to crotch.

Wrestling the boards was heavy work, hard on arms, back, legs and trousers. After fighting it for two days in a row, I noticed that another handler, Bill Craig, had been watching for several minutes. When I paused and stared at him, he said deferentially, lifting one hand, "Now it ain't like me to tell another man how to do his work."

He paused. I said, "Yeah?"

"There's an easier way."

"How?"

"I'll show you."

He went into a shed and brought out a saw horse which he set between the pallet and the car door. It ran at right angles both to boards to be loaded and to those already in the car. He grabbed an end of the top board on the pallet, swung it over so that it hit the horse with one third of its length toward him and two thirds beyond the horse. He pushed his end down hard, and, using the horse as fulcrum, swung the board around and up until its far end pointed into the car door. Then a quick, two-handed shove jumped the board into the car.

"Swing, bounce, shove," he said. "That's all it is—but I don't mean to butt in."

"You're not. You're not. Thanks a lot."

He had taken four-fifths of the work out of loading.

When he was not on other assignments, we often worked together. Bill was a "native," not a "Frenchy," an immigrant from Quebec a hundred miles away. He was contemptuous of Frenchies—"trash trying to farm swamps and second growth timber and taking 'native's' jobs, couldn't hardly talk English. They even got the drug store to carry French Sunday papers."

But he boasted that his daughter had majored in French at UNH and was in Montreal now working on a Master's degree at McGill. "She talks like they do only better. When the War ends, she's going to go live in France for a while. We miss her, but we're sure proud."

I had been reading French since my freshman year at junior college in Missouri. I envied the Quebecois because they spoke French. Sunday afternoon at the drugstore I bought *Le Jour* from Quebec City. I skimmed articles on politics, found differences from American papers in war reporting, delighted in having *Little Orphan Annie* and *Joe Palooka* (*Jos Bras-de-Fer*) speak French. Carrying funnies and editorial page on the handlebars, I bicycled six miles on a loose gravel road, over into Maine, looking for shade and a creek. There were only scrub trees and poor farms, with pigs roaming freely and a few cows looking as if they wished they were somewhere else.

It was hot. No shade and no breeze, and the road was dusty. I opened my shirt to the waist as I rode to dry the sweat on my chest. I passed a girl with long brown hair, nice legs, and a narrow waist. She wore street shoes, not hiking shoes, though there was no house in sight. She was strolling along the shoulder. I slowed so as not to cover her with the dust even my slow cycling lifted in the quiet air. She heard me coming, turned and looked at me, at my bike and my open-fronted shirt. She was pretty, wide forehead, brown eyes. She had a good figure. She smiled, leaned back in mock admiration and said, "Wel-l-l-l!"

I blushed, smiled, said, "Hi" and rode on slowly. For half a mile I asked myself what should I have done? What could I have done? Then I turned and pedaled back, trying to look casual. The girl was gone.

Another handler, at least when he was not running one of the log saws, was Jim Lawrence. We were the same age—21. He told me, "I didn't quite finish high school. I was itchy. I bummed around on the rails for a couple of years, slept in hobo jungles, lived on handouts and odd jobs, saw a lot, worked harvests in Kansas and Nebraska. I hated the straw down your shirt collar sticking in the sweat and scratching, but the food was great. It was lonely, though. I came home and married Emma. We had been going steady before. I couldn't see much point in high school. We have a cute little girl. So I've traveled, got a job and started a family, and here you are still in school. You've never done anything."

He startled me. I was generally on track, fearful only that the War might end without me. Before MIT I'd got a degree in math from William and Mary and a Phi Bete key. He didn't know that. He did know I was studying engineering, but it didn't impress him. Irrationally I wondered, what would he have done in his wandering years if that girl had said, "Wel-l-l-l!" to him?

The next Tuesday, after a quick lunch, I walked into Woolworth's to buy tape for the holes worn in the thighs of my jeans. The store did not have what I wanted, but I chatted with the clerk, a thin, pleasant high school girl. She said, "You're not from here."

"No, I'm on vacation from engineering school. I work at Studley's and room at Mrs. Dolan's."

"There's a junior prom next Saturday. Would you go with me?"

She had told me she was a junior in high school. High school seemed so long ago to me. I had cast myself as a wanderer and watcher for that short break from reality and was enjoying the role. Unwilling to hurt her feelings, I said,

"I wouldn't know anybody. I don't have any good clothes, just these clodhopper work shoes, another work shirt and another pair of jeans. Of course, that pair doesn't have these big holes."

"That would be all right. People wouldn't care. I wouldn't care. You would know me."

"I don't even have a razor. I'm not planning to shave until next month."

"We sell razors, but you would look OK even if you don't shave. That would be all right, too."

"I don't think so. I would feel funny, stranger and all, and looking like a bum—but thanks a lot."

"All right, but if you change your mind before Thursday come tell me."

"OK. Good bye."

"Good bye."

All Rochester was within walking distance. I only used my bike to ride out of town. I chatted and kidded with guys at work—both natives and Frenchies—and knew by name those I ate with and where they worked—mostly at Studley—but I saw them only on the job and at meals. I wrote weekly to my parents and brother and sister, but spent more time reading Mark Twain's *Pudd'nhead Wilson* and, in French, stories about Arsène Lupin, master thief.

The Fourth of July was coming up, and I wondered whether Frenchies would celebrate, but not enough to stick around. A week before the holiday, I gave notice. Brown said, "You just got here. Not five weeks yet. Work too tough for you?"

Only then did I admit that I was going back to school. He shook his head and said, "This damn war."

Then with a shrug he surprised me with a smile and said, "Well, good luck. I'll have Claire get your hours and pay you up to the minute when you leave, so we won't have to send a check. The super says you did a good job."

Saturday evening I said good-bye to Mrs. Dolan and Mrs. Nelson, grabbed my laundry bag, biked to the station and bought a ticket to Boston. I left my bicycle in the baggage car and slept through most of the ride. From South Station I pedaled into the setting sun to Brookline, looking forward to telling the guys about loading boxcars. I had $50 more than I started with, and my month-old beard would keep them talking until classes started.

Canoe Incident

One sultry Saturday afternoon late in June Dan Sirney and I were loafing in a canoe on the Portage Lakes south of Akron. Dan was a tire development engineer like me. Both of us were new to the tire business. We were unwinding from a 44 hour week of expediting critical military orders. Akron was spewing out tires for armies in Africa, Russia, the islands of the Pacific and now Europe. His draft board, like mine, had let him finish his mechanical engineering degree, but probably would not wait much longer. Summer 1944 held off reality for us.

In three months of working at Firestone Dan and I had become inseparable. Neither of us had a car. We walked around town and talked about the war and New Deal politics. We compared Akron where big factories were organized by the United Rubber Workers and Pittsburgh, where Dan grew up and the Steel Workers were the big union. Housing was critically short, but each of us had a room in a nice home. We ate in cafés and walked the mile and a half to and from work. Street cars and buses worked but were usually crowded.

Saturday afternoon was a relief from the noise, heat and hurry of the tire plant. Out at the end of the bus line we had found a canoe livery on the lake. From it we paddled away from crowded beaches and swam off the canoe. At three the sultry air cooled and a welcome breeze sprang up. We saw clouds to the west. As we sat watching, half a mile from the livery, the storm front hurried in. The wind strengthened. Waves developed. The sky darkened. Dan said, "Let's go back."

"Let's don't," I shrugged. "It's not a big lake and it might be fun out here."

Clouds swirled over our heads. White tops capped the rising waves. Dan said, "We can't get back. Let's try to beach over on that sand."

I really did not want to. It was raining hard, but I had been in canoes in rain, even capsized for fun. The waves were up. Already there was no practical possibility of beaching. Exhilarated, I headed the canoe into the wind, now blowing a gale. Dan paddled furiously with me. Control was already dicey when a gust flipped us over. I grabbed my glasses and paddle and swam toward the overturned canoe, of which only the bottom was visible. A seat cushion and a shirt floated off. I caught the shirt, but as I headed back, the canoe, with Dan hanging on, was moving away from me. That lake, which had been placid, now had a strong current. Wind was piling water, pushing it through a narrows into the next lake. The bottom strut of a bridge over the narrows, a bridge we had planned to canoe under, was now only inches above the water.

As we swept towards it, I shouted, "Grab the girder. We'll hold the canoe with our feet!" We both got good hand holds on girders and hooked our feet on gunwales, but the current dragged the upside down canoe like a parachute in a high wind. As we slowed its movement, the pull of the current dragged it down and under. We let go of the bridge and, free of restraint, the canoe bobbed up. We floated beside it.

Five minutes later the wind was gone, clouds were clearing, and we had all our gear except one cushion. We pushed ashore and emptied the canoe. As we paddled slowly toward the livery, Dan said quietly, "Axon, I know you thought that was fun. You're still grinning, but listen!

"My parents immigrated to Pittsburgh from Czechoslovakia before I was born, when my brother was six. He was fourteen years older than me. *His* name was Daniel. *Mine* was Michael. He loved canoeing. When he was eighteen, he and a friend were over on the Youghiogheny. It has rapids, but they were good canoers. Somehow, though, they got caught. After they went over one fall, an eddy pulled them back in. Understand that! *They were through, but the eddy took them back.* The other guy swam out. My brother drowned.

"My folks were crushed. So many of their hopes and expectations for the new world had centered on him. They did something Americans never heard of. May be Czech. They rechristened me, even though I was four years old. They gave me his name. They called me Daniel.

"I always thought the waterfall came after my brother. When the canoe flipped today, I *knew* another Daniel Sirney was going to drown."

We paddled slowly back to the canoe livery launching beach, saying nothing, pretending to look for the cushion. The canoe livery man said, "Boy, am I glad to see you. Never mind the cushion. I started worrying when I saw that storm line and you out in the middle of the lake."

I was afraid Dan would not sit beside me on the bus, but, without looking at me directly, he did. Neither of us spoke. It was a long ride back to town.

The Man Who Eats Snakes

Most of my early experiences with snakes were at scout camp. We had garter snakes, black snakes and, infrequently, copperheads—the most common poisonous snake in Missouri. A man visited the camp once with a timber rattler in a box, so I heard it rattle, but I saw none in the wild. Missourians in general, whether Boy Scouts or farmers, identified every swimming snake as a cottonmouth water moccasin. There were a few real ones in that part of Missouri, but I never saw one. Most swimming snakes were not poisonous.

My friend, Jimmy Parsons, knew and liked snakes. Once as we walked down the steep rocky path to the Maries River to swim, a three foot black snake emerged from the underbrush and moved sinuously across in front of us. I looked for a stick to pin it down, but Jimmy didn't wait. He grabbed the snake by the middle. Predictably, I thought, it turned back on itself and bit his thumb.

"Let go of it," I said, gaping. "Do you want me to hit it?"

"Oh no. No. It'll turn loose. But I can't go swimming right now. I have to take it back to the cabin. I have a cage all ready for it."

As I watched, the snake worked its lower jaw and its teeth lost their purchase. I went back, too. Jimmy dropped his prize through a little trap door into a screen cage at the head of his bed and threw in leaf mulch so the snake would feel more at home. Jimmy's thumb did not need first aid—there were two or three tiny drops of blood—so we headed for the rope swing and the drop into a deep spot in the river.

We fed the snake little toads and handled it frequently. It did not bite anymore. On Sunday one visitor was Patty Dawson, a pretty girl in my class in junior high. Her little brother was in the cabin I was in charge of. I took her to Jimmy's cabin and brought out the snake. It wrapped around my forearm. Instead of the horror or admiration I hoped for, Patty reached out and said, "Let me hold it."

I did, but I was disappointed.

Years later in a nature preserve on the Outer Banks of North Carolina, I saw a sign:

> CAUTION This is cotton mouth water moccasin country. If you see a water moccasin, remember that. This is his country not yours. If you stop, he will probably go away. If he does not, you go away. Turn around and go back along the trail. This is his country not yours.

I saw no water moccasins, but I loved the sign.

Twenty years ago we bought a half interest in a cabin on a few acres of woodland half an hour's drive from our home in Ann Arbor. I like sawing and chopping, and Shirley had joked for years about finding me a wood lot. Now I had one. The cabin is isolated, surrounded by a state park, the Pinckney Recreation Area. When our close friends and co-owners, the Caplans, moved to Bethesda, Maryland, they left us effectively in sole possession. We cook and heat with wood. I fell dead oaks and hickories and carry or drag them in as logs to cut to stove lengths.

In my timber cruising and hiking, I occasionally meet snakes. Most are garter snakes, but we also have black snakes and, once, a blue racer. Second most common are northern water snakes, a name I dislike because of its total lack of imagination. Garter snake says something. So do cottonmouth, copperhead, blue racer, rattler, even black snake, but northern water snake? They are a blotchy dark brown, bigger than garter snakes, but smaller than black snakes. To catch a snake I hold it down with a stick—or my foot if no stick is handy—and grab it behind the head so it can't bite. In Michigan only the little Massasauga rattler is poisonous, and I've never found one of them. For other snakes you don't worry about poison, but their bite is startling enough to avoid. When you grab a northern water snake, it not only tries to squirm away, it tenses its muscles and broadens and flattens its body, becoming perceptibly wider than it was on the ground.

Visitors to our cabin react differently to snakes. Many, perhaps most, abhor them. Others find them curious but unattractive, yet quite a few, including our children and grandchildren, like them. We have a picture of our seven year old granddaughter, Isabel, smiling at a garter snake she holds. The snake's tail curls over her left shoulder and twists around her blond braid.

Years ago Shirley and I took a walk through the woods near the cabin on a sunny but still chilly early April day with Bob and Anita Caplan and their ten year old son, David. Trees had not begun to leaf out, but everything was near bursting. It was just right for finding snakes. First and most spectacular was a blue racer, little more than an inch thick but nearly five feet long. Ordinarily they are almost as dark as black snakes, but this was a light, milky blue, because it was preparing to cast its skin. The skin we saw and handled still adhered tightly to the body but would shortly slough off.

A few minutes later we met a black snake nearly as large—shorter but a little fatter. Bob and Anita are committed amateur naturalists, but more curious about than fond of snakes. Out of good fellowship, however, Bob handled and Anita admired both big snakes. David hung back, standing behind Bob when I approached to let him look closely. Asked if he wanted to hold the black snake, he said, "NO!" I let it go and it slithered away under the leaves.

I talked to him, told him those were nice snakes, nothing to be afraid of. They would not attack him and would get away if they could. While I spoke a garter snake appeared almost at our feet. I grabbed it. It tried weakly to bite but my hand was too big for it to close on. It was only fifteen inches long. I passed it to Shirley and the less than eager Caplan parents. David wanted no part of it. I said, "It won't hurt you. It's completely harmless. Look!"

I brought it to my mouth, grasped it with my lips rather than my teeth so as not to hurt it and lowered my hands. Bob took a head shot of me holding the garter snake in my mouth. Everybody laughed including David, who was delighted. He finally reached out and touched the little creature before I let it go.

The Caplans sent us the print and wrote that back in school David had told his buddies that they had a friend who eats live snakes. When they hooted, he produced a picture of the man with a snake in his mouth. Then they half believed him.

BARBARA BACH

I was born in Boston, Massachusetts, in 1935, lived in West Newton until the age of seven and then Wellesley Hills until I was married. After graduating from Vassar College in 1956 with a child psychology major, I taught school in Sharon while my husband completed college on his GI benefits. We moved to Norwood and had two children: a daughter, Lucinda, born in 1958, and a son, Peter, born in 1961. I was a busy homemaker and community volunteer. My activities included remodeling and decorating our home, learning to sew and cook, creating and producing two documentaries on mentally retarded and emotionally disturbed children for WGBH/TV, founding a cooperative nursery school, facilitating church youth groups, and baby-sitting for my sister's children.

Following my divorce in 1968, I headed west with my kids to Ann Arbor, where I have now lived for over thirty years. In Michigan, I pursued a number of careers, reinventing my life several times over. I first completed a Master's degree in Education at the University of Michigan and took on four part-time jobs in order to survive, finally landing a position at Eastern Michigan University supervising student teachers. After a four-year marriage to a University of Michigan professor, during which we lived abroad and completed a trip around the world, I began my next incarnations. Again I was a single mom, but now with a high-schooler and a freshman going to college. In my first new job, I was a manager of a national political campaign. This led to a turn about—two and a half years as a co-founder and co-owner of a French catering business, the Moveable Feast. Needing benefits and income for my college bound children, I then took a job as a Legislative Aide and began many years of commuting to Lansing as well as traveling all over the state of Michigan. I worked to change public policy relating to job training, education, and economic development. My last employment was as the director of an organization founded to assist inventors and aspiring entrepreneurs.

In 1991, diagnosed with breast cancer, I made another shift. It began with no more commuting, ever, which gave me a lot of new time to read for my own pleasure. Following this, I experimented with creating art and ran for local public office. Currently, I serve on several local boards which reflect important interests of mine: theater, child care and our urban environment. I particularly value how important outdoor space and our physical environment are to our health and for our community.

My son died in 1982 from Hodgkin's disease. My daughter is married and has inherited two lovely step-daughters. She teaches in the English Department at Salem State College in Massachusetts. With my daughter, my brother, my nephews, nieces, and their families all living on the east coast, I travel there frequently. I am also enjoying adventure travel (most recently to the Galapagos and Peru), art workshops, the many cultural events here in Ann Arbor, and having time to reflect.

Halfway Up the Stairs

Halfway up the stairs
Is the stair where I sit.
There isn't any other stair
Quite like it. . . . .

When I was a child, halfway up the stairs was as special a place for me as it was for Christopher Robin. The staircase in our Wellesley house had a landing with the last four stairs turning to the left, allowing a perfect place to sit down almost hidden from view from below. And just in case someone walked by the stairs from the living room to the kitchen, it allowed for a perfect line of retreat. If I scrunched over and went backwards up those last four stairs, I could back right into my own bedroom.

When my brother was still young enough to have me as his companion, we could both sit there and back up together into my room and then, if it was serious, like "Someone is really coming upstairs" to fetch a coat or go to the bathroom, or our mother was "checking on things" and someone actually ascended the stairs, my brother could get right back into his room, too, because his room was accessed through mine. This meant fast action on our parts to remain unnoticed and safely panting and listening to our own heart rates calm down in our respective rooms.

It was this landing in our Wellesley house that drew us during my parents' parties. My mother's laugh—embarrassing to us kids and especially to me because no one else's mother laughed so high, so loudly and explosively—could be heard above everyone else's. But then, there was my father's laugh—more like a chuckle—and an occasional guest exclaiming "Oh, Peggy!" or "Oh, A. D.!" Here were my mother and my father giving a party and being the *life* of it. Their laughter together brought us the tonic of enjoyment. I remember giggling inside just because their laughter and fun was intoxicating and catching. My eyes still crinkle when I remember the overtones of their parties.

First came the games. They came early in the evening, before the singing. There was the button game. I was allowed to help hide these buttons ahead of time so I knew where each one was. Each guest was given a descriptive list of all the buttons. Thirty buttons of different sizes, colors and shapes were hidden all over the living room. The rule was, you mustn't touch anything—they were hidden in plain sight. There was the leather toggle button sitting on a Florentine leather box; the rose-pink button perched on top of the rose-pink damask-covered love seat; the ivory flat button tucked in the corner of the piano keyboard on the last white key; the etched silver button carefully balanced on the etched silver trim of the letter opener. After a specified length of time, the one who had checked off the most buttons had to show where each one was. This often brought on more hoots when the "winner" couldn't remember where one of the buttons was located!

Then there was the straw-and-tissue-paper-fish relay race. Each team had to carry a three inch tissue paper fish on the end of a straw, by sucking it tight to the bottom of the straw, then running the length of the living room to deliver it to the next teammate. This meant continually sucking through the straw in order to keep the fish attached. This got me really giggling, listening to the hoots when someone dropped their fish and then had to get down on the floor to reconnect with it. Imagining grownups on the floor sucking up their fishes sent me off into great spasms of muffled laughter!

The last but the best game for us listeners was the spelling game. My mother would prepare words beforehand, the number depending on the number of guests. She would create two teams, husbands and wives on different teams. Each team member donned a 12 by 12 piece of cardboard with one huge letter on it. The cardboard was equipped with a loop of string to hang around one's neck. The team members would scramble around among themselves to form the word and the first team to do it right got a point. This was the best game to listen to because we knew what was going to happen. The team my father was on would invariably spell the word backwards and the great hoots of laughter would announce the inevitable: my father's dyslexia had co-opted his teammates again!

My most favorite part of the party began when my mother was urged to play the piano for a group sing of "old favorites" and current hits. Again we could always hear mother's voice above the others. She was a trained mezzo soprano and had a voice that could carry. She knew all the tunes and could follow the words as she played. I would listen for my father's voice—a mellow tenor that delighted me. My father, the silent presence at home, came alive then, romantic and participatory at those moments, and my mother, the executive director, seemed human, lovable and talented in her musical glory. She played the piano easily, skillfully embellishing the written music with broken chords, ragtime basses, trills and octaves. She could sight read anything. She and their guests would leaf through sheet after sheet of current musicals. Whenever my mother and father went to a new show, my mother would buy the sheet music of the hits. My father loved musicals and they both thoroughly enjoyed the romantic love stories and lively comedies of the day. My father, however, often had trouble either reading the words or remembering them. I can still hear him da-da-da-ing along through some tune or see him raising his head to look through the bottoms of his bifocals over my mother's shoulder, straining to see the words on the sheet music—and my mother quickly raising her hand to point to the measure to help him find his place. Of course, if he misread a word there might be another break for laughter.

When they got to the oldies the voice volume seemed to increase ten-fold—voices contending as if for first place. "Tea for Two," "Smoke Gets in Your Eyes," "Blue Moon," "Indian Love Song" were popular. Phrases of other songs stick in my head, like "'Don't sit under the apple tree with any one else but me," or "Three iddy fishes and the mama fishy too. . . And they swam and they swam all over the dam." There were World War I songs: "And the caissons go rolling along," "Over there, over there," "K-k-k-Katy," "Mademoiselle from Armentières," and "The Yanks are Coming." World War II songs: "The Last Time I saw Paris," "I'll Be Seeing You," "Lili Marlene," "The White Cliffs of Dover," "Praise the Lord and Pass the Ammunition," and the battle song of the marines, "From the halls of Montezuma to the shores of Tripoli." The most unusual song that was most often played last, was the "tinkling" song in which every one had to have a glass of water filled to a different height and something with which to tap it. There was much scurrying around to get the instruments in place. It would start off OK; but like an amateur bell choir, someone would make a mistake and great hoots of laughter would ensue. Pretty soon the evening would be over.

It's the memory of their laughter that draws me back to when I felt safest as a child. Laughter and safety became partners for me. My world was OK on the evenings I could hear my mother laughing at my father's goofs, my father's good-natured responses, and the animated voices of their guests. I could recognize most of their friends by their laughs. The warmth of friendship surrounded them and infused our house . . . streaming up the stairs to the landing in Wellesley or filtering up through the floor boards in Manomet. These were not sounds to lull us to sleep. These were sounds to absorb and to remember for good. Whether it was after dinner game parties in West Newton, dinner parties after the war in Wellesley, or house parties in Manomet, it didn't matter if I was alone on these sojourns or with my brother. The same dialogue occurred, either in my head or whispered out loud to my brother: "That's Mommy's voice," or "That's Daddy's voice." It was an identification mixed with astonishment—"They don't act like that with us"—and pride—"They do have fun together."

My Sister's Gift

Closeness was what I yearned for as a child—as a sister and as a family member. So my sister's death when it occurred was a particularly devastating experience for me. Patsy and I were six years apart. I have an early memory of being thrilled that we had matching sister dresses and I have family photos of us together, yet we were never playmates. I was aware of her, but I didn't know her, nor she me, when we were youngsters. We were always in different schools and living in a large house didn't help. Because she had been an only child for so long, she had a special relationship with my mother. My mother would tell me how she trusted Patsy because Patsy told her everything. That left me out. When I was young, she was intimidating—a stranger—another remote adult—and worse, she might tattle on me. In my teens I admired her, at least from a distance. As she matured, she developed a natural beauty—thick, slightly wavy, light brown hair, large hazel eyes, a debutante slouch she acquired in her teens, and a hearty laugh that I hear now in my daughter. She was an average student, better in history, English, and music than in the sciences. She particularly loved English history and knew the names of all the kings and queens. She could do the *New York Times* crossword puzzle and somehow get out of doing dishes. She was liked by her peers and her teachers and always seemed to have a steady supply of boy friends to bring home. She blotted her deep red lipstick on pieces of paper and left them lying around. Sometimes she let me watch her get dressed for dances. By the time she was in college, she smoked. Not only did she smoke in front of my disapproving parents, she inhaled the smoke up through her nose! Though I don't remember her being a leader in her crowd, I viewed her as loyal and principled.

It wasn't until I got married in 1956 that Patsy and I began to have something in common: houses, husbands, in-laws and babies. We lived fifteen minutes a part in different towns—she in a middle class suburban town and I in a working class, lower income town. In my head, I can still drive the back route short-cut to her house. One year I earned my own pin money as her regular once-a-week babysitter when she volunteered at the Women's Lying-In Hospital in Boston or went to the church to play the organ.

By 1963, Patsy was thirty-four and had three children and I was twenty-eight with two. She had had the first grandson and I had the only girl. We shared decorating tastes and began to relate our personal experiences of growing-up. After all, we did have the same parents. We always shared holidays and family weekends at our parents' house. I was eager to have her as a friend, though it was hard to get past feeling like an awkward younger sister in her presence. But to my delight she began to become an ally as we developed into what our mother called her "young matrons." We always shared holidays and family weekends at our parents' house. We even, occasionally, had a night out as couples.

The week before Thanksgiving of 1963, President Kennedy was killed. For the entire holiday week, the whole nation was plunged into a black mood—an all consuming gloom. Here was a young man tragically cut down in his prime. Alert to every news bulletin, drowning in grief over the fate of the president's young widow and her two children, we as a nation were glued to our black and white TVs. Boston, Massachusetts, was Kennedy's home.

He was one of us—Republicans and Democrats alike. We watched endless reruns of every event: the motorcade, the shots, the confusion, and then Jackie in her blood-stained suit standing by Lyndon Johnson as he was sworn in as our next president. Kennedy's death was the beginning of a long dark weekend.

As the stories of the assassination unfolded, we took breaks from our TVs, called friends on the phone, took walks and fed our families. On one of my walks with my two children, Cindy, then five, and Peter, two and a half, we found a stray kitten under a bush. A tiny buff kitten mewing loudly. I let my children bring it home. It was so little and warm to hold and it was so alive. We could feed it and love it. It would make us smile. We needed such small comforts.

We had double need, for Kennedy's public death foreshadowed our own private loss. While we were agonizing with the rest of the country over the Kennedy tragedy, our family was also agonizing over its own more intimate bleak drama. Patsy was terminally ill—about to be cut down before *her* time, leaving family members who needed her, leaving me. No one had said how many weeks or months she had to live, but we all knew there was no cure. The week that Kennedy died, I could see that Patsy had begun to fail physically, and at the same time a curious kind of numbness and dread was beginning to invade my own body.

My sister and I commiserated over the phone about Jackie's loss, her fortitude, and her new task of bringing up two children alone. We both had children the same ages as Caroline and John-John. As young mothers, we could identify with Jackie, the mother. Then Patsy said that she couldn't *think* of being Jackie the mother and managing. Patsy was glad that she didn't have to be Jackie the widow. Her statement hit me hard. My chest burned, my mind blanked out, and I had to concentrate to breathe. 1 suddenly realized that *I* would be the "widow". I'd be the one left when Patsy died.

I wondered whether her comment was only expressing sympathy for George, who'd be the widower. Did she know how much *I'd* miss her? Or was the comment her way of recognizing how hard it would be for any one left? I wanted her to tell me directly that she knew it would be hard for me. I wanted her to say that I meant a lot to her, and that she knew how much she meant to me. But we didn't expand on the subject. If the country was overwhelmed with grief, I felt as if I were in a black hole, peering out at the activity around me.

Thanksgiving dinner, as always, was at my parents' house, but this year Patsy was staying home. My husband Hoppy and I and our two children, Patsy's husband George and their three children, all joined my mother and father. That made five adults, and five small children aged two to nine. Bob, my brother, was not coming home. He had decided to go sailing over the Thanksgiving weekend. I'm sure I had called ahead to see how Patsy was doing—not so well—but George and the children would still come and we would all do what we could to focus on them.

I still see that dining room in the late afternoon light with its eggplant rug, sea green wails, full length gold drapes and Colonial pewter chandelier over the mahogany gate-leg table with its extra leaves inserted. The table was properly draped in a white damask linen tablecloth, set with Ritz-blue water glasses, sterling flatware, gold-rimmed china, and the centerpiece, a huge half of Hubbard squash dripping with grapes and walnuts and almonds in their shells. The room was cast in the rusty-oak and gold-maple light of a late November afternoon—the kind of light that doesn't enter a room through its windows but somehow seeps through the outside walls, attaching itself to the opposite inside wall, which glows ever so dimly. It was the time of day when your eyes keep wandering outdoors because it's still lighter outside than inside. Even though light is needed, turning on the lights doesn't help much.

You can still see outside, but inside the light is closing down and emptying out of the room. It's the time of day when hugs and quiet are what you most want next as you anticipate the coziness of a warmly lighted room surrounded by soft darkness, allowing your full attention to be inside and close at hand.

Patsy's children were on either side of George, their Daddy. This was the first holiday meal Patsy had missed since she had been diagnosed with cancer—Hodgkin's disease—eighteen months earlier. She was at home and in bed—too weak, too uncomfortable to come. My plan was to visit her on our way home from dinner. The conversation at the dinner table was not much to remember. Our efforts, of course, were to interact with the children and lighten, as best we could, a very heavy meal. It was difficult to stay focused. Our hearts were grieving as we chewed on special tidbits of crisp brown turkey skin, made craters in our whipped potatoes for gravy, and mashed our feelings down on our plates. Thank God for toddlers who know how to spill milk for a welcome diversion.

After we left my parents' house, we stopped as planned to see Patsy, but Mrs. Colpitts, the Nova Scotian housekeeper who had cone to live with them, greeted us with concern. Patsy had stumbled getting out of bed during the day while we were at dinner. Mrs. Colpitts wondered whether Patsy's new medication was too strong. George called her doctor. I went up stairs to look in on her with my children. She stirred and responded to me with a groggy greeting. Then we went home, grim and silent, for there was nothing for us to do.

It was a scattered time both mentally and physically. I had no idea what to expect. Was she dying? The rest of the weekend was "covered," as my mother would say. She would take the older boys Friday and Saturday, freeing up George to come and go as he wished. Mrs. Colpitts would have her watchful eye on Patsy and on Tommy, who had just turned two. The weekend dragged on and on with more Kennedy TV.

Monday came. My usual weekly visit with Patsy was Monday morning through lunch. This was what she had named her toughest time—the first day after the weekend, when everyone left for work or school. I'm sure it was the most lonely time of the whole week for her to contemplate the shortness of her life.

On her bedside table Patsy kept a copy of Frankl's book on the meaning of life, which reflects his thoughts while confined in a Nazi prison during World War H. He had survived by planning lectures about his incarceration that he would deliver sometime in the future to his students. Patsy and I had talked often about his strength and his existential ideas. It seemed to give her comfort and kept me preoccupied intellectually. We listened to organ music on her record player, which was perched along with me on the other half of the king-sized bed. Just before she had been diagnosed, she had taken up playing the organ in a serious way and played for the children's service on Sundays at the Needham Congregational Church, but now she had lost the strength to play. And we talked about her discussions with her minister and the deep questions she shared with him.

Of all the subjects that she had needed or wanted to talk about in those last few months, there were two that seemed to me were the toughest. First, leaving her family was tough. How very hard it was for her to think of leaving her three boys—Stuey nine, Stevie seven, and in particular her youngest, Tommy, who had just turned two. She knew Tommy was too young to be expected to remember her, but he had brightened up her days with his newly acquired walking skills, his soft affectionate nature, aud his winning smile. The others were at school with the unfair burden of knowing she was failing. Patsy assumed George would remarry, and realized that her boys would all be brought up by another woman—

someone she would never know—someone who would replace her. The thought of not being able to see her children get married or go to the wedding of my daughter Cindy, the only girl grand-child at that time, would make her cry. Second—and the worst part about dying, she would say—was dying and not being known. Then she would cry, tears would fill my eyes too, and we'd both fall silent.

Somehow, I could do more with words on the first subject. We'd fantasize about her children and how her friends would be part of their remembering—how their talents and looks would al-ways reveal part of her and that any mother in her circumstance would feel and think the same way. On the second subject, I don't think I was much help. If she needed to say to someone that she feared not being known, I was willing to be that someone. If she couldn't say this to her husband because it might be too painful, I could understand that it wouldn't be an easy topic. The little I knew about intimate talks on death between husband and wife was about the size of a lentil. Her concern has stayed with me as an ex-istential issue throughout my life.

Patsy's concern was both deeply moving and deeply unsettling to me. Can anyone ever know someone else fully? Was she asking me if I really knew her? Didn't I have this painful question myself? Here perhaps was a measure of the closeness that I yearned for as a child. Patsy was now willingly revealing her vulnerability to me. She was trusting me with her innermost fears. I had several re-sponses at once. Suddenly I wasn't her "little" sister, but someone she was looking to for a response and understanding. Suddenly I realized that this shift must mean she was feeling even weaker, that she might be dying; and with a jolt I realized I couldn't answer her question because it was mine, too. We both had the same fear of not being known—of not being somebody—of not recognizing our own selves. At that moment, I desperately wanted to do something for her and ease her inner pain. Anything. But how could I share with her the fact that I felt the same fear? I had to be strong! I couldn't burden her with my fears—but to whom could I reveal my vulnerability? When I couldn't think of anyone, fear and anxiety rose inside of me. I reined in my panic, as I had done in the past, giving her what I could of my time and attention.

I expected to be there with her as usual on the Monday after Thanksgiving, but that morning was to be different. I got a call from George or my mother telling me that Patsy was now at the local community hospital and that my father was going to be with her in the morning. George had taken her the night before so she could be monitored more closely. Would I visit her in the late afternoon and be there until George got home from work? Sure. But my calm cooperation hid my alarm. This was the first time Patsy had been hospitalized and hospitals to me meant death. I must have arranged baby-sitting for my children. I saw her that evening in the hospital for what turned out to be the last time.

I still ache wishing I could recall each word of our last conversation and remembering only how very scared I was that afternoon and evening. I think she referred to me affectionately as her "little sister." I think we expressed our love for each other. I think she said something like she was glad we had gotten to know each other. I think she expressed her appreciation for the time I had spent with her during her illness.

She got up to go to the bathroom by herself. I leaped up to be with her. She declined my assistance. I could tell by her gait that she was quite heavily drugged but still under her own control. I smile now as I think of that small act of independence.

When George came, I stayed awhile and as she was snoozing—drifting in and out of awakeness—I left. With a very heavy heart, I got in my car and cried all the way home. Seeing her in the hospital made it clear that she was very, very sick, but I still didn¹t let myself think of her as dying.

I called George the next morning to see how she was doing. He asked, Hadn't my mother called me? No, she hadn't, nor had my father. No one had called me. That's how I found out that Patsy had died just after I had left the night before.

A mixture of feelings and thoughts began to brew the moment I knew she was dead. Anger at her leaving me when I was just trying on my own closeness-suit and developing that much wished for bond of sisterhood. Fear that I couldn't function without her support. Fear of admitting any competitive feeling that I had had towards her. Anxiety about the responsibility of now being the only daughter, a big responsibility with my mother. Gratitude that I had known my sister, for a while anyhow, as an adult. Pride in her accomplishments and successes. Appreciation of our developing friendship and shared family jokes. Pleasure in the knowledge that we gave our parents anniversary parties together, even though I had unresolved feelings about automatically having them at her house. Delight that I could borrow her clothes when I needed something fancy and that she could borrow mine. Gladness that we could share ideas about home decorating and raising babies, if only for a few years, though I wished she had visited me more often. Thankfulness that I had connected with my nephews as each one came along and that I could baby-sit for her children as her sister and their aunt And finally, I felt honored that she had wanted me by her side at the end.

I had not anticipated that Patsy's death would unleash such a host of feelings and unresolved childhood issues that I had never identified before. Understanding was to come much later. But right then I had to struggle with managing my own pain and the immediate reality of my sister's death. Writing this, I understand that in our talks about wanting to be known, Patsy was expressing that deep human yearning for connection and for a legacy. To be understood—to have mattered. It doesn't matter whether one is dying or living. That yearning will bubble up after any loss, accompanied by anger and sadness. It's just around the corner from understanding and acceptance—and on the other side of joy.

Nearly forty years have passed and Patsy is gone, but she is not unknown. Cherished and loved, Patsy touched us all: her boys, her husband, our parents, her friends, our younger brother, and me. We knew her as best we could. I continue to see her in her boys who are now adults, and I am grateful for that connection and legacy.

But the most lasting memory for me is of that moment when she revealed herself so nakedly. When she shared her fear of not being known, I realized that she was not only sharing her own deepest concern, but was also putting into words a deep fear of my own. And with the recognition of that truth I felt our sisterhood. Her parting gift to me—the one I treasure most—was that experience of closeness that I had yearned for as a child.

ALICE BOLEY

I was born in a little cottage surrounded by roses in California in June of 1914. I grew up with loving parents and my precious twin brothers, nine years younger than myself. Our lives changed significantly when my father died during my senior year in high school.

I attended Carleton College in Northfield, Minnesota. Most of my working years were with Michigan Bell and telephone work in general. I lived in Vermont during World War II and my first marriage ended following the war. My little son and I struggled. A second marriage ended with the death of my spouse after only three and one-half years. I had a little daughter, too. Then I lost my son at age 28 in a tragic accident on the basketball court. His two daughters were raised in California and I have been fortunate to stay in close contact with them. My daughter and her family now live in Helena, Montana, and my three grandsons are there.

I love the arts and in recent years have revived an interest in writing that I had in college. So now, in my eighties, I enjoy our writing group and my poetry group. Painting is also important in my life, something I discovered in middle age. I have been an active member of the Ann Arbor Women Painters. So I feel blessed with family, good friends, and so many wonderful things to do.

My Hemingway

When I was in the sixth grade we lived in Oak Park, Illinois, in a stucco house with a large sun porch across the front. We had to walk about a mile to school, up and down the tidy streets; and every day as I went on my way, I had a continuing story going around in my mind. One story could last for weeks and was like an old friend as I added yet another chapter. They were usually adventure stories about damsels in distress, but there was always a happy ending. Sometimes I would walk with other children, but I never minded the days when I was alone because of my stories.

Right on a corner, about a half block from Holmes Elementary School, stood another big rambling stucco house. It was well known to us children because there was a place to buy candy in the basement, but we had no idea we were trading in a famous house—the home of Ernest Hemingway. After school many of us stopped by. We went down about four steps and entered a little room where a single wooden case contained an enticing assortment of gumballs, jujubes, black licorice, and tootsie rolls, as well as stick candy. There was a lady in charge who was always cheerful and thoroughly enjoyed our coming. She even knew some of us by name. Somehow we managed to hold onto our pennies through a day at school and then, on the way home, crowded into the small basement space, eager to make a choice. For the most part we were well behaved. In all the biographies of Hemingway nothing has been said about the penny candy in the basement, and they certainly haven't mentioned how he spoke at our assembly and I had the honor of introducing him.

My passion for stories was given an added impetus when I became part of this special event. In English class we had a contest to see who could write the best story. It was hard to put my thoughts down on paper, but I really worked at it, and was pleased when I won. That is how I earned the honor of introducing Hemingway when he came to talk to our whole school.

I practiced my speech for hours in front of my parents. It was brief, but I mentioned his military service as well as having been a correspondent for the Toronto *Star*, and touched on the books he had written. This was 1925, and Hemingway was just getting started on his writing career. He published *The Sun Also Rises* in 1926. I ended my little introductory speech with a flourish, and said, "It is with the greatest of pleasure that I present Ernest Hemingway."

My father sat in his big brown leather chair and was an appreciative and proud audience. Mom was concerned with what outfit I should wear on that day. I was just becoming acutely clothes conscious and wanted to look my best, so Mom and I went over my meager choices. She believed in having just a few well-chosen practical outfits and never went in for fashionable items. In the end Daddy sanctioned the purchase of something new for the occasion. It was a lovely blue wool dress with a plaid scarf. Hemingway was already well-known, though still quite young—only about twenty-six years old. Still, on the day of the assembly the reality of his presence was overwhelming. He was tall, vigorous, and very handsome. My heart was pounding, but I somehow managed to make my little speech, while looking up into his tanned face with the large black moustache. He smiled at me and shook my hand. I felt weak in the knees and was glad to retire to a chair at the side of the stage. My big moment was over quickly, but I am not likely ever to forget that day and my brush with Ernest Hemingway.

Sugaring Off

In the long ago time when I lived in Vermont during World War II there were few occasions for celebration. But every year when March came around, the whole village of Craftsbury turned out for something called "Sugaring Off." It was the annual harvest of maple sap out in the country where they make maple sugar best. Perhaps I should feel guilty about saying that because I am well aware that maple syrup is also made in Michigan, and I have been a Michigander for a long time. But I have yet to see and taste any syrup here to compare with the pale amber elixir made in Vermont. The highest grades of maple syrup are very pale.

During the winter Vermont is under a perpetual blanket of snow, but some time in March you can see patches of brown dried leaves in the woods. Although the nights remain very cold, daytime temperatures rise. Perfect weather for the sap to run. The maple orchard I visited was on a little country road, and in among the trees was a wooden structure with a smokestack. That was the Sugar House where the sap was boiled in large shallow pans to the correct point to become syrup. I liked to go past the orchard and see the buckets attached to the trees after they were tapped. The farmer had a horse-drawn sleigh to gather and carry the sap up to the Sugar House. Then when the harvest was complete, the fun began.

The "Sugaring Off" was at night, and sweet smoke curled overhead and vanished into the starlit sky. There were people everywhere—young and old. Some came in cars, some in sleighs and some on foot. I could hear a fiddle playing somewhere in the darkness. Most of the young men were gone, involved in the war, but there were teenagers laughing and little children running around and elderly folks. Many of them were active farmers and their wives, in their seventies and eighties, still running their farms and doing an amazing amount of work. I developed a lot of respect for Yankee durability.

The night was chilly and people were stamping their feet and gravitating to the warmth of the fire in the Sugar House. There in long pans snow was piled and when the sap had boiled down it was poured carefully over the snow, where it thickened to the consistency of soft caramel. When the syrup was just right the visitors would take a fork, wind some of the delicious confection around it, and indulge in a delightful treat. Some of the ladies served plates of homemade doughnuts with pickles to clear the palate so that we could eat more syrup. There were also steaming cups of coffee made in a large galvanized pot. It was a rare bright spot in our lives during the war, and every year when March arrives I think of it with an affection that goes way beyond the taste of maple syrup.

On Our Own

B ack in the late Forties my son and I were starting our long saga of "us against the world." I had taken the job of running the telephone exchange at Mendon, Michigan, because it was the only one I could find where my son could be with me. It was an interesting time in a tough sort of way, and the beginning of my philosophy which guided me through many difficulties: "Nothing is impossible."

Our office was in a storefront right on Main Street, and our living quarters were in a large, empty room behind it. Mendon had five hundred telephone subscribers, so the office was a busy place. Most townspeople came to the office to pay their bills and our pay phone was very popular. Not everyone had a telephone at home in the Forties.

My son, Ray, was ten months old and spent a lot of time in a playpen when we arrived. I had counted on the safety of the playpen to last a couple of months while I learned the ropes. After a very short time, however, he started walking and climbing, and the playpen had to go. Somehow I managed to teach him to stay away from the mainframe with its circuits and wires. In those days the mainframe was right in the office. In exchange, he had a few favorite toys to play with. He was so unbelievably good and he had a wonderful smile. He was a hit with the locals and he loved the attention. Ray had his first haircut in Mendon, and the barber prided himself on making the first cut a good experience. He did such a great job that Ray started teasing to go to the barber.

Things were going along fairly well. I had organized my day. I had to leap out of bed at an early hour, put Ray's bottle on to heat, dash down to the basement to tussle with the huge coal furnace, bathe and dress Ray, fix a hasty breakfast, dress myself (neatly if possible) and be prepared to open the office at eight o'clock in the morning. Sometimes people were outside waiting. Then I was on duty until my high school helpers arrived to take over for a few hours, around four or five p.m. I got eighty dollars per week to run the show, and whatever was left after paying my help was mine. Not a whole lot was left.

From five to nine in the evening was my special time with Ray. We had supper together and story time before I tucked him in. At nine I wheeled my folding bed into the office, parked it next to the switchboard and slept—with one ear open for calls and the other for Ray. If this sounds impossible, it almost was, except that I was young and determined to succeed.

Because I was young and fresh from a devastating divorce, I received many off-color calls and some downright obscene ones. It made me wonder some about my predecessors. How to handle this? Some were well-known people right in town. Ignoring most of it, hanging up on them and holding my head high, I eventually convinced the populace that I was not interested in any kind of hanky-panky.

The big boss came down from Muskegon only about once a month, I was pretty much left on my own with very little training. I introduced a lot of courtesy and the townspeople appreciated that. At Christmas time we were overwhelmed with gifts and two Christmas trees. Once the big boss arrived and while we were going over our little operation, said that he thought Ray's toys shouldn't be in the office. Well, that did it! I told him that if Ray couldn't have a few toys, then they couldn't have me either. In fact, I remember really sounding off and then I started to cry. Working around the clock seven days a week had worn me down.

Well, the boss backed down in a hurry, promised a new furnace and a raise if only I would stay and stop crying. So I did for a while. We had a very serious ice storm that winter and a lot of the wires were down. The storm went on for days and I ran the switchboard by cranking our emergency setup. That switchboard would now be "Exhibit A" for an antique store. And we had a tragic fire which kept me up all night handling emergencies.

One time, when people were lined up paying their bills, I noticed the name of one of them—Glenn Tallman. Out of curiosity I asked if he had any relatives in Iowa. Surprisingly, he did and wonder of wonders, he was my father's cousin. From then on he and his wife, Clare, brought us water. Local water was bad and they had lovely well water on their nearby farm. We managed to get away sometimes on the weekend for a few hours on their farm. Glenn was the same gentle and kind sort of person my father had been. These people made all the difference. We had found family in a very unexpected place, and I will never forget them.

This was all very long ago in a different world, but overall it makes me smile to think of it.

The Bath Street Sale

There are a few annual garage sales in Ann Arbor that should not be missed and the Bath Street Sale is one of them. It's not just because of amazing bargains. Bath Street has a certain ambience that is hard to beat. This is a dead-end street just off Seventh near West Park. There are ten to twelve houses; trees are large; and some of the houses are far from fashionable. But it is obvious that the owners have put much loving care into refurbishing them, and I think it must be wonderful living there.

There is another reason I look forward to this sale. Right down the street is the small cottage where I came to live in Ann Arbor with my little son a half century ago. It was in Professor Spurlin's back yard—and it's still there.

On this day a traffic jam has developed on the narrow street, which tells one and all that this is something special. And it might be best to be patient about a parking spot or it will ruin the whole experience. There is a feeling of adventure the minute you step out onto the sidewalk. A chatter of friendly conversation greets your ears and blends with dogs and baby strollers as people walk around and visit the various items for sale.

The owners are out in force, smiling and genuine. Here is the difference. They seem really involved, and they want to make this sale festive and memorable. One lady is serving coffee and dough-nuts. I spotted a young woman sitting in the lotus position in a chair in front of her house. There was a table almost empty nearby—only some hardware and old records left. Obviously her sale had been successful. I admired her tulips and lovely violets, and she told me how earlier a truck had backed over some of her flowers. She didn't seem upset. Perhaps that is why she was meditating. At any rate, it is evident that people on Bath Street are used to doing their own thing.

I moved on to a most eclectic assortment displayed at the house next door. Here were decorator items for the home: old books, clothes, a teakettle that I really favored, and the owner was telling stories about some of the objects. A charming lady.

Across the street I found the buy of the day—a four-part container for microwave cooking, in good condition, for a dollar. A gentleman helped me with this transaction and I left happily, clutching my "find."

I ambled on in a blissful trance. Boys on in-line skates dodged around. I suppose the slight hill and dead-end make Bath Street ideal for skating. The original sunniness of the morning was fading and it looked as though it could rain. I made a few more stops and breathed in the special atmosphere of Bath Street, knowing full well that all good things must come to an end. Then I left and it did.

AAA

It was a lazy Sunday morning recently and I took my time over the Sunday paper and listened to church services on the radio, instead of hustling around and going to church. Of course, it wasn't nearly as good. Then I listened to an analysis of the week's events, so it was early afternoon when I ventured out with plans for the rest of the day.

I slid into the driver's seat and started to back my car out. It seemed strangely tipped and not at all as usual. I started down the street and it was laboring, steering very hard, and I knew something drastic must be wrong. Still I persisted around a couple of corners, then realizing it must be a flat tire, I pulled over.

Yes, the front left tire was completely flat. My car tilted to one side. It looked sad. I hadn't had a flat in a very long time and I was amazed. The set of tires on the car was fairly new, and although I often worry about various parts of my old car, tires haven't been one of my problems. Until now.

I walked back to my apartment and called AAA. They said it would be as much as 45 minutes. How could it be so long? I went back to the car to wait. Of course in due time the welcome sight of a wrecker came into view, and the driver took a look at my tire.

"It's been slashed," he said. "No hope of fixing that one." He showed me the four-inch gash in the side of the tire. My heart sank at the thought of vandalism and all that it implies. Did some one have it in for me? What would they do next?

The driver was noncommittal and said he had already serviced seven flat tires and it was only 2:00 p.m. He tried to open my trunk. The lock wouldn't budge. He pounded on it, twisted the key this way and that, squirted something on it—all to no avail. The driver became discouraged and started preparations to tow me. Then at the last minute he realized that he could fold the back seat down and enter the trunk that way.

But on this day, nothing was going to be easy. How could I have so much stuff in my trunk? He kept pulling items out—things that I had completely forgotten. How about the old basket, that tangle of clothes hangers, empty boxes, a large piece of plywood, and Dick's old kit from the Navy. There was the pile on the pavement—so very embarrassing. But then he put his considerable bulk to the task and finally emerged with the spare tire. I felt like cheering! It was brand new, but so small! I didn't even know about "donuts" and realized this must be the first flat for my '86 Nova.

Well, the rest was predictable. I hurried to Firestone because they close early on Sunday, and purchased a new tire, and had it installed. Then I went home to think about the consequences of having my tire slashed. When night fell, I turned on all available outside lights, and didn't sleep well. How could I with some one lurking out there?

On Monday I reported the event to the management in my complex. There were three other people on the far side of the complex who had had their tires slashed and cars broken into. The police felt it was a normal thing—probably teens on a spree. They thought some other complexes had been hit also.

When I reported my event to the police I got some one who was obviously bored and said it was mainly for insurance purposes that they even took the information. When I said my insurance wasn't going to cover it, they almost hung up. I asked if they could do anything about protection. She said maybe the cruiser could come by more often. I hung up with the feeling that slashed tires are run-of-the-mill, so ordinary as to be almost a given. I must be out of touch. Still, I ran the light bill up to alarming proportions the following week, then gradually settled back to more or less normal.

The management where I live felt sad about all this and they waived a month's rent to help compensate for the tire. They have always been good to me and none of this is in any way their fault. The part I don't understand is how slashed tires get to be so *unremarkable*.

MARAJEAN BROOKS

I was born in Rockford, Illinois, and lived there until I came to Ann Arbor in 1998 to live near my daughter, Chris. My husband, Chad, and I met in grade school, started dating after high school, and were married during World War II. After the war he went back to college and I worked in the Publications Department at the University of Iowa. We returned to Rockford where he worked for the Rockford Newspapers and I enjoyed the challenges and rewards of raising our three children, whose interests were very different from one another. They became a professor of law, an electrical engineer, and a computer program developer. Chad's working at night gave me time to be creative in cooking, sewing, and gardening and also time to be involved in school and community activities.

I became active in the Rockford Art Association and spent many years on its board, organizing exhibits and fund-raisers, and developing the Picture Lady Project that introduced famous painting reproductions to elementary students. This work, together with Sunday School teaching and Great Books groups for grade school students helped me decide to return to college for a teaching degree when my youngest child was in sixth grade.

At age 48 I graduated and started teaching sixth grade, going on to teach almost every elementary grade during the next nineteen years, enjoying both the subject matter and the students. It is a demanding job but gives such satisfaction when the class begins to work together, absorbing any problems, taking pleasure in the learning activities, and being responsible enough to work up to their capacity as individuals and also in group productions. I taught long enough to have former students come back and tell me they had decided to become teachers because of me.

I have always loved to read and to travel, especially with Chris and her family who will spend hours in art museums or exploring neighborhoods with me. After my husband and my sister died in 1997, I decided I needed to live near one of my children and here I am, making new friends and exploring the multitude of possibilities in Ann Arbor.

The Long Way to Kokomo

When one of my eighth grade English assignments was to write a ballad I knew that my trip home from a visit with my grandmother was a good subject. I remember only the first two lines:

> We got upon the trolley when we should have caught the bus.
> The trolley did just shake and sway until it shook up us.

I had just had my thirteenth birthday and my sister Laurella her eleventh, when we were left in Indianapolis, Indiana, for a two week visit with my grandparents. My parents drove us down from our home in Rockford, Illinois, for our usual summer visit, but this time we had my new baby sister Vonnie to show off, and the three of them went home without us. With nine cousins living nearby, we had a busy and wonderful time, going to the amusement park, the Boy Scout carnival, parades and fireworks for the Fourth of July, a riverside cottage, and a working farm. Indianapolis was a "southern" town to us and just being at my grandparents' house was much more exciting than being at home.

When it was time to leave because my sister was to be the flower girl in a wedding, Mother planned for us to return home by taking the bus to Kokomo, Indiana, where my Aunt Tressa recently had been transferred by her company. She would meet our bus and accompany us on the train to Chicago and then to Rockford. The only thing I had heard about Kokomo was that it was a small town with the railroad track running down the middle of the main street.

We got up early and Grandmother took us downtown to catch the Greyhound bus to Kokomo. On our way Grandma remembered that this was the last year for the Interurban to run, and since we had never ridden on the Interurban, she thought it would be nice for us to have the experience. Instead of going to the bus station, we went to the car barn where she settled us into our seats, had the motorman put our suitcase up on the luggage rack above our heads, and received assurances from him that he would be sure that we got off at Kokomo. We said our good-byes and watched her hover outside the window until we took off.

The Interurban was a trolley, running on tracks and powered by an electric wire which ran above the tracks. A bent arm on the top of the car had a roller on the end, placed to roll along this wire to get the electric power. It was much like a streetcar but built to go at a much faster speed. The slippery old woven straw seats were designed so that the back could be pulled over to the other side when the car reversed directions. The seats were stiff and hard and we had to brace our feet, but eventually we adjusted to the shaking and swaying as we careened through the countryside. The day was hot but air rushed in through the open windows. The trip seemed to be taking a long time. My grandmother had not taken into account the fact that we could only follow the tracks which ran in a circle linking many small towns in north central Indiana. I checked the name of each town, concerned that the motorman was forgetting about us.

Meanwhile, the bus was scheduled to arrive almost two hours earlier than the Interurban because the bus could follow the new highways and go directly north. We were scheduled to catch the train at one o'clock. My aunt met the bus when it arrived at ten o'clock but we were not on it! She made inquiries about the next bus and ran home to call Grandmother in Indianapolis and then Mother in Rockford. Although in the depression year of 1937, long distance calls were still considered an expensive luxury, only used under special circumstances and limited to the three minute minimum rate, this was an emergency! But since Grandmother had been downtown early, she had gone shopping for the day, so there was no one at her house to answer the phone. When Aunt Tressa called Mother in Rockford she had no idea why we weren't there.

It must have been almost noon when we arrived in Kokomo. We were using my Dad's worn and battered old leather suitcase, and as the conductor jerked it down from the rack, one end of the handle broke loose. The only way I could carry it was to pick it up with both arms and hold it in front of me. We were surprised that our aunt was not there. After looking around I finally asked the station agent when the bus had come in. He explained that the bus came in at the bus station which was ten or twelve blocks away. He said, "Walk down this street for seven blocks and turn left. Keep going until you see the bus station." We set off for the long walk with the heavy suitcase in my arms.

The curb at the first corner was extra high and since I could not see the ground over the suitcase, I fell and dropped the bag. After I blotted my skinned knee and picked up the suitcase I discovered that it had fallen into some chewing gum and I had put my hand right in it. I wiped off my hand as well as I could and put my handkerchief over the gum on the suitcase. As we walked down the street at the edge of the business district we passed empty or closed store fronts, seeing no people and no cars. The dilapidated town seemed deserted. My sister was getting a little weepy, worried that I could not find the bus station, but I was the oldest and used to being responsible and I reassured her that we were going the right way. I knew my job was to find the bus station and I thought I could do it. After all, I had had the experience of walking the two miles to Junior High every day during the last year. It was a hot day; the bag was heavy; and I was anxious, too, because we were late and because the place seemed so empty.

I fully expected Aunt Tressa to be at the bus station when we arrived, but she wasn't! There were many bored people sitting around waiting for the next bus and all conversation stopped as they took a good look at the two hot, dirty, and bedraggled girls. This was a welcome diversion for them and they listened as I talked to the station manager. He said that our bus had come in a long time before and there had been a woman looking for two girls. How were we going to find Aunt Tressa? We didn't know her address! Then I remembered that she had written Grandma a letter verifying our plans. That letter might be in the bottom of the suitcase if I hadn't thrown it away when I packed.

I put the suitcase flat on the floor and knelt down to unbuckle the straps. When I released the clasp, the lid popped up and the contents burst forth. I had crammed in every memento, including my sister's plaster dogs, her feathered Kewpie dolls, my miniature loaves of bread. The audience seemed to be quite interested and amused as I dug through the clothes and junk to the bottom of the case. Luckily I found the letter and the return address! The manager said it was not far and gave me directions. I refastened the bag, picked it up in my arms, and we set out once again.

Aunt Tressa rented rooms in the upstairs of a widow's home. As soon as we knocked at one of the doors a strange woman opened it and started screaming, "Tressa, your girls are here! Tressa, your girls are here!"

We went up the stairs to the hot apartment where Aunt Tressa was very relieved to see us at last but obviously agitated because there was not much time. Still she insisted we eat a few bites of a sandwich and some milk while she quickly changed from her wrapper to her traveling dress and hat and grabbed her gloves, pocket-book, and the suitcase. The landlady ran to get her car and was waiting with the motor running when we dashed out the door.

In those days trains merely hesitated at most small towns, just long enough to throw off one mail sack and pick up another. If there were no passengers, they didn't stop. As we pulled up to the station we heard the train whistle. We jumped out of the car and ran down the platform as Aunt Tressa called to us, "I don't have time to buy the tickets. Just get on the train and I'll buy them from the conductor."

We climbed on the hissing train and it pulled away. The conductor wired ahead and asked the station agent to hold the Rockford train so we could make the connection in Chicago. Luckily we didn't have to change stations. It was my first train ride and I don't remember a thing about it, probably because I was so glad that we had made it in time and, as I listened to my aunt negotiate with the conductor, relieved to turn over the responsibility of the trip to her.

Months later, at a family gathering, I overheard my mother and aunts saying with customary exasperation, "You might know that Mom would want to do things her own way."

"Those Terrible Americans!"

In the summer of 1999 I visited Paris with my daughter Chris, my son-in-law Jay, and my sixteen year old granddaughter, Emma. We were having a great time visiting art museums and historical buildings, and traveling around that beautiful city, but Emma was a little homesick for her friends, so to cheer her up Chris promised to take her to the Paris Disneyland. This was the opportunity for Jay and me to go to the Musée de l'Armée in the Hôtel des Invalides. Jay has read extensively in history, particularly military history, and he had just finished *The First World War* by John Keegan. He tried to find a tour to its battlefield areas but none was available. I was interested because my father was in the U.S. Marines during World War I and fought in France in most of the important battles of 1918. I grew up with the ominous European news on the radio every night and my father's worry that there would be another world war. Also, my husband had been in the Army Air Corps during World War II and I could remember well the news and tensions of those years as well as the impact of the war on everyone's life in the US. I had visited the wonderful Imperial War Museum in London and was eager to see France's memorial to that momentous time.

We arrived at an impressive complex of buildings, including a majestic church with Napoleon's tomb and, over to one side, a veterans' hospital, still in use. We reached the army buildings by going down long halls and through colonnaded courtyards behind the church. The first rooms we entered contained colorful displays of uniforms from the campaigns of North Africa, showing both the French and the African uniforms. Then we found the beginning of the exhibit about Napoleon which was marvelously complete, taking up most of the rooms on the two floors. It even contained his saddled horse, preserved for posterity, and the tent he used, with folding table, chairs, desk, and cot. Because of my work in the wardrobe department of an historical museum in Rockford, Illinois, I was particularly interested in the uniforms, their fabrics, and how they had been preserved. Some showed signs of extensive wear and damage, but were carefully displayed to show them at their best. The hats looked very stiff and heavy in pictures, but they were of a relatively pliable felt, steamed to a very deep crown, with a brim all around that measured from eight to twelve inches in width. The soft brim was merely folded up in the front and the back, with no visible support—only the stiffness of the felt. I imagine that in the event of rain it was folded down, at least in the back—a very practical design. Jay was interested in the different campaigns and the weapons they used, and the detailed maps which helped him follow the explanations of the battles. We spent almost two hours going through room after room filled with displays commemorating Napoleon's triumphs.

In World War I, more than one thousand French cities and villages were destroyed and another twelve hundred had only half the buildings remaining. World War II was even more destructive to the northern half of France. Both wars devastated the French countryside and killed most of their young men, as well as causing millions of casualties of military personnel from many countries.

When we looked for the World War I exhibit we found only two or three rooms with a tank, field artillery, pistols, daggers, guns with bayonets, and several French officer and infantry uniforms. There were two British uniforms and one of an American doughboy, fully laden with field equipment. A table had a small model of the trenches, showing them only two lines deep and only the French side. (I recalled the huge British model showing both sides with the tangled No Man's Land in between, crossed by barbed wire and shell craters. Before seeing that I had thought of a trench as a straight line, and the intricate maze of open tunnels had shocked me.)

There were photos of the French generals and a few photos of the destruction of forests in some battle areas. A display of medals included the Croix de Guerre with oak leaf clusters like that which France had awarded my father. I was disappointed that there was no mention of the American Expeditionary Forces and the US Marines, but I kept telling myself that this exhibit was for the French people and the authorities and the people who designed the museum wanted them to feel good about their history. Jay, just completing Keegan's book, was also expecting a more complete display.

The World War II exhibit opened with mannequins of a French Air Force officer and an officer and sailor from the French Navy. (Their air force was destroyed by the German invasion and the fleet scuttled soon after.) No mention of the Maginot Line! Nothing about the Vichy government! I had read several books about the French underground and recognized several names of the resistance agents in a display of their photographs with a brief description of their backgrounds and what had happened to each. Most of them had been shot or tortured and imprisoned by the Nazis. Several portable short-wave radios were displayed, each one in a nondescript suitcase to fool the Germans. One was set up with the antennae, ready to transmit messages and there were also code books, messages, weapons, poison capsules, and other equipment smuggled in or dropped to them by parachute. Photographs showed the German army in Paris rounding up people for deportation to prisons or concentration camps.

Another room had one uniform each of the English and of the American infantry, and some photographs of destroyed towns and villages. There was the uniform of a paratrooper, and some leaflets which had been dropped by planes. Prominent was a giant map which covered the wall at the end of the room. It was of France with lines showing the invasion of the northern coast and dated lines showing the progress of the battle fronts. They started out about a week apart and then a longer time apart until they reached Paris. There was one label, "Allies," for the whole invasion. The lower part of the map had a wide red arrow, the base of which encompassed France's Mediterranean coast. It was labeled "US," and a pale, short blue arrow on either side was labeled "Free French." The solid red mark tapered up to a point, piercing into the heart of Belgium, blotting out the south and east of France. The red color and the solidity and boldness of the arrow seemed to mean a bloodbath of death and destruction. This map may well have been in the history text of our French AFS student. Suddenly I understood her reaction when the subject of World War II came up. "Those terrible Americans! They invaded Southern France! Our beautiful country!" When we tried to ask her about her father's or grandmother's memories of the War, she could just sputter, with great bitterness, "Those terrible Americans!" Later when I said to my husband that I could not remember any invasion of southern France, he explained that it had been planned as one of the many decoys to fool Hitler and draw German armies away from the north. The Allies did make a landing but they didn't battle their way north because there was no opposition to what became known as the "Champagne Campaign."

In a room at the exit of the exhibit there was a short film of scenes of the war. After scenes of the Germans occupying Paris, the movie showed tall, erect, somber French General de Gaulle striding through the streets of Paris, liberating the city and being swamped by mobs of cheering citizens waving flags, overjoyed to be free of the German invaders. Another scene showed him liberating another French city, then another, and another until, by the end of the film, all the large cities of the country had been liberated by General de Gaulle.

I was furious!

I came out of the building really steaming at what I considered a travesty of history. I know the Allies brought de Gaulle back from exile in the hopes that he could form a non-Communist government, but I was accustomed to seeing French citizens being liberated by tanks and soldiers from many countries.

I knew I had seen newsreels and photographs, heard radio news, and known many soldiers who had fought in World War II. Were these facts true or U.S. propaganda? I almost began to doubt my memories. When I was back home I recalled that Walter Mason had been in France in the US Army, so I asked him what he knew to be fact. He had been with the infantry which had fought to reach Paris, and he said that they were ordered to wait outside the city until de Gaulle was brought over from England to enter with the armies.

Two weeks later, I met my kindergarten friend and her husband at an airport when they came out to have lunch with me during the lay-over time I had. George had been a pilot in the Air Force during and after World War II and I wondered what he would think of my reaction at the museum in France. George told me that after the war he was assigned to pilot the US Army general who was going around France accepting and dedicating the land the US Air Corps was allowed to use for airfields. George also wrote the speeches for the American general, who instructed him never to mention the war, but to write about how grateful we were for being allowed to use this land, and how wonderful the French people were for allowing us this privilege. Because England and the US wanted to establish a non-Communist government in France and to build up the morale of the people as quickly as possible so the country could recover from the devastation of war, it seemed imperative to promote De Gaulle as a powerful leader in France's past and future. He was the only pre-war leader of the country who had escaped death or dishonor at the hands of the Germans.

What did I expect in a French museum? I expected them to show how many countries were involved before the wars could be brought to an end and how much destruction was caused. Couldn't they show how the French citizens suffered terror and privation at the hands of the Germans? I expected them to give more importance to the years of peril when France's liberation and the defeat of Germany's military menace became the focus of much of the western world.

They must look upon their defeat by the Germans and subsequent occupation as so humiliating that they want their citizens to completely forget about it. I must remember that when I see or hear stories of history, I must consider *who* is telling them and *when* he is telling them.

JAY CARP

When I was born in Boston, Massachusetts, on December 24, 1927, I was not aware of the two handicaps that I had been given. The scope of my disadvantages only became evident when I was continually told that I had been born a day too early in a very backward part of the country. Nevertheless, I did grow up in Greater Boston and, until I graduated from high school and was drafted into the army, I never left New England. I had what I thought was an ordinary childhood with some happy and some sad experiences. Because I was uncomfortable with the sad experiences, I pretty much locked out my childhood. In the last few years, though, I have begun to think about the past.

While I was in the army I got rheumatic fever and was bedridden for seven months. While I was recovering I learned that I could go to college under the GI bill. After I was discharged, I was accepted at the University of Michigan and came to Ann Arbor in 1948.

I stayed in the Ann Arbor-Detroit area for ten years. During that time, I got an education; I got engaged and disengaged; I got a job; I got married to Virginia; and I begot a family. Two of my three daughters were born at University of Michigan Women's Hospital.

We ended up in Boston, of all places, where I took a job with Sylvania Electronic Company which was bought out by General Telephone and Electronics (GTE) just after I was hired. For over thirty years I worked for GTE as an engineer and as a manager on several military electronic systems. Most of my career during the last twenty years was spent on the Minuteman Missile system. During this time, I made frequent trips all over the continental United States, troubleshooting problems and attending technical meetings.

In 1991 Virginia unexpectedly died while visiting my daughter Julie. After the death of my partner of 37 years, I lost interest in my work and asked to be laid off. GTE complied and I headed for retirement to the home that Virginia and I had purchased in California while I was the GTE site manager at Vandenberg Air Force Base. On the way to California, I stopped to see a friend in Ann Arbor. That weekend, I met the woman that I had been engaged to forty years before, and I never got to retire in California. My plans just burnt up and shriveled away in the emotions that rekindled and engulfed Ruth and me.

Ruth and I married in 1993 and we had the sweetness of four years together before she died of breast cancer in 1997. And that takes me up to the present.

Honk If You Love Jesus!

In 1972 I was living by myself in Silver Spring Maryland when spring arrived. It was a welcome change to the cold, raw, damp, days of winter. The dirty snows of winter begin to melt slowly as the warmer days shyly make their appearance. At first, the sun lingers a little longer each day. The cold changes to cool, and winter coats, as they become unnecessary, begin to feel hot and bulky. The air becomes moist and perfumed with the smell of vegetation coming alive after being dormant. The birds begin to put heart and gusto into their calls. The spring flowers, jonquils, iris, lilies of the valley, and bluebells, stand up and proudly display their brilliant reds, yellows, blues, and whites. Spring in Maryland brings the promise of new life in every breath you take.

One of these rare and precious days occurred on a Saturday in early April. It was on a weekend that I was not driving to Massachusetts to see my family, so I had almost nothing to do. I decided that I would enjoy the day and revel in being alive. I left my room very early in the morning and drove on back roads and country roads as slowly as I could. I stopped and watched brooks running, horses gamboling, and a farmer chopping down a tree. It felt good to breathe the hint of hope and happiness that early spring brought.

And I needed a hint of hope and happiness. Two years earlier, I had been laid off by GTE (General Telephone and Electronics). At the time, that was neither unique nor hard to do; thousands of engineers were out of work in the New England area. What was hard to do was to find a job. There were men with doctor's degrees driving cabs in downtown Boston; the electronic sector of the economy was in bad shape.

My layoff, after thirteen years with the company, took me totally by surprise, but there was absolutely nothing I could do about it. I needed money as I had three young daughters, a wife, a mortgage, two automobiles, and a lot of debts. Unemployment compensation did not begin to cover my expenses; I needed to work as many jobs as I could for the money. My motto became, "Anything for income."

The first week of my layoff, I went to the Foxboro Town hall and filled out an application for the highway department. The highway department supervisor attended the same church my family went to, and I knew that he was always hiring. His crew was primarily made up of high school dropouts, marginal alcoholics, men with minor criminal records, and underachievers. He had a high rate of turnover. So, I was not surprised when I was hired; after all, compared to his other applicants, what could he lose? He knew that, for however long I worked for him, he would have someone who was dependable. He made a dump truck available to me so I could learn to drive it, and I practiced for hours. When I had learned the necessary skills, I passed the Massachusetts driving test and was promoted to truck driver.

After about a year with the highway department, Vitro Laboratories in Silver Spring, Maryland, contacted me. They worked for the U.S. Navy testing submarine Intercontinental Ballistic Missiles (ICBM's). Vitro offered me a job as a test engineer. I parked my dump truck, took a hot shower, and returned to the missile world.

Although I was thankful to get this job, it posed a terrible dilemma for my family and me. At the time I accepted their offer, Vitro offered to relocate my family to the Silver Spring area. After discussions with Virginia, we decided to delay moving the family. My oldest daughter was starting her senior year in high school and Virginia was very reluctant to leave her home and friends. So, I asked for, and Vitro agreed, to postpone my relocation package for a year.

When I arrived at Silver Spring that late spring, I rented a room in a house that was near Vitro Labs. For the first three months I would drive four hundred miles to Foxboro every Friday night, and four hundred miles back to Silver Spring every Sunday night. After that, for the next eight months, I drove home every second or third weekend. By then, I was tired, the car was tired, and the gas embargo made it hell getting gasoline.

To make matters worse, the personnel office at Vitro wrote me a letter saying that, if I had not relocated my family and furniture within the year that we had agreed to, Vitro had no responsibility to pay any expenses. I couldn't argue, but it did mean that we were facing a real deadline. We knew that we would have to move, but Virginia really wanted to stay in Foxboro. We were as frozen as the winter weather, looking for a thaw, but fearful of what the thaw would bring. We were uneasy and unhappy. And yet, in the midst of our slogging through our problems, changes were on the way. We did not sense them, but they would profoundly affect us. And the first of these was the loosening of the cold, raw winter weather and the sweet arrival of spring.

By mid morning I was lucky enough to be lost on a small, winding road that had no traffic and didn't seem to go anywhere. As I rounded a bend, I saw a car ahead of me, going in the same direction, but moving more slowly than my car. As I got closer I could see that the car was an old station wagon that had its rear window down. The bottom panels were rusted out and the entire car was caked with dirt and grime.

When I got about thirty feet from the car, a boy and girl suddenly appeared in the back compartment facing in my direction. The boy was about six years old and the girl was about five. They were both tow heads; the girl had her hair braided, and the two braids hung in front of her. The boy had long hair clumped in spikes. Judging by their looks and coloring, they were probably brother and sister.

I could see them talking and, finally, the boy raised his hand and gave me a small wave. I smiled, put my hand out of the window, and waved back. Immediately, he grinned, and his second wave was much larger and more vigorous than his first. When I responded to that one, he really began to wave. His sister, who had been watching us without moving, joined in and began to wave. Within a minute or two, both of them were laughing, waving, and cheering.

When my car got about fifteen feet from their car, I noticed two legible bumper stickers in the back. One had a picture of the stars and bars, the Confederate flag. The other had the printed motto, "Honk if you love Jesus." Since I figured that was well within the spirit of the game that we three children were playing, I gave the horn three gentle, quick taps. The horn beeped no longer than a hemidemisemiquaver, a 64th note.

I saw the woman driver's blond head move to look out first her rear view mirror and then her side mirror. She slowed her car even more and lowered her driver's side window. She put her left arm straight out of the window, and then she bent her arm at the elbow, straight up in the air. Slowly and distinctly, three separate times, she gave me the finger. After that, she stepped on the accelerator with such force that the two children rolled on the floor, and she roared off.

I laughed so hard that I had to pull over to the side of the road so as not to lose control of my car. From that day to this, I never use my automobile horn to express any religious views whatsoever.

Oddly enough, it was the Monday following this incident that I got a call from GTE asking what it would take for them to be able to rehire me.

❧

Lambeau Has His Ups and Downs

During the thirty-five years I have known Edward Lambeau, he has often left me shaking my head, either in total wonder or in complete dismay. Yet, for the first two or three months after I met him, I paid hardly any attention to him. We talked almost daily, but they were brief conversations and only dealt with specific details of our jobs. Ed was working the counter in our stock room and he would supply me with whatever equipment I needed. I was busy and he seemed busy, so our talks were usually short and impersonal; Ed seemed aloof.

When I returned to Massachusetts, after fifteen months in North Dakota, I was assigned to Sylvania's Minuteman test beds as Test Supervisor. It was at the main test bed where I met Ed Lambeau. Whenever test equipment was required, I would go to the stock room and make sure the equipment was available. The stockroom was thirty feet long by forty feet wide, and it contained row after row of twelve-foot high shelves containing thousands of items, each one catalogued and specifically located.

The person I dealt with was a red headed man who introduced himself as "Ed." After a couple of months Ed said to me, "I'm a little busy. From now on, reach inside, unlatch the door, and come in and get what you need. Just let me know what you are taking. You know what you want, so why should I wait on you?"

That is how I happened to be in the room, about two weeks later, when the phone rang and Ed answered it. I was close enough to hear a man's voice on the other end, but I couldn't hear what he was saying. The tone was short and angry. Ed listened for almost a minute and then he replied just as angrily, "No, damn it. I said no and I damn well mean no."

My first thought was that this was a personal phone call and that I should not eavesdrop, so I started to leave the stockroom. Then Ed said very slowly, "Screw the General." I stopped immediately. Now I was all ears; this was not a personal call.

"I said, 'Screw the General,' he continued. "Until SAC tries what I suggested, I am not going out to look at this problem again. I have been out to that site twice. Going out there once more won't change my mind. I don't have to go again to know what the problem is."

Later, I found out that the phone call was from The Strategic Air Command (SAC) headquarters in Omaha, Nebraska. The Air Force was having a problem with our equipment in Montana. When they had asked Sylvania for help, Lambeau had been dispatched. He investigated the problem, and, based on his suggestion, Sylvania made a formal recommendation to fix it. The Air Force, disagreeing with the recommendation, had ignored the advice. Now, when the Air Force asked him to return and look at the problem again, Ed eloquently declined the invitation. After I heard the story behind the phone conversation, I decided I had to find out more about this "stock clerk" who could give a general such clear, specific instructions. I enjoy people who like to tweak the system.

Ed Lambeau was not a stock clerk. He was an engineer from our Needham plant who had helped design our equipment; he was hanging around the stockroom in Waltham because he was feuding with his boss and needed a place to stay. His office in Needham was so cluttered with junk that no one, including Ed, could get into it. It looked so disgraceful that his boss told him to either clean it up or keep the door shut. He just took his largest tank of goldfish out of his office and moved up to Waltham.

Ed was unique. When he was a senior in high school, he declined a total scholarship to M. I. T. to attend a smaller engineering school in Boston called Northeastern. He turned M. I. T. down because they stressed theory and discouraged their students from touching equipment. Northeastern was different; it was a co-operative engineering school that encouraged its students to work with equipment.

Theory came so easily to him that he also wanted hands on experience. Ed loved hands on; he could not keep away from equipment whether it was electrical, electronic, or mechanical. He just had to assemble or disassemble everything he saw. At lunchtime, he would be out in the parking lot, in coveralls, working on secretaries' cars. He would time the engines, repair the radios, or fix the air conditioning. Many times I have seen someone from Sylvania pull him from under the hood of a car to explain a missile problem to a visiting Air Force officer or an engineer from an aerospace company. They would stare in puzzled amazement, as he would explain everything completely to their satisfaction and then go back to working on the car.

He had almost total recall when it came to blueprints or schematics. The division of Sylvania that made televisions and radios would call him when one of their dealers had a problem that they could not fix. He would ask the model number and the year of manufacture. He would then ask what the problem was and what they had done to troubleshoot. After listening, he would suggest, from memory, replacing a particular component, such as a transistor, a diode, a capacitor, a resistor, or a thermistor. He would give the component he was referring to the specific number it had on the schematic. Most of the time, that would solve the problem.

He became interested in photography and began taking still life pictures of scenery and flowers. He won so many prizes that the walls in the Needham corridors were covered with his prize winning pictures. About this time he earned a Master's Degree in programming by attending night school.

Ed Lambeau was a cornucopia of technical intelligence and ability. That was his positive side. His negative side could be equally impressive. For example, if he lost interest in something, he would walk away from it. That was part of the reason that his office looked like an abandoned junkyard. His office was stacked with toasters, televisions, blenders, radios, stereos—items that he had promised his fellow workers he would repair. If he didn't fix it in a few days, it could sit for a year. He was the same way in his own home. A heavy television antenna sat on the dining room table and prevented his family from eating there for almost two years. He left a motorcycle he was repairing in the middle of the kitchen for almost six months. He finally moved it when his wife, Tracey, threatened to slash the tires.

Ed was thrifty and frugal to the point of being cheap. He was obsessed with saving money. Many times I would be driving with him in a car and he would ask me to stop. He would get out and return a few minutes later carrying some cans and bottles to recycle for five cents apiece. I didn't mind, but his bosses would feel a little uncomfortable when one of their lead engineers would show up late for a meeting carrying a bag full of clanking empty cans and bottles.

Ed was very sloppy about paper work. Even though he was a friend of mine I denied him access into any of our test sites unless I gave him permission. He was allowed in only after he had an engineer and a quality control person to accompany him. Their job was to write down everything that he did while he was on site. Friendship or not, no one was allowed to deconfigure Air Force equipment. I slowed him down because that equipment had to be kept exactly in the same configuration as the real missile sites in North Dakota and Montana.

Ed's guilelessness drove his bosses crazy. He would do things on the spur of the moment without thinking of the consequences. For example, we were out at a meeting at Hill Air Force Base and we went into a fancy restaurant to eat dinner. Near the end of the meal, while he was still at the table, Ed took a citizen's band radio out of his pocket and started to talk to any trucker he could contact. His bosses squirmed and couldn't leave the restaurant fast enough. Socially, they avoided him as much as they could and referred to him as an idiot savant.

Luckily for him, his wife filled in some of his social gaps. Tracey Lambeau was also, in her own special way, an outstanding person. She had been in an automobile accident when she was young, and as a result, she had to have plastic surgery done on her face and she had a glass eye. That accident did not lessen her zest for life. Her formal education had initially stopped when she graduated from high school. She started to work as a nurse's aide, and, by going to night school, she became a registered nurse. She completed her education while raising a family of seven children; eight if you count Ed.

My favorite story about Ed concerns his buying a station wagon that Sylvania traded in on a new one. It had been used, and abused, by everyone at the test bed for four years and it was in fairly bad condition. That did not bother Ed; he could fix it up. He wanted it for Tracey because it had a tailgate that opened either to one side or from the top down. Tracey could use it to haul groceries and it was cheap. Ed followed the sale of the station wagon closely. He found out which automobile agency was supplying the new station wagon and how much trade-in was allowed on the old one. The day the test bed got the new station wagon was the day that Ed bought the old one. He paid fifty dollars above the trade in value and got it in an "as is" condition. Tracey loved it. She could go shopping, buy a week's worth of groceries for her family, and load it by opening the rear door either way, quickly and easily. She enjoyed shopping when she had that big station wagon.

One day, the rear window got stuck one third of the way down. With the window stuck partially closed, the tailgate would not open in either direction. Grocery shopping became a nightmare for Tracey. She would have to open the side doors, lift the grocery bags over the rear seat, and put them on the floor in the rear compartment. When she got home, she had to retrieve the groceries the same way. The rear window was not down far enough for her to put her groceries through it, but it was down far enough to let in rain and snow. Sometimes, her grocery bags would get wet and split when she unloaded them. Then she would have to lean over the seat and individually retrieve the grocery items from the rear compartment.

Tracey complained about the window to Ed. As months went by, and he did nothing, her complaints got louder and more bitter. Ed did nothing to fix the window, but he always promised to get to it shortly. It was almost a year before Tracey got completely fed up and figured out a way to get his attention.

One morning Ed got out of bed to get ready to go to work. In the bathroom was a yellow post'em stuck on the medicine cabinet mirror. Written on it was a very terse message.

"If that rear window does not go up and down, I do not go up and down."

Edward Lambeau arrived late for work that day because he spent the morning making sure that the window went up and down. What I do not know is whether Tracey reciprocated.

Lost in the L. A. Airport

Vandenberg Air Force Base, in California, is an oasis of beauty. It has almost forty miles of coastline left in its pristine state. Every time I went there, I would drive along the almost deserted coastal roads and ocean gaze. Occasionally, I would see herds of white tailed deer and wild boars amidst the ground cover of beautiful native flowers. The weather is delightful. Usually the morning fog burns off by 10 A.M., leaving the sun shining in a cloudless blue sky. The sunlight warms your skin, your bones, your heart, and your soul. The temperature rarely goes above 85 in the daytime and under 60 at night. Since I had spent 15 months in North Dakota and almost a year in Thule, Greenland, I always looked forward to visiting Vandenberg. It was my payback. This trip, though, was a little different from my other visits. I had been on the road for three weeks before I got there and I had a strong yen to go home. This had been a hard trip and I wanted it ended. Everything went smoothly that week, and on Thursday the meeting at Vandenberg concluded.

Friday morning I went to the Santa Maria airport and boarded a two engine propeller airplane, a puddle jumper, to fly to Los Angeles. I checked my luggage, except for a small leather briefcase, through to my final destination, Boston. When the puddle jumper landed at Los Angeles I started to walk from that terminal to the United Airlines terminal to board the plane that would fly me home. The schedule originally listed the departure of the Boston plane as one hour and fifteen minutes after the puddle jumper landed, but there had been a forty five minute delay in Santa Barbara, so I had only a half hour between flights. That would give me enough time to get to the United terminal, but it was tighter timing than I liked.

As I was walking down a long corridor I noticed the crowd ahead of me moving around something, or somebody, like a river flowing around an island. When I got closer, I could see that it was not a something; it was a some one who was moving very slowly. And when I got directly behind this person I had to stare because I couldn't quite believe what I was seeing. A big, black woman was inching her way along the corridor. She was tall, broad shouldered, and had heavy hips and thighs; more muscular than fat, but very chunky. She was wearing a blue sleeveless shirt that was soaked with perspiration. In her left hand she carried her purse and an overnight bag; in her right hand was a large valise and a draw string for a duffel bag which was lying on the floor. She would slowly take a step with her left foot, slowly take a step with her right foot, and then she would pull the duffel bag forward. Left foot, right foot, pull; left foot, right foot, pull. It was painful just to watch her. With every step she kept repeating, "Oh, sweet Jesus, please come and help me, Oh sweet Jesus, please come and help me. Oh, sweet Jesus, please come and help me."

I walked even faster as I started by her because I did not want to get involved. I might have made it, but I glanced at her face. Tears were streaming from her eyes. I kept on going. Thirty feet in front of her I said, "Oh shit," and stopped. I must have spoken out loud because five or six people looked at me. I didn't care; I was furious.

I was not angry with this woman. Who could be mad at anyone in such misery? I was not angry because I was going to miss my plane; I knew that would happen the moment I stopped. I was angry because I had tried to walk away from someone who needed help. Well, I was going to make amends.

Facing towards her, I waited until she came up to where I was standing. When she reached me, she stopped and said quietly, "I has got to go the bathroom."

"Beautiful," I thought. "What a great way to start a friendship." Looking up and down the corridor, I saw rest room signs just ahead of us. I pointed them out to her and she said, "Thank you, oh, thank you." She left her luggage at my feet and she went, very quickly, to the ladies' room. While she was in there, I moved her luggage closer to the wall, out of the traffic flow, so we could talk.

When she returned, she asked, "Mister, would you please help me find my airplane? I wants to get out of here and back to my Momma in Louisiana." She was much younger than I had first thought; she was in her early twenties at most. Her name was Cleona. Her Delta Airline ticket was from Los Angeles to Baton Rouge, Louisiana, and her plane was scheduled to depart in seven minutes. I did not even bother to tell her that the plane would be departing without her.

I said, "Come on, Cleona, I'll get you to the Delta ticket counter." I picked up her valise and duffel bag; she carried her purse and her overnight bag. We started walking; we had quite a way to go. Cleona thanked me, and as we walked, she told me how she came to be in Los Angeles.

She lived in a small town called Catahoula, and since her graduation from high school she had not been able to find a steady job. She wanted to be a bookkeeper or an accountant, not a counter clerk at McDonald's or Arbie's. So, her mother and father and six brothers and sisters saved their money and bought her a ticket to Los Angeles. She was going to live with her aunt while she looked for a job.

Leaving Catahoula was a mistake and coming to Los Angeles was a disaster. Cleona was homesick for her family and she did not like Los Angeles. She was going to go back to her mother and father and stay in Catahoula and find a job even if she had to drive to New Iberia. She finished her narrative as we arrived at the Delta terminal.

We stood in line until it was her turn to show her ticket. The ticket agent was bald, pudgy, and he wore half glasses, which he peered over to look at Cleona. He glanced at the ticket and said, "Why, this flight has departed. Do you want to wait and be booked on tomorrow's flight?" He did not seem particularly concerned.

I told him, "No, she can't wait. She needs to get to Baton Rouge as quickly as she can."

He looked over his glasses at me and then he began typing on his computer keyboard. "Oh, here it is," he said after a while. "We can get her on a plane in three hours for Chicago. She will have a five hour delay at O'Hare airport and then she can catch a plane for Baton Rouge."

"Wait a minute," I said. "She is going to fly to Chicago, wait for five hours, and then fly to Baton Rouge? A detour of half a continent? Isn't there any other way of getting her there?" I was specifically thinking that Delta might transfer her to another airline.

Now, he really stared at me. He asked, "Sir, what is your interest in the passenger?"

For the second time that day, I got angry. I leaned forward and said slowly, "I do not like that question, I do not like that insinuation, and I do not like your attitude. Please call your supervisor."

A tall thin man, who was standing behind the counter, heard our conversation and he came over to the ticket agent. "Paul, is there a problem here?" Paul peeked over his glasses and cocked his head at me.

"Are you the counter supervisor?" I asked.

"Yes," he replied. My name is John Wesley. What can I do to help you?"

Pointing to Cleona I said, "This young lady missed her plane to Baton Rouge. Your agent suggested a flight to Chicago, a five-hour layover, and then a flight to Baton Rouge. That's a long dogleg to travel. Isn't there a more direct route with less waiting, either with Delta or another airline?"

John Wesley looked first at me and then at Cleona. It was a professional look without any malice. "That does seem like a long way for her to get home. Let me look."

He kept punching and punching at the keyboard. After a few minutes he said, "Paul was right. Unless she takes tomorrow's flight, Delta has no other way to connect her for the same fare except through Chicago. And that is ridiculous. Rather than rescheduling her on another airline, I will upgrade her ticket, at no cost to her, to first class through Dallas-Ft. Worth. She will have a two-hour delay and then she will fly directly to Baton Rouge. Will that be satisfactory?"

"Mr. Wesley, that is more than satisfactory," I said. "That is a very decent gesture. I do not believe she will understand what you are doing, but I do and I appreciate it. I thank you."

He took her old ticket, issued her a new one, and tagged her luggage. Cleona was ready to return to Catahoula.

I walked her to the gate; I was taking no chances on her getting lost again. "Cleona," I said, "You have to call your family, tell them that you missed your plane, and give them the information on your new flights."

"Mister Jay," she said, "I am going to call them and tell them how you and the Lord Jesus helped me."

We found a pay phone and she placed a long distance, reversed charges, call to her family. She explained her misadventures to her mother and, after much repetition, gave her the new flight numbers and arrival times. Before I left her to straighten out my own travel plans, I happened to think of something else.

"Cleona, when is the last time you ate?"

"Why I had breakfast at six o'clock this morning, Mr. Jay." It was now four in the afternoon and her plane did not leave for another three hours.

I handed her a ten dollar bill and said, "Listen, Cleona, I am going to leave now because I want to go home too. You will be all right. You must be hungry. Get yourself something to eat."

"Oh lordy, I surely am Mr. Jay. If you ever get to Catahoula you look us up. My family will be wanting to thank you."

I replied, "If I ever get to Catahoula I will, Cleona. In the meantime be careful and ask directions only from people wearing Delta Airlines uniforms." We shook hands and I left.

When I got to the United Airlines terminal, I found that the only plane to Boston was a "red eye", which reached Logan Airport at six A.M. on Saturday morning. Even though I had a seven-hour layover, I was feeling good. I had helped someone who had needed help. I did, however, think it was ironic that the person who was responsible for my missing my plane was flying first class while I was stuck on an all night flight in cattle class. Who says there is such a thing as justice?

ASHO CRAINE

My life has been both blessed and burdened by a social conscience fostered by liberal parents. I was born in 1915 in Brooklyn N.Y. where my lawyer father worked for various political reforms. In 1933 he was elected borough president of Brooklyn with Mayor Fiorello LaGuardia and died while still in office in 1940. My mother, a woman of many enthusiasms, was an early supporter and friend of Margaret Sanger. Her spontaneity and adventurous spirit added zest to our lives, but when her unpredictable demands led to clashes I would turn to my father for consolation. He helped me gain perspective and always elevated my self-respect. I adored him.

Being in the first class at Bennington College was an exhilarating experience. Following graduation in 1936 my most interesting work was with a consumer-farmer milk cooperative. This led to a job in the Department of Agriculture in Washington. There I met my future husband, Lyle Craine, who was working in the Bureau of the Budget. Within seven months we were married, in March 1942. He spent the war years at the War Production Board while I started raising our children: two sons followed by a daughter.

After the war Lyle headed a small staff in the Secretary of Interior's office coordinating its programs in several major river basins. When his job was abolished by the Eisenhower Administration we came to the University of Michigan where he obtained. a Ph.D. and taught in the School of Natural Resources. Because family life was fulfilling and I had financial security, I lacked the incentive to pursue a career. Instead I became active in the League of Women Voters and more recently with the Gray Panthers. I also did volunteer tutoring and once ran for school board. Lyle and I never regretted our move to lively Ann Arbor where we enjoyed forty years together.

Childhood Summers on Duck Island, 1922–1932

The acquisition of Duck Island was a stroke of good luck that fulfilled my parents' dream of owning their own place in the area where they had rented for a dozen summers. For the four of us children, it was an idyllic place for exploration and adventure. Lying directly across Northport Bay from the Centerport house, Duck Island is not really an island, but rather an offshoot of Asharoken Beach connected by a half-mile of causeway. The causeway and Duck Island itself gracefully extend the curve of the beach on the bay side. On the other side lies Duck Island Harbor formed by Eaton's Neck which projects northward into Long Island Sound. The island, like the causeway a half mile long, has wooded bluffs at either end and a low, narrow center section. All told it covers forty-four acres.

One day in the spring of 1922 Henry Ingraham, who had a beach house on Asharoken, phoned my parents to tell them that Duck Island had just been put on the market at a bargain price. Knowing that his sister and brother-in-law, Edith and Miner Crary, who were also my mother's brother and sister-in-law, were looking for a summer place, he saw Duck Island as ideal for our two families. Mother and Dad quickly conferred with Uncle Miner and Aunt Edith who agreed to the purchase. Together our two families, the Crarys and the Ingersolls, set up the Duck Island Corporation to own and maintain the entire property. Then we bought from the corporation the existing house at the near end of the island and the Crarys bought the undeveloped bluff at the far end. We soon found that our well had turned brackish. It had been dug six hundred feet deep back in 1890, but eventually sea water had seeped in. We managed to dig three shallow wells which lasted until we got town water in 1929, although in dry spells we had to resort to using rainwater from the cistern to flush the toilets. Water proved to be a more difficult problem for Uncle Miner than for us. After all attempts to reach fresh water at their end of the island failed, the Crarys had to wait for the town hook-up before they could start building.

Until they did, we had the freedom to enjoy their unspoiled woods. A steep narrow path led up to the point, the destination of our walks and pony rides. There we came out onto a small clearing and a wide view of Northport and Huntington Bays. Below us an old seawall, topped with a layer of red sandstone, circled the point. It was fun to walk along it when the tide was high and came half way up the wall. In a heavy wind the waves would dash spray so high we could see it from our house. That far end of the island seemed much larger and steeper before the house, garage, stables and graded driveway took up much of the space. There was more extensive marsh too before the Crarys dredged out the tidal pond to form their garden and ball field.

In those days Duck Island was, in proportion to my size, a vast territory inviting exploration. When we moved there in the summer of 1923, I was eight and Jerry was twelve. He was the instigator of adventures, and I his happy follower. Four-and-a-half-year-old Raymond and three-year-old Marion tagged along when we let them. Sometimes Jerry led me into situations that were scary. For instance there was the wild ride down the gutter. At the time we moved to Duck Island, a new concrete gutter had been made beside the road which went up the hill from the beach. It was about three feet wide and gently curved. That gleaming white path cried out for travel, but what could we use for a vehicle? The only thing available was the younger children's kiddy car. Jerry found he could sit on it with his legs out straight in front of him. He had me give him a push, and off he went. After one or two spills he mastered the technique and made it safely to the bottom of the hill.

Then it was my turn. Jerry instructed me not to over steer and to be sure to keep my feet up so they would not trip me. Fearful that I would let my legs sag, I held my whole body tensely rigid. He gave me a little push. Sure enough, I found myself going too far to one side and I over corrected by steering too far the other way. The zigzags widened as the momentum increased. I was totally out of control. Before I knew it I crashed. In spite of scrapes and bruises I was thankful to be off that runaway kiddy car.

Another risky activity was melting lead. Of course we knew we needed to be very careful because it was extremely hot and could cause a severe burn. However, we were innocently unaware of the dangers of lead poisoning. What the lead was doing there near the garage, I don't know, nor what sort of fire Jerry used. He handled the whole operation, while I was just an observer. As the dull lead came to a boil it turned bright and shiny like the quicksilver we used to catch in a glass jar whenever a thermometer broke. We knew mercury was poisonous and were careful not to touch it. Jerry used to sing a cautionary song on that subject to the tune of "The Last Rose of Summer."

Little Johnny had a mirror, and he chewed the back all off,
Thinking in his childish terror it would cure the whooping cough.
Some days later Johnny's mother, sobbing, said to Mrs. Brown,
'Twas a chilly day for Johnny when the mercury went down.

Once we had melted the lead, we looked for small containers to serve as molds. Seashells were good for this purpose, especially scallop shells. Sad to say, when the molten lead cooled it became dull again. I'm sure some adult soon put a stop to our enterprise, but not before we made several scallop shell paperweights. Mother kept one of these for years.

All this reminds me of how much fun we used to have catching scallops in the early days. Unlike the more prevalent mussels, clams, and oysters which stay on the bottom, scallops swim. Their two symmetrical, fan-shaped shells are hinged at the base and are connected in the center by a strong muscle. This wedged-shaped muscle is the part we eat. It enables the scallop to swim by rapidly snapping its shells together. The eyes are a row of many brightly colored dots in the fringe of soft tissue. Scallops fed on eel grass which grew low on the bottom of protected waters like Duck Island Harbor. Our search for them was near the narrow section of the island across the road from our dock and bathing beach. At about half tide we would wade in with our buckets and butterfly nets. If we were lucky we would come across a bunch of scallops. They would swim around our legs so fast that we had to act quickly before they got away. We would reach down and pick them up with our hands or scoop them up with our nets. Come to think of it, their fluttery motion is something like that of butterflies, only they don't open up as wide.

Jerry was our expert cleaner of scallops. He would pry open the shell with his knife, slice off the muscle close to the shell on one side, scrape the innards away, and then slice the scallop off the other shell. He could do this in record time as documented in one of our first home movies. Those small, delicate scallops, sauteed and served with bacon, were delicious. Unfortunately, the eel grass disappeared from the bays and harbors of western Long Island in the early thirties, and the scallops with it. There still were plenty of clams, though, both soft shell for steaming and hard shell for chowder, as well as mussels and oysters.

In calm weather when the tide was halfway out the clammers would appear on the bay, several right off our shore. Each clammer stood alone in his small rowboat working a pair of long-handled rakes. These had curved tines which fitted together to make a basket. When he had raked together a load, the clammer would lift it out of the water and dump it in his boat. These were hard shell clams. Now-a-days the clammers use bright-colored tarpaulins for sails and drag a basket along the bottom. Oyster beds were marked by stakes further out in the water. They were leased from the county and seeded by an oyster company whose motorboats would harvest them at the proper time. The oysters are gone, but we can still dig for soft shell clams at low tide right on our own beach and gather mussels off the rocks at the Crary's point.

Walks along the beaches presented a fascinating variety of shells. I was particularly fond of some small, translucent, yellow and gold ones. Most were shaped like little bowls, but some were simply flat disks which we called toenails. We called another sturdier little shell a boat, because it had a shelf at one end like a seat. We found these, along with various snail, clam, oyster, mussel, and scallop shells, on the beach in front of our house. The Sound beach, whose finer sand made it seem like an ocean shore, gave us special treasures. The most beautiful was the whelk. It is like a conch with a tapered stem. Dried whelk egg cases made fine rattles. They were coils of paper-thin disks with tiny baby whelk shells inside each one. Egg cases of the skate, black rectangles with long spikes at each corner, were aptly named devil's purses. Then there were razor clam shells and dried starfish.

Back on the bay side, in the tangle of brown bladder kelp which marked the high tide line, we often found horseshoe crab shells. The top is like an inverted shallow bowl and hinged to it is a tapered section ending in a long spike of a tail. The shells come in all sizes since the crab discards them as it grows. Naturally I preferred the delicate little ones. Sometimes we found dead horseshoe crabs, unattractive as they stank. My visiting friends were thoroughly repulsed by the dead ones and terrified of the live ones. The latter are rather startling when they appear as a dark shadow sliding along the bottom, but they won't hurt you because their claws are underneath. Jerry would even pick one up by the tail, placing it upside down on the beach so we could watch how it used its tail to right itself. It would stick its tail in the sand, arch its back, rotate sideways and flip over.

While the ugly horseshoe crabs looked threatening but were harmless, the beautiful pink umbrella jelly fish trailed mean stinging tentacles. Painful experience quickly taught us to avoid them, but we could play with a colorless variety which floated like an elongated ball with faint white streaks. These glowed with phosphorescence on August nights. When we scooped one out of the water it collapsed into a slimy glob. The same was true of the fragile forms of seaweed such as green sea lettuce and several branching types in shades of red. A neighbor, Cora Carter, used these to decorate stationery and greeting cards. She showed us the technique. First you soak the seaweed in fresh water overnight. Then you arrange a few pieces in a shallow dish of clear water. The trick was to slip a card under them, and then carefully lift it out without letting the seaweed slide off. As the card dried the seaweed would meld into it, but my clumpy creations never achieved Mrs. Carter's artistry.

We tried fishing off the float at the end of the dock. Once Jerry had been pulling in several flounders, when much to my surprise I found one on my line. At dinner that evening I proudly ate my first fish, but it must have been my last as I can't remember ever having caught another. My brother Ray reminds me how the blow fish would puff themselves up with water to look fierce when we frightened them. We would herd them toward the shore where they would become stranded on the beach, collapsing as they spluttered out the water. He also tells of Mr. Steele, our caretaker, skinning eels. He would hammer a nail through the eel's head to the side of the barn, make a cut in the skin just below the head, and then, using a piece of sandpaper to grasp the slippery skin, he would pull the skin down like rolling off a silk stocking. I'm sure I avoided that scene.

The most unusual marine creature we ever encountered at Duck Island appeared soon after we moved there. One day the collie who belonged to Mr. Steele came limping up to the house with a bleeding leg. We wondered how he had been wounded. A few hours later we saw a strange lump, like a large stone, slowly moving across the front lawn. It was a huge turtle nearly two feet long. It stood high on sturdy legs, not flippers like a true sea turtle, and it had a domed back. Nevertheless, we presumed that it was a sea turtle, rather than a land tortoise, and that it had bitten the dog and followed the trail up to the house. When we saw how easily it snapped a stick in two, we kept a respectful distance from its powerful jaws. We kept him in the fish pond by the dining room porch for a few days. Then he disappeared. I would like to think it was returned to the water, but suspect that Mr. Steele may have cooked it up for soup.

When we moved to Duck Island of course Poppy, our speckled Indian pony, came with us. She had a paddock along the side of the road between the end of the garden and where the tennis court was eventually built, at which time a new paddock was fenced off behind the garage and stable. Poppy was strong-willed and clever. For instance, she soon found that a certain apple tree had a low, horizontal limb just high enough for her to go under. Whenever anyone except Jerry rode her, she would make a bee line for that tree and dash under the limb, effectively pushing her rider off on to the ground. After a few tumbles I learned that if I paid close attention and used all my strength on the reins, I could keep her away from that trap. Visitors, even though forewarned, usually got dumped.

For a while we had a second Indian pony, named Marble Cake, because of his large, brown and white patches. He *was* more docile, but slow and reluctant. When Jerry became too big for ponies, we traded Marble Cake for a horse. Woody was a high-spirited bay with a silver mane and a silver tail. We were told he had played polo in his younger days. He was a challenge, even for Jerry, and eventually for me. At some point I too outgrew Poppy, so we sold her, to a caring family I trust, and bought another horse. By the time I reached high school and Jerry was away at college, that horse too was gone. All we had left was Woody, my solace and soul mate.

During Jerry's high school years riding provided us with a very special companionship. We would keep the horses at a trot along the causeway, but when we reached the shore at the east end of the harbor, away we would gallop. On our return we would always slow down when we came to the lone cedar which had acquired a Japanese look. We rode all over Eaton's Neck where dirt roads ran through woods and past fields. Our destination might be the lighthouse or the old sand excavation which we called Sand City. A favorite spot was the sluice near Winkle Point where the tide rushed in and out through a narrow channel. We would sometimes tie the horses to a tree, and take a swim in the current. Eaton's Neck had only a scattering of summer homes then, but now the entire area has become suburbanized.

I was always impressed by Jerry's superior knowledge and glad when he passed some of it on to me, such as how to tie a square knot instead of a sissy granny knot. I completely trusted him, except when he teased me. An example of my trust was the time we camped out on the Crarys' point. I had already settled into my sleeping bag when Jerry realized he had forgotten some essential item for breakfast. He would have to walk the half mile back to the house to get it, but first he asked if I would be afraid.

"What is there to be afraid of?" I asked.

"Nothing." he replied.

Assured that there was no danger I sent him on his way. Later Mother told me how proud Jerry was of me for not being afraid to be left alone so far from home. Though pleased by his praise, I was puzzled that he should think me brave when he had told me I was quite safe, and wasn't Mother herself always fearless?

Jerry trusted me too, though once I was not completely trustworthy. One day I discovered two perfect little hiding places in my bedroom. After removing the small drawer from the step at one of the doors, I found a little compartment on either side of the opening. I shared my secret with Jerry and let him have one side in which he hid a box marked "Private, Keep Out!" Well, of course curiosity got the better of me. Guiltily I opened the box to take a peek. There, to my surprise, was a booklet on the anatomy of sex. My curiosity came to an abrupt halt. Handling the box like a hot potato, I hastily returned it to its hiding place, and never touched it again.

Early on, Jerry learned the way through the attic to the trap door to the roof and soon had me following him. Stairs in the back hall led to a floored attic under the high pitched roof of the dining room wing, but the area under the flat part had no floor boards and only a dim light at the near end. Stepping very carefully on the beams so as not to break through the ceiling below, we would grope along until we came to the ladder. What a relief when Jerry climbed it, pushed off the lid and there was the bright sky! It was a thrill to be way up high looking out over familiar territory from this new perspective.

The flat section of the roof was covered with copper. It was an area about ten by twenty feet over the center parts of the front hall and living room. Wood shingles sloped off the two sides and the west end to the living room chimney. At the east end was the start of the peaked roof of the dining room wing. At first it was excitement enough just to be up there, but after a while we found that we could slide down the short distance to the living room chimney. With our feet braced against it, this was a comfortable hide-out as the shingles were not as hot as the copper roof. This was plenty good enough for me, but Jerry felt compelled to venture out to the dining room chimney, which required straddling the peaked roof and hitching oneself along for quite a distance. It really did take courage to follow him as the ground on either side looked mighty far away. The thought of rolling down that steep roof kept me from trying it again.

When Mother saw what a good time we were having on the roof she decided to improve access so she and her guests could enjoy it too. Fortunately the ladder in the attic was directly above the hall leading to the west bedrooms, so it was an easy matter to put a trap door in the ceiling and install a set of steps that could be raised or lowered by a pulley. In addition to its fine view, the roof was a great place for star gazing. I remember especially how Mother would settle down with blankets and pillows to watch the August meteor showers.

Those early summers at Duck Island gave me welcome relief from city and school and, more precious, the freedom to discover myself and the world of nature. As we grew up and left home, Duck Island was the locus of many family reunions—a happy place for our children to experience some of our childhood pleasures. My father died in 1940, leaving Mother to preside over the big house until her death at ninety-one in 1972. Fortunately, Ray and his wife Elex had built their own house in nearby woods twenty years earlier, to which we continue to return with joy and gratitude.

The Outsider

John Dewey's philosophy of education greatly influenced my parents, especially as Dad had known Dewey in the "X Club." They were interested in the new progressive schools where Dewey's theories of "learning by doing" and "educating the whole child" were being tried out. When the Smileys, a Quaker family who ran a resort at Lake Mohonk near New Palz, NY, opened a boarding school for boys there in 1920, my brother Jerry was promptly enrolled, although he was only nine and the youngest in the school. Likewise Raymond, at age four became a charter member of The Brooklyn Ethical Culture School down the street from us on South Oxford. Marion followed him there but at fourth grade transferred to Woodward, recently established by my first grade teacher from Friends School and only two blocks from our new house on Clinton Ave.

My turn to be volunteered as a guinea pig came when our next-door neighbors on South Oxford, Miss Silver and Miss Goldsmith, started Shore Road Academy in a spacious house in Bay Ridge overlooking New York Harbor. On its beautiful grounds was a greenhouse where each girl could have the hands-on experience of cultivating her own little garden plot. Perhaps that's what sold my parents.

The school started at fifth grade, but the fact that I was only at fourth didn't trouble anyone. My January birthday made me a borderline case anyway, and it was assumed that somehow or other I'd learn long division and whatever else is covered in fourth grade. A more serious difficulty was the distance, considerably farther than Packer on Brooklyn Heights where I had been the previous two years. Instead of a short ride on the street car or a half hour walk with my father on his way to work, I would have to take the subway. The nearest BMT station was a ten minute walk down Hanson Place across Flatbush Avenue to Pacific Avenue. The ride to 82nd Street took about a half hour and from there it was a short walk to the school. At least I would be going against the rush hour traffic and Jerry could help me learn the way. He was at that time attending Poly Prep and got off at Dykker Heights, the next stop after mine at the end of the line.

Nobody seemed concerned that I might miss my friends at Packer, perhaps because I hadn't shown evidence of strong friendships there. Most of the girls at Shore Road came from the area, so those who didn't already know each other had the possibility of getting together for play after school. I felt like an outsider even though we were all of us newcomers. For the most part school work went pretty well. In fact I got along better with the teachers than with the other girls. In their eyes, no doubt, I was the teacher's pet which was another obstacle in my social life. For instance, there was the matter of my winning a prize for the best garden.

It all happened by default. Each girl was assigned a small section of greenhouse bench for her garden. We planted calendulas, nasturtiums, baby's breath and other flowers. The sweet peas were always at the back of the plots where strings for them to climb on hung from a wire strung down the center of the bench. Variations in layouts were achieved by miniature paths separating the flower beds, but by mid-November, when our seedlings were only an inch or two high, there was little to distinguish one plot from another.

Then one girl got the idea of decorating her garden for Christmas by placing small ornaments along its borders. Others followed suit. The competition escalated. Soon stars, Santas and angels dangled from the sweet pea wires. Some girls even covered the soil with artificial snow, smothering the parched seedlings. Meanwhile, because I couldn't think up a stunning display to impress my classmates, I silently continued to water my plants. Besides, I had no opportunity to shop for decorations and surely would not think of asking Mother for some.

Just before Christmas vacation the prize for the best garden was announced. Much to my embarrassment, mine was declared the winner because it was the only one with healthy vegetation. I felt like a hypocrite. Those teachers didn't know how gladly I would have abandoned their pet project for the silly decorating game if only I had been invited to join in.

My real triumph at Shore Road came that spring. We were studying the ancient Greeks, and our teacher had been reading aloud *The Children's Homer* by Padraic Colum. She suggested that we put on a play about the Trojan War. When it was time for us to try out for the part of Achilles, she selected the scene where he is sulking in his tent after Agamemnon took away his captive maiden. When Odysseus comes as an envoy to try to persuade Achilles to rejoin the battle because it is going badly for Agamemnon, Achilles replies, "Deem'st thou I grieve for Agamemnon's griefs, Odysseus?" After each girl had stumbled over this line, in a good-little-girl voice, the teacher would protest, "No, no. Don't you see he is angry?" While waiting my turn I worked myself up to such a state of imagined rage that my face flushed red as I sputtered out those archaic words. That is how I landed the part of the heroic Greek, the height of my dramatic career.

Last Memory Letter to Lyle

[Following is the last of some forty imaginary conversations in letter form that I wrote to my late husband over a period of nearly two years. They ramble among memories of our life together before a cerebral hemorrhage left him wheelchair-bound and practically speechless; his four and a half years in a nursing home prior to his death in April 1993; and events in my life at the time of writing. Mario is my sister.]

March 4, 1998

Because it was simply out of the question, I never told you how often I wished I could have cared for you at home. If you had been able to put weight on even one foot to help in transferring from bed to chair we might have managed, but there was no way I could handle that Hoyer lift alone. I witnessed enough mishaps to be nearly as scared of the contraption as you were. We would have needed round-the-clock help, but even so it would have been a difficult undertaking. I can imagine that my preoccupation with responsibilities and details of your care would have constantly infringed on our companionship. As it was we had enough of such distractions at the nursing home.

Recently I had an experience that reaffirmed this conclusion. Mario and I were halfway through what was supposed to be a relaxing and carefree vacation in the Yucatan, when, not noticing a stone step in the sun's glare, she fell and broke her foot. We were staying at The Blue Parrot Inn on the north edge of the town of Playa del Carmen right on the beach looking out across the blue-green Caribbean to the island of Cozumel in the distance. The inn's several small thatched roofed buildings were in various stages of repair, and for the first three nights we stayed in the most decrepit one. Dark and shabby, our room barely had space for two double beds, a small table and one chair. Quantities of sand blew under the ill-fitted door while more sifted onto our beds through the screen of the unglazed window. I had suspected that the place would be on the seedy side, but Mario was shocked. You would have been as distressed as she, though we should have been forewarned by the low rates and the fact that it was recommended by Jon's favorite guide book.

Nevertheless, when not in our miserable room, we enjoyed some delicious swims in the surf, barefoot walks along the shore and strolls down the main avenue of the town lined with colorful shops and restaurants. At night we joined the throngs of pedestrians who took over the street. On the third day we were moved to a bright and spacious bungalow complete with a combination sitting room/kitchen and verandah. Once settled, we felt our vacation had really begun. You can imagine how glad we were to be able to fix our own breakfast of instant oatmeal and raisins brought from home. Afterwards I enjoyed a solitary walk far up the beach beyond the last buildings and another great swim with Mario. We were looking forward to devoting the following day to the extensive Mayan ruins of Chichen-Itza and our last three to leisurely companionship. I was even tempted to try parasailing, where a parachute is pulled behind a boat, but have since learned it is banned in the U. S. because it is unsafe.

So much for our dreams of an idyllic vacation. Mario's fall that afternoon suddenly changed the whole picture. The management of the inn gave her prompt attention and whisked us off in a cab to their doctor's clinic. Three hours later we were back at the Blue Parrot with a green cast on Mario's foot and stitches in her elbow. It took three men to carry her in her wheelchair over the soft sand to our bungalow where she was confined for the next two days. There we each faced problems of coping: she with learning to maneuver in and out of a wheelchair and to hop her way on overlong crutches through the narrow bathroom door, and I with helping her, foraging for food and attending to various tasks involved in rescheduling our return home. In spite of frustration and exhaustion we tried hard to be good sports and not dwell on our disappointment. However, even though I found time for a walk the second morning, I didn't go far because my heart had gone out of it. Neither had I the spirit to brave the surf alone.

We planned our day of departure with ample time to return the wheelchair and crutches to the clinic and reach the Cancun airport by noon. After the eager helpers who carried Mario to the waiting taxi succeeded in fitting the chair and our four bags into the trunk, we took off through the barren back streets of Playa del Carmen whose cinder block buildings glared white in the bright sun. In less than ten minutes we reached the clinic only to discover that the crutches were missing. Nothing to do but race back to the inn hoping that someone had turned them in at the front desk. Our driver wisely returned to the spot where he had picked us up and there, to our great relief, stood our crutches leaning against a small tree! One more trip to the clinic and we hit the road north and even arrived at the airport as planned, two hours ahead of our plane's scheduled departure. Even so those were a stressful and sweaty two hours as I tracked our bags through customs, negotiated the change in our tickets, tried unsuccessfully to exchange our money, and worried whether someone would find us a wheelchair in time to board the plane. One appeared all right, but it took Mario only to the door of the plane where she would have to hop her way inside until she reached the seats and could then brace herself on the arms on either side of the aisle. I didn't see how she would manage to hop all the way to our seats when a kind passenger sitting alone in the last row of first class took pity on Mario's plight and relinquished his seat. Never have I appreciated luxury so much as I did those comfortable seats and the cozy blankets offered by an attentive steward when the welcomed air-conditioning cooled us off too fast. Finally I could begin to relax and we could enjoy unhurried conversation. In Saint Louis, where we changed planes to go our separate ways, I managed to exchange our money, phone Dick Fernandez to confirm his time of meeting Mario, and bring her a cup of coffee. I was sad to leave her, though she was assured of wheelchairs both to the door of the plane and a narrow one that fits the aisle, and I knew she would be well cared for by Dick and in her retirement home. As it turned out her doctor took off the cast because they now believe her kind of break heals better by bearing weight. She tells me she is making good progress with walking in spite of some mild pain. Needless to say we were both sorry that our long anticipated trip had such a disappointing ending. It has taken us both some time to regain our spirits.

However my three days' stint of care-giving made me aware of my limitations both in terms of stamina and anxiety. Of course ten years ago when you were stricken I had more energy than I do now, but worry and being rushed has always made me feel harried and irritable, a mood certainly not conducive to intimate communication. Looking back now I think the nursing home was not only a practical necessity in your circumstances, but an opportunity for more peaceful interludes together than we might have had at home.

There was an advantage to my coming to you each day with fresh anticipation. I was always glad to see you and felt a special lift when you greeted me with sparkling eyes. A few times early on you surprised me by saying, "There you are," and once in your last year you exclaimed., "Hey, there's my girl!" In my eagerness to re-connect with you I often found myself annoyed at things that needed attention before we could settle down to enjoy each other's company. How I might have handled that difficulty if you had lived at home I do not know. I do know that your attitude of acceptance had a calming effect on me. You were able to articulate it one time when I was fretting over some wheelchair problem that the occupational therapist had not yet resolved and you wisely advised, "We'll let them take their time."

Once we were alone, I would tell you the news of the day in-cluding whatever had given me pleasure, as I felt a strong need to enjoy life for both of us. Most of all I cherished our intimate mo-ments when I lingered after you had been put down for your nap. Then I would indulge in some sweet talk and remind you of the countless times you used to tell me you loved me. On rare occa-sions you echoed my declarations by saying, "I love you too." Sometimes, when you were crying, I might try to express what I suspected was making you sad at that moment or, if I missed the mark, we'd cry together about your whole predicament. I marvel that we seemed to be on the same wave length so much of the time. I guess that's what half a century of living together does for two people who love each other.

Though I still grieve that you had to suffer those long years of confinement I want you to know how grateful I am for what you gave me. You taught me to be patient, to accept ambiguity and to trust my intuition. You helped me discover levels of understanding that don't require words. Above all, the gifts of your peaceful and courageous spirit and your love sustain me now and surely will help me face whatever the future may bring.

Did I ever tell you of the dream I had about my wedding ring? It came to me in the first year or two after your stroke and I think it sums up what I'm trying to tell you now. I dreamt that while I was staring at my hand my gold wedding ring transformed itself into delicate filigree. Then I showed it to someone, it was not clear who, and said, "You see, this ring is my marriage. There are holes in it because much has been taken away. But it is still beautiful!"

SHIRLEY FERRIER

In 1925 I was born in the newly finished house that Mama and Daddy had built for them in Dearborn, Michigan, and I lived there all of my life until college days. I was married shortly after graduating from Albion College. We both were working. We bought a lot on Belleville Lake and, after all its high price was paid off, began building our house We raised our three children in that house. After our last child was in the first grade I found I needed something more to do, so I decided to get a teacher's certificate at the University of Michigan, followed by a job teaching school.

In 1988 I left my home of 37 years and moved to Ann Arbor and the following year I retired from the kindergartens in Van Buren Township Schools. I like Ann Arbor so much I never want to leave! Ever since college days I had hoped that some day I could go to school just to learn what I wanted to learn, and I seized the opportunity at the University of Michigan by sitting in on various classes, with permission of the professors, and loved it.

Now writing, gardening, watercolor lessons, grandchildren, volunteer jobs in several organizations, and the ever-present housekeeping chores don't allow enough time for three times a week classes, but I hope to remedy that some day. At this stage of life I like to say I am born again—born to retire!

The Wallet in the Snow

The snow had already been trampled hard on the sidewalks and big flakes were still trying to lighten the darkening sky as Ella and I headed to the dime store to buy birthday presents for Charles, a neighbor boy. Charles was much younger than both of us. Ella was ten, I was nine, and he must have been two years my junior, so it seemed odd to me that we had been invited to his birthday party, but we both were pleased by the invitation. Even though we were due at the party in about an hour we didn't hurry, instead choosing to dawdle along, enjoying catching the fluffy flakes on our tongues or scuffing up the snow piled beside the sidewalk. When we were passing Ned's Firestone store and service station Ella called my attention to a worn wallet lying on the packed snow. We looked it over, saw money inside, and knew at once we should try to return it, so we asked a man who was working at the gas station what to do. He told us to take it across the street to the police station. No discussion was necessary. We just took off at a run.

The police station, city hall, fire station and a large park with a fish pond in a sunken garden occupied an entire city block. It was familiar to all the kids in our neighborhood because on our way home from school we often walked through the park and would look up at the police station's second story windows with the bars on them, hoping, with fear in our hearts, to see a jailbird's face appear. None ever did. We would enter the police station by the lower level back door off the garden and felt free to explore the upstairs and downstairs office areas, but we never ventured into what we considered the working area where we could see the policemen through a large archway. But this night was different; we were on important business and marched right through that archway! I was stunned to find myself looking up at the same high desk that I felt I had seen in many movies, and there was the ever present officer in uniform peering down at me from atop that desk, too! But this was not a movie. This was reality, and I was standing in what I had considered the off limits area of a familiar haunt. We handed the wallet to the man behind the high desk and told him that we had found it. As other uniformed officers began to appear on the scene he looked at the identification inside the wallet and dispatched one of them to take a squad car to the man's home to get him. He asked us to wait, which pleased me because I wanted to watch whatever was going to happen next. This was exciting and I never considered that I was being detained by the police; in fact they were very friendly.

In a very short while the squad car returned with the man who had lost his wallet. He was a Ford Motor Company employee named Fred W. Bullen, very old, with white stubble on his chin. He was wearing a dark shabby coat. He had already discovered a hole in his pocket and his loss, and since fifty-three dollars, almost his entire pay, had been in the wallet, he was frantic, but hadn't told his wife about it. Of course the return of his money was a great relief to him and he gave each of us a dollar bill as a reward. Meanwhile, one of the policemen had the idea that this event should have newspaper coverage, so someone called the Detroit *News* and a reporter and photographer were sent out. It seemed to take them forever to travel from Detroit to Dearborn and I wondered if we would ever get to the party. When they arrived the photographer took a picture of the transfer of the wallet from two honest little girls to a grateful old man. Then the reporter asked us some questions, one of which, and the only one I remember, was, "Who saw the wallet first?" Ella didn't reply, so I said I guessed we both did. After the excitement was over and we were released we hurried down the last block of our trip to the dime store, picked out the birthday presents, rushed home to wrap them and arrived late at the party, but with a great story to tell!

The photograph, with the heading "Honesty Pays a Big Dividend in Happiness," and accompanied by an article telling about our deed, appeared in the next evening's newspaper. A short time later an envelope addressed to Ella and to me arrived at our house. It contained a congratulatory letter from a Detroit *News* columnist. His Spencerian handwriting in the letter was the most beautiful I have ever seen! Mama asked Ella to take the letter to show it to her folks, with the understanding that it was to be returned so Mama could save it. She also saved the newspaper article, and to my dismay, my reward dollar, keeping all three in a small carved wooden chest that sat on top of her chest of drawers. l didn't mind her keeping the mementos but I did mind her keeping my reward money. Ella bought roller skates with her dollar but I didn't have the pleasure of deciding how to spend mine and I didn't think it was fair for Mama to insist that my dollar bill be a keepsake. In my opinion all dollar bills were alike and brought pleasure only in the spending. But my greater disappointment was with myself, because I knew that Ella saw that wallet first, and I knew that she knew it, but I never told anyone until I set pen to this paper today.

My Southern Roots

It was 1932, Depression times. I knew little about the Depression except that it was happening. When the man who lived upstairs bought a new car we all went outside to admire it, but he was ribbed with remarks like, "Why did you buy a new car now? Don't you know there's a depression?" That confused me. I didn't see why if he had the money for a new car he should not buy it because of the depression; it wasn't some kind of sacred holiday. Anyway, in spite of the hard times and the risk of being ribbed, that same summer Daddy saw his way to a new maroon Ford sedan. In August we took the first of two trips to Arkansas, Mama's home state.

Mama had been something of a traitor and had left her southern roots, come north, and even married a Yankee! While I was growing up I asked Mama questions about her childhood and she told me a lot about her life in the small town of Clarendon, Arkansas, where her Papa, as she called her father, was an attorney. A hired cook prepared their meals, and she had a pony. What I experienced on our visits to the towns and small cities, and especially the farm wasn't necessarily typical of her life in the south, but it did show me a way of life that was different from what I was used to.

I was almost seven and my brother, Leland, was one and a half. Aunt Cavett and Uncle Braswell, Mama's siblings, went with us.

Daddy did all of the driving because he was the only one of us who knew how. It was probably a more peaceful trip than some of our later ones, because Leland was too young to participate in fights like the ones we had in subsequent years—fights for which I was always blamed. But we were a car full! And the car had no trunk! There was a platform fastened on the rear behind the spare tire. Our few suitcases were tied onto it.

When we reached the rice-growing area of Arkansas we had rainy weather and got hopelessly stuck in the mud. It was getting dark, so Uncle Braswell rolled up his pants legs, walked bare-footed to a farmhouse and asked for help. By the time the farmer had harnessed his mule and got to us the car lights were needed so he could see to hitch the mule to the car. The mule pulled, Uncle Braswell pushed; Daddy steered; I was scared as heck. Finally we were released from the mud's grip. Daddy gave the helpful man some money and we were on our way again.

Mama's Uncle Davis Parker's plantation near Holly Grove was our destination and we arrived later that night. Uncle Davis, Aunt Laura, their son Sam and his wife Neoma all lived there. The place did not fit my idea of a plantation at all. Plantations were supposed to have huge houses with tall white pillars marching across the front. This was really more a broken down farm surrounded by cotton fields. The cotton fields came almost up to the picket fence around the front yard. The white frame house had a porch across the front with the traditional rocking chairs and hanging swing, I loved that swing. It was like the one Grandma had on her porch in Highland Park. Swinging in it made me feel grown up. There also was a porch that zigzagged across the back of the house but nobody sat on it—it was a way to get from one part of the house to another—sort of an outdoor hall. A third small screened porch was called a sleeping porch. The front wing of the house had a breezeway right through the middle, with screens and screen doors on both ends, but no provision for closing it in. The farm was not electrified, but there were gas chandeliers in all of the rooms.

Also there was no running water. We were served by a pump near the kitchen door. Opposite the door to the dining room a shelf fastened to the porch railing held an iron-bound wooden bucket full of water with a metal dipper hanging from a nail. This was our supply of drinking water. I thought it curious the way nobody drained the dipper but always flung the last bit of water on the bare ground in the back yard, sometimes scattering chickens when it hit. The water was rich in iron and I hated the way it tasted. Mama thought that Leland shouldn't drink it because he was so young, so they procured better tasting water for him. I was jealous because I wasn't allowed to have the good water. We took sponge baths in our bedrooms where basins and pitchers were an essential part of the furnishings. Once at least I had a bath in a large metal tub which was brought into the kitchen. The cook and Mama were there to help me, but I was used to taking my bath alone and I was uncomfortable with the lack of privacy. And of course there was an outhouse out back.

Although I was used to the conveniences of city life I found the place had its compensations, like the rooster who stationed himself on the back porch to wake us every morning with his crowing. But the advantage my relatives had that impressed me most was a full time cook. And cook she did—three big meals every day! There was usually delicious fried chicken, bowls of mashed potatoes and other vegetables, and for every meal hot buttermilk biscuits. The cook was a middle aged, short Negress who lived alone in a small building behind the house. I liked to visit her in the big kitchen and asked for jobs to help her. Probably I was more hindrance than help, but she usually found something for me to do unless it was getting close to meal time, when she would shoo me out of there. As far as I was concerned she performed magic in producing all of those meals. Needless to say, it was all done from scratch, which in this case included catching, killing, scalding, and plucking the chickens. She grabbed the chicken by the neck with one hand, swung it around and around above her head, then let it go, and the chicken flopped around on the ground until it died. I didn't understand how anyone could do such a horrible thing, even though I had watched my mother's friend Manon scald and pluck chickens in her basement. I tried to avoid this almost daily event, but my appetite for that fried chicken wasn't diminished!

Since I liked the cook I went in search of her one evening when I had nothing to do. I found her sitting in the dimly lit kitchen eating soda crackers. She told me she wouldn't eat the chicken she fed us because the chickens were allowed to run wherever they wanted to, eating anything they came across and she thought it made their meat nasty. I was astonished and didn't understand why what they ate would matter. Besides, I knew they were fed chicken feed every day—I liked to help throw it to them. But I commiserated with her by eating some soda crackers, too, although I would have preferred a cold piece of fried chicken. These days free range chickens command a premium price.

As far as I know, the families who lived in the very small houses in various places on the farm were hired to do the work in the cotton and other fields and to tend the few animals—some pigs and mules are all I remember—that Uncle Davis kept; I'm pretty sure they weren't share croppers. One of them was a woman named Lavinia who lived across the road from the farm. Even though her house and Uncle Davis's house were separated by a large cotton field, Neoma (Uncle Davis's daughter-in-law) would stand on the front porch and call, "Lavinia, Lavinia," until Lavinia heard and answered her. Usually she was being called to come and get some leftover food or to do a chore. Lavinia also did our laundry. We were very amused when a pair of my socks which had elastic in the cuffs came back all stretched out because they had been ironed! Nothing was said to her about it, for which I was grateful, and the socks were discarded.

The pace of life on the plantation was slow but I found things to do. Cats were living in one of the outbuildings and I became very concerned about their welfare. Realizing that absolutely no one else around there cared a thing about those cats distressed me. I begged milk and scraps and a dish for them from the cook. She considered it pure nonsense to feed cats, but usually gave me something for them. Even Anne, Uncle Davis's and Aunt Laura's granddaughter who came to visit for a few days was not sympathetic to those cats' needs!

Anne was a little older than I and she did promote some adventure. She secretly took me into the cook's house. I felt we were doing something sneaky and was afraid of being caught, but she said it was all right. While we looked around the one room Anne had an idea. We would do something to spruce the place up a little as a surprise for the cook. When I told Mama about our plans she let me know in no uncertain terms that we would do nothing of the kind and that I was not to enter the cook's private space again, so our project ended. The two Goldilocks would have to look for something else to do.

One of the out buildings served as a commissary where supplies and non perishable food were kept locked up. It was for the convenience of the employees, who were allowed to purchase from it, as well as for the family's use. I suspect it served the same purpose back in the days of slavery. However, I don't think that this farm had been in our family that far back, because Uncle Davis's family was originally from Tennessee. I went to visit the commissary a few times with Neoma and managed to get safely past the mean turkeys who lived in the enclosure surrounding the building, but when I ventured in there alone one day a turkey chased me so I never entered his domain again.

One morning I discovered that the fields in front of the house were full of straw hatted people dragging very long strong canvas bags from shoulder straps. They were picking cotton and putting it in their bags. How exciting! I begged to go out there and join in the fun and when my pleas were denied I was most unhappy. The next morning the field was empty and not as tempting but again I begged to pick cotton. This time someone found a cotton bag for me and out I went dragging it behind me. In no time at all I realized this was not fun. The bag was heavy, there was little cotton left on the plants and getting it off wasn't easy; the sun was hot and worst of all I was all alone. The camaraderie was what I had wanted most. I didn't last long and returned to the house feeling the victim of a dirty trick.

Sometime later I discovered that the grown-ups were making plans for a fish fry. I'd never been to a fish fry and was curious and anxious for the day to arrive, even though I didn't like fish. The fish fry was to be held beside a river, where those who wanted to could swim while others fished. The help would build the fire and cook the meal. On the day of the fish fry we were joined by several cars full of other relatives. I rode in the middle front seat of a car that had a windshield that opened at the bottom for ventilation. Mama, Leland and another woman rode in the back seat. Beside me was an extremely fat woman who had been hired as an extra cook for the big occasion. She held a big stack of china dinner plates on her lap. The day was already hot but the breeze that came through the open windows was pleasant. All was fine until a snake dropped out of a tree, landed on the hood of the car, and came speeding through the open space under the windshield. The fat cook, still holding the pile of plates on her lap, rose up out of her seat with a mighty "Who-o-o-p!" The snake went under her and disappeared into the back of the car to the accompaniment of shrieks from its occupants. The surprised driver stopped and everyone got out of the car in a hurry. Everything, even the seats, was removed from the car; the boxes and baskets were searched; but the snake was not to be found. At last we continued our journey and had a wonderful day. For many years afterward, Mama, who was absolutely terrified of snakes, told that story with a great imitation of the whooping cook.

One evening a dance was held in the living room. The furniture was moved to the edges of the room, the gas lights were low, some of the Negroes played various instruments while the white folks danced, and refreshments were served. I'd never seen anything like this before. I thought it was wonderfully grand but I wished I could participate.

Our second trip to visit relatives in Arkansas was in the summer of 1937 when I was almost twelve years old and Leland was about six and a half. Again we stayed at Uncle Davis's house, but Aunt Laura had died between our two trips. My most vivid memory of this visit was the night a Joe Louis boxing match took place. The farmhouse was electrified then, but the workers' houses probably were not. Uncle Davis took his small radio out to the front porch. When it was getting dark the male Negroes began to gather quietly around, some sitting on the steps, others standing in clusters on the grass. Joe Louis was their hero and they were excited about the upcoming fight. They may not have had electricity in their homes but they brought plenty of it with them that night: I could feel it in the air. When the fight began they all edged in closer to the radio, listening anxiously, but they didn't do much cheering until Louis had won. Then of course there were cheers and grins all around. I was fascinated and stayed outside to watch until it was over and they began to drift homeward. Life was so different here, I thought!

One early evening when we were returning to the farm after a trip into town we heard singing as we neared one of the farm workers' houses. Maybe half a dozen singers were gathered on the tiny porch. Their music was beautiful. Daddy stopped the car so we could enjoy it. I was entranced and wanted to get out of the car and move closer to them. Daddy and Leland were spellbound, too, and Daddy was rather profuse in his appreciation—perhaps too much so for Dixie-raised Mama. She didn't like their music, didn't think we should be so enthusiastic about it either, and was anxious to move on. Although I knew that her upbringing had taught her that we were being too friendly with Negroes, I was upset about having to leave. But Daddy started the engine and drove away.

Another memory of this second trip is of a visit to a woman Mama referred to as Aunt Mary Capps. She wasn't really Mama's aunt, but they were related. She lived in a tiny place called Capps Corner, named for her family, in a large old two-story red brick house that had belonged to her family for generations. It had high ceilings and she showed us the high water mark that was left by the latest flood they had suffered. Just before we left Aunt Mary Capps delighted me when she told me I was a very pretty girl, but when we were alone Mama really burst my balloon by telling me that she shouldn't have said that; people shouldn't tell young girls such things. Mama said this in a kindly way, with a smile that told me she knew it was true, but her attitude took away the glow. I needed that! But Mama just couldn't give it.

After we got back to Michigan I drew a picture of the front of Uncle Davis's house and used water color on it. Mama said it was good enough to send to him and was sure he would appreciate it, so I sent the picture and was thanked. I wish I could see it now!

These trips have given faces and places to some of the stories Mama told me. The friendliness and outgoing qualities of our relatives and others I met have given me a feeling of rapport with the southern part of our country—a rapport that otherwise I might not have had.

The Baron Takes Off

Good Friday, 1988, was a beautiful, unseasonably warm, sunny day and I was in great spirits with a week's vacation stretching ahead of me. I began the day by scooting around town on various errands and then piloted my beloved 1982 Le Baron back home. That car had been my pride and joy for the previous six years and I had no interest in replacing it yet. I monitored it carefully, checked its hoses, wires, and fluid levels and added fluid when necessary, had the oil changed regularly, changed the air filter when needed, examined the engine and wiped every thing under the hood with a damp cloth fairly often, and I loved to wash it. I had never before felt much responsibility for car care nor taken great joy in a car, but this was the first car that was really mine. I picked it out and made all the decisions; it was black, beautiful, had fine red striping and deep red luxurious velvet upholstery, a vinyl roof, the best silhouette on the road, and I enjoyed the many compliments it brought. There are still a very few of these Le Barons around in 1996 and whenever I see one I react in much the same way that I do when I see a tricolor collie—something like, "Ah, memories! How are you, old friend?"

As I entered my driveway I remembered that I wanted to take a close look at a new spot I'd noticed on the garage floor—could it indicate an oil leak? This was a nice, bright day for such a chore so I pressed the in-car garage door opener, stopped just short of the garage, shifted the car into park, left the engine running and the driver's door open while I went into the garage and briefly examined the spot on the floor. Out of the corner of my eye I noticed something moving and when I looked up I was stricken with panic to see my car very slowly moving backwards. I gave chase but found that I couldn't get to the driver's seat by the most direct route, because the driver's door that I had left open was about to hit my small side porch, thus blocking my way, so I knew I'd have to go around the back of the car.

As I ran past the other side of the car I heard the door crunch against the brick porch and its metal railing. When I reached the back of the car it was picking up speed, because the driveway at this point became steeper. I allowed extra room to get around the back of the car, reached the open door and managed to get one foot inside the car, aiming at the brake, then realized with horror that this was much too dangerous because the car was now moving so fast I couldn't keep up with it, and I would have to let it go. As I tried to turn around to get away from it the open door hit me, knocked me to the pavement, and passed over my head. Fortunately no part of my body was in the path of the front wheel. Being hit by an automobile was not as terrifying as I had always thought it would be, probably because I didn't have any time to realize that it was inevitable.

As I picked up my head in disbelief to see what my car was doing I saw that it was aiming at the picture window in the house across the street, but then an amazing thing happened! The car, still traveling backwards, began to turn slowly into the street in front of my house, and then I knew I was in real trouble! Where would it stop and what kind of damage would it do?

"Oh, help!" I uttered weakly, as I ran across my lawn in pursuit of the runaway car, but no one was around to hear.

As the car passed in front of my house it looked as if it was aiming at my next door neighbor's new car which was parked on the street in front of his house, but no, my lovely car was apparently intent upon completing a circle rather than smashing itself into another automobile, so it started up my neighbor's driveway. The incline slowed the car's speed as it continued its circle onto my front lawn where I was able to hop into it and step on the brake before it could hit the house.

As I sat in the driver's seat feeling overwhelmed by this chain of events, my first inclination was to leave the car where it was and go into the house to regain my wits, but immediately I rejected that notion. I was not going to leave my car parked on my front lawn with its wrecked door dangling open to amuse or intrigue the neighbors and gawkers. Not a chance! I stayed in the car and, holding the door partially shut with my left arm, retraced the circular route the car had just pioneered. *Then* I went into the house; but before I let myself collapse I got the yellow pages, some ice cubes for my damaged knee, and propped my leg up on the sofa to think about what had to be done next. I was determined to bring this whole thing to closure. It took me almost no time to locate a nearby repair shop that "did" doors, and the man who answered the phone said they could start working on it immediately. By now my adrenalin level must have been subsiding, for I began to feel limp and relatively helpless, and I asked if someone could please come to get the car. It was agreed and a short time later two sympathetic men arrived. One of them got in the driver's seat and the other tied the door shut and my much babied car was off to get a change of doors.

I felt dazed and made my way back to the comfort of my sofa to ponder the rapid-fire events that I had just experienced: the discovery of impending disaster, the choice of action, the realization that I had put myself in too much danger, abandonment of my original plan, the series of threats from the car, each one necessitating a new plan, and the final outcome. Wow! And no one was there to witness this misadventure!

❦

ROBERT HAMMONDS

❧

I drew my first breath in Wolverhampton, a town in the West Midlands of England, on the 31st of August, 1927, the youngest of five sons born to Frank and Jane Elizabeth (Oakley) Hammonds. I was educated fn the County Borough School System and Wolverhampton College of Arts and Crafts.

From its beginning in September, 1939, I endured the long ordeal of World War II and served in the Royal Navy from 1945 to 1948.

In 1951 I emigrated to the United State, with my fiancée, Rebecca M. Brackstone. We sailed from Liverpool on the Cunard liner Britannic, *arriving in New York City on January 31st. Together we traveled to Michigan to join my aunt and uncle, Monica and Fred Harland, on their farm at Wolf Creek, eleven miles west of the town of Adrian. I married Rebecca at St. Mary's Church in Adrian, on July 28th 1951. In November we settled in Ann Arbor, where I worked as a designer and pattern maker in the sign and display business. Rebecca worked as a secretary in Ann Arbor Public Schools Administration.*

On the 25th of May, 1960, 1 became a naturalized citizen of the United States of America, taking the oath in the Washtenaw County Courthouse.

In 1969 I established a business of my own under the name of Hammonds Signs and continued successfully until retirement in the year 2000.

My wife Rebecca and I raised four children, one girl and three boys. They in turn have rewarded us with five lovely grandchildren.

In addition to my chosen vocation I have enjoyed travel, gardening, reading, writing, and woodworking. I derive great pleasure from music, the theater, movies, and educational television. I have a deep reverence for life, love people, places and things, bright colors and the sounds of nature in the countryside.

Discovering Spring Head

O ver the hills and not so far away, up towards Sedgely, a mile or two from our house in Wolverhampton in the English Midlands, was the very favorite place to roam and play for my brothers and me in those carefree days of our childhood in the early 1930's. There were fields to run in, abounding with wild flowers, trees to climb or carve our initials on, long grass, short grass, bushes and hedgerows and so many birds: sky larks, finches, thrushes, swallows and all. There were hills and valleys with rocks and boulders, the very best place for playing soldiers and war games with our hand-crafted wooden guns, ideal for a session of cowboys and Indians or Robin Hood and his merry band of out-laws with our home-made bows and arrows, swords and shields. There were plowed fields and pastures with grazing cattle, fences to climb over and barbed wire to crawl under, patches of bramble where luscious blackberries could be had for the price of a few scratches on eager hands. An occasional hazelnut tree in between the hawthorns along the hedgerows yielded its crop of sweet nuts in season.

There were rabbits and squirrels by the number and an occa-sional fox. We knew a place, an abandoned coal mine, with some of the tumbled down sheds and rusting old engine parts for us to climb on and explore. The mine shaft was covered with heavy wood boards but there were spaces between the boards wide enough to shout into and hear your voice echo down to a great depth. We would drop stones into the dark pit and listen for an amazing length of time before the sound echoed back when hitting the water at the bottom.

Then there was the brook, the very thing that held the greatest attraction for us and possibly gave us the most pleasure, playing around, along and in the brook. Ours was like the one in Tennyson's poem "For men may come and men may go but I go on forever."

Running water holds a unique fascination for everyone, I think. We as children were drawn to it perpetually. We would wade in the brook, sail and race our toy boats in the fast flowing stream of crystal clear water. There were only small fish in our brook, minnows and sticklebacks. We caught them with small nets, took them home in a jam jar and kept them in a goldfish bowl until we got tired of looking at them.

If you walked along the banks of the brook you would come upon places where it was narrow and you could take a running jump across to the other side. Then again there were places where the brook was wide and shallow and you could cross on stepping stones, but sometimes, when the brook was deeper and swollen from heavy rain, the stepping stones would be below the surface and of no help in crossing over.

On a warm, lazy day, when there was no school, Peter and I and our older brother Ken, were playing in the brook, trying to build a dam with stones, mud and dead tree branches, hoping to make a pond where we could float a raft. I think Kenny got the idea from reading *The Adventures of Huckleberry Finn*. Though our brook was no Mississippi River, we had little success in holding back the insistent flow and eventually gave up the endeavor.

"I wonder where it comes from?" I asked of the others.

"What do you mean, where does what come from?"

"The water," I said, "all this water, where does it start?"

"Oh well, probably miles away, up in the hills, I suppose," said Ken, the older, wiser one.

"Let's find out," I suggested. "We could follow the brook all the way to where it starts."

"We may never find it, but I suppose we could try, as long as we can get home before dark," Ken agreed, so the three of us set off up stream.

The first thing to consider, as always, on such hiking expeditions, was to select and cut a stout straight stick from the hedgerow for each one of us, achieved with the help of Peter's indispensable pocket knife. The sticks were walking aids essentially, but they also had other uses, such as whacking nettles and prickly things, beating a way through tall grasses and reeds along the water's edge to scare away snakes, rats and other such undesirables that might be lurking in the underbrush as we made our way forward.

We were on an expedition, like Sir Richard Burton a hundred years before, when he set out to discover the source of the Nile river deep in the continent of Africa. But we didn't need a Royal Commission or a charter from The National Geographic Society. We didn't expect to encounter head hunting savages, get bitten by tsetse flies or come down with malaria. The worst that could happen to us would be to get severely scratched by thorns, or thoroughly wet and bruised from falling into the water.

The first mile or so was to us familiar territory. There was the place of the stepping stones, and further along the marsh at the foot of the meadow, the muddy bank where the cows came to drink. We then followed the brook through the field where our annual Sunday School picnic was always held. The farm house and barns stood at the top of the hill facing Sedgely Road. We came to a place where the brook disappeared beneath a thicket of overgrown bushes that forced us to detour. A wide, shallow pond at the other end of the thicket supported a good patch of watercress.

We must remember to pick some to take home on the way back. The ground was wet and spongy underfoot here, the water coming up over the tops of our shoes with every step that we took, but the land was pretty with bright yellow marsh marigolds and periwinkles pushing up out of the almost floating carpet of wet grass.

The brook began to narrow as the ground started to rise into the hills. The banks were steeper now, the water having cut its own channel into the softer ground. There were fewer trees and bushes here, just tall grasses and reeds close to the water's edge. Stones and pebbles now formed the stream bed, whereas before it was sandy or muddy. The noise of the water rushing and tumbling over stones and pebbles was now quite distinct, a happy, soothing liquid melody.

We crossed over a farm lane, where the brook was bridged over with stone slabs; then it flowed beneath a wooden fence, hardly any obstacle for our youthful agility. On up the gently sloping hillside the three of us pursued the ever narrowing brook, turning this way and that, following the natural course of the land in its obedience to the force of gravity. Birds rose up, startled as we approached, disturbing their feeding on gnats and other insects that hovered above the tumbling water and the soft, waterlogged earth at the edges of the brook.

As we followed the stream into a valley with gently sloping sides, the landscape changed quite abruptly. The lush vegetation diminished to a few hardy shrubs and weeds as we moved up the valley; the grasses and moss of the marshy low land from whence we had come changed now to stones and gravel. It was quite evident that the sides of the valley had, over the years, receded and stony material had fallen from the sides to form the floor of the swale. Our bonny brook was now a shallow wash of clear, fresh water sparkling in the afternoon sun, meandering between and around boulders and banks of sand and gravel.

"Hey! look at this!" Peter shouted. We went over to where he was bending down peering at some object that he had picked up from the rubble of stones. Ken took the curious piece and eyed it for a moment or two and announced his findings.

"It's a fossil. What you have is the remains of what was once a living creature millions of years ago."

It was somewhat like a clam shell that you would find at the seashore, now petrified and set into a larger piece of sandstone. For a while our original quest was delayed while we all three hunted for other samples of fossilized prehistoric life. We found several, but none so big as Peter's find, and pocketed them as souvenirs of our adventure. They sat displayed on top of the chest of drawers in our bedroom for a number of years. In primordial times this whole area would have been covered by ocean waters and the creatures therein, when dead, sank to the bottom and became fossilized. Then the waters receded over eons of time. We had no knowledge of the science of geology or the phenomenon of glacial recession at that age, but surely we learned something new every day of our lives.

Now we could see the high end of the valley. Our brook was little more than a trickle, like that in a rain filled gutter after a brief shower. We followed it up the slope until we came upon a small pool of bubbling water, not much bigger than a wash basin in a bathroom. Pure water came pouring out of the sand on the side of the hill about ten paces from the top rim of the valley. We put our hands over the flow to try to stop it, but the little fountain would not be denied and appeared again just a few inches away in a new outlet. We put a large stone on it, but nature had its way and within seconds the stream found a new outlet and continued on its appointed way. So here, without a doubt, was the beginning of our brook, its very source, a natural spring on a sandy hillside no more than three miles from our starting place. We all took a long drink of the sweet, clear, cold water, refreshing on this hot day, congratulated each other on our discovery, then set off on the shortest way home, away from the meandering brook. In diminishing daylight we walked through the little village of Spring Head which lay at the lower end of the valley of the fossils, grateful that the path would be down hill all the way home

Saturday Night Dance

It was Saturday afternoon and I was wondering how we were going to spend our precious free time on this particular weekend. I walked over to Hudsons where my close and eternal friend Billy lived, just two doors away from us at number 39, Parkfield Crescent. Bill saw me from the front window of their house as I approached and we met at the garden gate. The year was 1943. The turbulence of war continued unabated and the workshops and factories of England were running along at full capacity in the manufacture of every kind of war material. Bill worked on assembly in a factory. He was seventeen, a year older than I. I had graduated from Wolverhampton School of Art about a year before and was employed in an apprentice program for engineering drawing at Turner Manufacturing company which made parts for aircraft, including the renowned Hurricane and Spitfire fighter planes, and the landing gear for Lancaster bombers.

"What shall we do tonight?" I asked Billy.

"I don't know, what do you want to do?" he countered.

"Well, we could catch the early picture show at the Odeon, then go over to Mary's place and shoot some pool."

"What's showing at the Odeon this week?"

"I think it's a musical, *Moon Over Miami*. Betty Grable's in it."

"Betty Grable's OK, but I'd rather not sit through another one of those Technicolor musical extravaganzas. I still haven't dried out from the Esther Williams fabulous underwater spectacular we saw at the Colosseum two weeks ago. What's on at the Savoy?"

"*Key Largo* with Bogart, I think. I'll get the newspaper, then you can see the whole list."

"Nah, don't bother. Got any other bright ideas? I don't have much money to spare. Had to buy shoes and I put a third down on a new suit."

"There's a dance at Saint Peter's Church Hall starting at seven. We might get lucky and pick up a couple of girls, take them over to the Youth club on Cleveland Street later, get something to eat, play ping-pong or something. What do you think?"

"Sounds good. Let's do that."

Bill finally showed a spark of enthusiasm, no doubt because I'd mentioned girls. Billy Hudson was an ordinary fellow, better than average good-looking, had a healthy mop of dark brown hair, and a tanned complexion. He was always well dressed. Bill was shorter than myself by about two inches. Billy was sort of brash and outgoing, adept in the technique of chatting with the girls and could dance quite well. I was rather quiet and reserved and could hardly manage a simple two-step across the dance floor without stumbling or stepping on my partner's toes, which restrained me when inviting girls to dance. Mrs. Hudson liked me. She thought Billy was a little rough around the edges and she supposed that I would be a good influence on him. She knew that the Hammonds boys used to attend chapel every Sunday and assumed that we must be devout Christians and perhaps civilised, so she encouraged our friendship.

Bill came over after tea. I was just about ready to go. The Westminster clock on the mantel shelf in our living room chimed on the half-hour; it was six-thirty. Bill chatted with my mother while I brushed my hair, put on a tie, and slapped a little cologne on my face. I had told my mother of our plans to attend the Saturday night dance and maybe go to the Youth Center afterwards.

"Well, don't be out too late. I'll stay up 'til you're home."

"Don't worry so much, Mom, it's Saturday night. We might be late getting home. You shouldn't wait up. If we miss the last bus we'll have to walk."

I assured her that we were quite grown up and responsible. She worried anyway. It's a mother's prerogative and it was understandable. She had endured much grief during the last few years. My father had died shortly before the war began. My older brother, Maurice, was with the Eighth Army somewhere in the Middle East. He had been on home leave only twice since the beginning in 1939. Brother Ken was in army service with the Royal Engineers in North Africa, and Peter was a petty officer on a Royal Navy ship somewhere in the Pacific. I was the last of my mother's sons still at home.

Mother devoted many hours each week to writing letters to my brothers. They responded whenever they could and told us whatever they were allowed to, so that we could learn of their well-being and about some of their experiences. At least the war was going better for our side by this time. German forces were fully occupied on the Russian front now. The bombing of Britain was much diminished; the infrequent air raids occurred mainly at night. When the warning sirens would sound we didn't go down into the air raid shelters as we did in the early days of the Blitz. However, the enemy had not neglected us entirely. They still had some awful tribulations for us to endure, one of several being the dropping of delayed action bombs which would have to be surrounded with a barrier of sandbags and carefully defused so they would not explode. Just this last week a German bomber had been shot down outside of town.

Many people grew weary of wartime conditions from overwork, stress, illness, and grief, so recreational activities and entertainment were regarded as essential to keep up our spirits and support our resolve. We enjoyed whatever outlets were available: the cinema, dancing, symphony concerts, athletic leagues, variety shows, and sing-alongs at union halls and social clubs, and of course that old, traditional British institution, the corner pub. (Strangely, beer was one of the very few commodities not rationed and was hardly ever in short supply.) All of these activities were shared with the many thousands of members of our own and allied armed forces that were among us. Never was there such cama-raderie and goodwill abounding between people as there was dur-ing those intense days of the war.

Bill and I walked toward the bus stop at the top of our street, Parkfield Crescent. It was the turn-around place where the bus would pause before starting back on the route to town center. We were early.

"I need to get some cigarettes. Let's go over to Thornton's. We have plenty of time," Bill said.

We walked the half block to the Pharmacy/News store. Mavis Thornton served us; she was always there. Her father was the pharmacist, or chemist as we called him. Mavis managed the newspaper, tobacco, candy, and other retail business. She lived with her widowed father in a small neat house on top of a hill be-hind the shop on Parkfield Road. Very nice people, permanent fix-tures in our neighborhood, almost like family. Mavis was about thirty years old, unmarried, a lovely, friendly lady, constantly cheerful. Bill bought a pack of Wild Woodbines and some lemon drops and I chose a ten-pack of Players and some spearmint gum.

"Where are you boys going? What are you boys up to, all spiffed up?" asked Mavis.

"We're going to the dance at Saint Peter's Church Hall down-town. Why don't you put on your best dress and come along with us?" Billy teased, knowing she couldn't leave even if she wanted to.

"Don't you think I'd just like to one of these days, eh?" Mavis replied good humoredly, and as we opened the door to leave, called after us, "Have a good time, boys. Be good."

Bill called back, "Don't wait up for us."

We made our way across Thompson Avenue to the waiting bus, climbed to the top level of the double-decker where smoking was allowed, dug into our pockets for coins to pay the fare, and lit up cigarettes. At the downtown terminal, we got off, walked across Queens Square, passed the statue of Prince Albert mounted upon his prancing horse, went through Saint Peter's Churchyard, across Wulfruna Street by the Technical College, and over to the Parish School Hall where the dances were held. We each paid the few shillings admission. The lady at the table put the money into a metal cash box, and issued pink tickets from a roll in return.

"Be sure to hold on to your tickets," she advised. "There will be a drawing for prizes at intermission."

The band sounded good, although not by any measure the "Glen Miller sound" which was all the rage then. Three or four couples were already dancing, and over in a corner several all girl couples were practicing their steps. We strolled across the dance floor toward the empty seats along the wall, looking over the girls for prospective partners.

Within half an hour the hall filled up. The band was more lively now, playing to the enthusiastic patrons. A mirrored ball, suspended from the ceiling and turning slowly, reflected moving specks of light across the room, like bright falling snow. The dance floor became crowded. All the couples moved in unison in a clockwise direction. Bill and I had already taken some turns around to an easy quick-step with two girls eager to dance. Both of us had been tapped on the shoulder and, we thought, rudely interrupted by competitors, but of course we were free to exercise the same privilege if we would choose to do so. We made our way over to the small cafeteria and ordered orange squash and a piece of Dundee cake, a generous portion I thought for the price. A layer of tobacco smoke hovered over the crowded hall, resembling an early morning fog over a dewy meadow. A female vocalist was singing "Green Eyes" as we resumed our places in the wallflower section. Very soon Bill invited a willing partner onto the dance floor and they disappeared quickly into the rhythmic throng.

A rather attractive girl coming towards me caught my eye.

"Wow!" I thought. "I'm in luck. She's actually going to ask *me* to dance with *her*. This is an unusual reversal of form."

She smiled and said, "Hello, would you care to dance with me?"

"Yes, of course," I replied with a morsel of suspicion. "I'll be delighted to."

"A certain fellow has been bothering me constantly, and I have to get away from him. I'm afraid he's a bit strange. If you pretend that we're together I don't think he will bother me any more."

"Certainly," I replied, gathering some enthusiasm. "I'm always willing to come to the aid of a lady in distress." I was also a little apprehensive because I thought he might turn out to be a heavy-weight, aggressive kind of chap looking for trouble. We waltzed around the floor for a while; then I noticed a slightly disheveled character moving stealthily towards me and I felt a tap on my shoulder.

"Excuse me, may I break in here?" the intruder requested in slightly slurred speech.

"Sorry, pal, we're together for the evening," I told him quite firmly, and he didn't persist.

"That's telling him," my partner said, as she drew me closer to her. "I don't think he'll try again." She was most forgiving of my clumsy effort at the inspiring Viennese waltz.

"My name is Bob," I said. What does your mother call you?"

"Phyll, usually. My name is Phyllis."

"I'm very pleased to meet you, Phyllis," I said sincerely. "You look vaguely familiar. Have we met before?"

"I have the same feeling," she said, "but I really can't say for sure."

My self confidence took a leap forward. I was hopeful that I might be at the beginning of a new friendship.

The MC announced an intermission and invited all present to patronize the refreshment booth where the ladies of the parish were serving and hoping to raise some revenue for their charity work. The congregation buzzed with conversation overlaid with occasional bursts of laughter. Every one nursed a glass of cold drink. Many puffed away on cigarettes adding to the thickening strata of smoke in the now overly warm and stuffy hall.

A drum roll and fanfare called attention to the Master of Ceremonies at the bandstand, where he announced the ticket numbers for the door prizes: a fancy box of Cadbury's Black Magic chocolates for the lady and a box of cigars for the gentleman, welcome treats in those days of scarcity and austerity. We had no luck in the sweepstakes.

The music began again; the dancers returned to the floor. It was a mixed assembly. Lots of uniforms, men from the big RAF base at Cosford, a few allied soldiers from Poland and The Netherlands, some American GI's, some British Army and Royal Navy lads, most likely on home leave, but still a predominantly civilian crowd, slightly more male than female. Phyllis and I took another turn or two around the floor. Then I suggested that we leave the dance.

"Have you seen the German bomber that was shot down last week?" I asked her. "It's on display in the Market Square."

"No, I haven't," she replied, "but my brother told me about it."

"Would you like to go over there and see it?" I proposed.

"Yes, that might be interesting. Why not?"

I found my friend Bill sitting with his new partner and told him that I was leaving with Phyllis. "We'll catch the last bus home. See you at the bus stop, eleven-thirty, all right?"

"So long, then," Bill acknowledged with a nod and a thumbs-up sign.

Phyllis and I retrieved our coats from the cloakroom and walked out of the hall into the fresh night air. The dance music faded as we made our way toward North Street which would lead us into the market square. It was about half-past nine. We walked close together and exchanged small talk. We were of similar height. Her honey blond hair was almost shoulder length, and I supposed we were about the same age though I thought she might have been a bit older because she danced so well and seemed to be more confident than I at making conversation; but I didn't dare to ask.

There in the corner of the broad, cobblestoned market square was the downed German bomber, mounted on a huge flatbed trailer. The street lights were dim but still cast enough light for the few interested onlookers to see it all. The idea to put it on public display was, of course, a morale builder, an opportunity for us to meet the enemy face-to-face as it were, and to prove that he wasn't invincible.

"I wonder where it dropped its bombs?" Phyllis asked.

"Probably Liverpool or Manchester, since we haven't had any raids around here for a week or two." I answered. I knew that the plane was a Heinkel 111 because I had taken a mandatory course in aircraft identification, fire fighting, and first aid while in school. The plane was somewhat smaller than I had envisioned, quite sleek and streamlined in design, painted entirely an ominous dull black except for the white double cross insignia of the Luftwaffe on both sides of the fuselage. Both of the outer wings were broken off; the three-bladed propellers on both of its engines were twisted and bent out of shape; and there were some holes in the main body of the plane, no doubt the result of anti-aircraft gunfire. Otherwise the plane was undamaged. The unlucky plane had probably been hit and brought down while homeward bound and had belly landed in farm fields outside of town, the surviving injured crew members taken as prisoners of war.

Phyllis commented, "I've lost a cousin in a plane crash in the RAF, 1940."

"I'm very sorry," said I. "As a matter of fact, I've lost two cousins in RAF plane crashes, first year of the war—one in Egypt and one in Kent."

"How awful," said Phyllis, as we slowly walked away from that vivid reminder of the frightful reality of the times. "It's a stupid, terrible war. I wish it was all over. How much longer can it go on?"

"Where do you live?" I asked my new friend. "I'd like to walk you home."

"Oh, not too far. Just where Stafford Road and North Street come together."

"Yes, I know that part of town, down by Christ Church. My grandparents live on West Street."

"Oh, really? Well, I'll turn off just beyond the church. It's getting late. I suppose I had better be heading for home anyway, and thank you for walking with me. I'd rather not be walking alone."

"Did you go to the dance alone?"

"Oh, no," Phyllis was quick to reply. "I was with a girl friend and like your pal Bill, she met some one and they left early."

I felt by this time we had established a certain fondness for each other and I took her hand in mine. We passed by the Bodega Inn where I could hear sounds of merriment within and a piano playing. I suggested that we go inside; they would be closing in half an hour, but she declined. "I really don't drink, and it's too noisy in there. Thanks, anyway."

"You're right. And the cigarette smoke can be pretty awful too," I added, "and anyway we have lots to talk about."

"Oh? What shall we talk about?"

"Anything," I said. "I just like to hear your voice."

"And what's so special about my voice?"

"Well, I think you have a special way of saying things, sort of gentle and agreeable."

She laughed as we strolled along. "Do you have a steady girl friend, Bob?" she inquired.

"No, no, no one at all," I answered, almost too hastily. "Are you involved with any one?"

"No, I was for awhile, but we broke up. I decided that he really wasn't right for me. He was too demanding and very selfish. Everything always had to be his way or he would pout like a small child."

"Oh, you're well out of it then. Probably a momma's boy."

"That's right, he was always talking about his mother, telling me how wonderful she was. I got to know her and really, I didn't think she was so gracious at all."

We walked slowly. I was wishing that time would stand still. We looked into store windows, all closed up for the night now. We laughed at our distorted reflections in the glass. We passed New Cross Street, both of us talking freely now about our jobs and some of the characters who were our friends at work.

"Would you like to go to the movies with me next week sometime?" I asked.

"I'd like to." She paused. "Would Wednesday night be all right?"

"Yes, that would be fine. We could catch the early show, then have supper at Reynolds Café afterwards."

"That sounds lovely. I'll look forward to it."

"Six o'clock on the steps at the Art Gallery then."

"All right, that's fine."

I put my arm around her waist. She looked at me and smiled timidly. We walked on slowly. I had a wonderful feeling about this evening. I felt good about myself. I was walking on air. I must be careful about what I say and do, be mindful not to offend, I thought, during a lapse in our conversation. I *do* like this girl and feel genuine affection for her.

Christ Church loomed large at the junction of Stafford Road and North Street, surrounded by tall stately elm trees. Its tall Gothic windows appeared dark and blank with no interior light to display the beauty of the stained glass that I knew was there. There were not many cars on the street and even fewer people about. We stopped near the church steps without speaking, and as if by pre-planned mutual accord, we stepped into the shadows near the stone wall of the old church. I held Phyllis close to me, put my cheek next to hers, so cool and soft, and whispered in her ear, "I think you are very beautiful. I like you very much."

We looked into each other's eyes for some moments of antici-pation, then I kissed her very gently on the lips. She didn't object or retreat, so I kissed her again, this time longer and more ar-dently. When our lips parted we breathed deeply. I started to speak, but she said "Shush! Don't say anything." She put a finger to my lips as if to say "Don't speak now." Putting her arms around me and holding me very close to her, she kissed me so very tenderly, her lips slightly apart, in a way that I had never experienced be-fore, so soft, so sweet, so warm. It was heavenly. At that moment I was madly in love, possessed by a deep feeling of elation, and I hoped that she also was elevated to the same level of happiness.

My exhilaration waned when we relaxed our embrace and Phyllis said quietly, "I had better go now."

"Not just yet," I pleaded.

"Really, I must. And you have to hurry to get the last bus home."

"Very well, but it's still on for next Wednesday then?"

"Yes, of course. Goodnight, Bob, and thanks. I enjoyed being with you."

"I had a good time, too. Goodnight, Phyll. I'll see you to your door. Which street do you live on?" I asked as we walked to the corner.

"Please don't bother. My house is just a little way down Nine Elms Lane. You must hurry."

"Say, I know someone who lives on Nine Elms," I said.

"You do?"

"Yes, my Uncle Jim."

"Jim who?" Phyllis asked, somewhat quizzically.

"Oakley," I said. "My mother's brother, James Oakley. Do you know the family?"

Phyllis took two steps backward, put a hand to her mouth, and gasped audibly. "Oh my God! You are Aunty Jane's youngest boy, Bobby! You are, aren't you?"

The realization that we were first cousins hit me like a bolt of lightning. I was at the same time both highly amused and utterly devastated.

"Yes, that's right, I am. Then you must be Uncle Jim's youngest girl, Phyllis."

"Yes. What are we going to do? Don't tell any one, promise! I can't believe it. I've been kissing my own cousin! Whatever you do, don't tell Flossie. She's sure to tell my mother." Flossie was Phyllis's oldest sister, the only one of the family apart from Uncle Jim himself, who was in touch with our family and then only on infrequent occasions. Flossie was a particular friend of my mother and had a reputation as a gossip.

When the initial shock subsided and the awful truth set in, I knew that any further intimate relationship would not be possible. On the one hand I was relieved to learn the truth, but on the other, terribly disappointed. We were both embarrassed now, couldn't even stand close to each other any more. We looked each other in the eyes and simultaneously broke into laughter.

"Never mind," said Phyllis. "I still had a good time tonight."

"Me too. A very good time," I added.

We touched hands. She walked away quickly. I called after her, "You're my favorite cousin, Phyllis." She turned back towards me, smiled, then waved goodbye.

The sharp sound of her half-high-heeled shoes on the stone pavement jarred the silence and echoed in the chilly night air, then diminished as she walked briskly away and very soon dissolved into the shadows on Nine Elms Lane.

I began the walk back to the center of town, all up hill now. I was bewildered and dejected. No longer did I want time to stand still. Quite the contrary. Suddenly I was alone and very lonely with plenty of time to contemplate the unusual chain of events in this extraordinary encounter. I passed two large canvas covered military trucks parked in Queens Square by the statue of Prince Albert on his horse, surrounded by a group of American soldiers waiting to be taken back to their camp out on Bridgenorth Road after their night on the town. Some were already in the trucks, some sitting on the kerb, others standing around talking casually and puffing on their favorite smokes, a few on the fringe saying their passionate goodbyes to Saturday night dates. A few white helmeted MP's were present, as usual, to keep things orderly. Their jeep was parked in front of the transports.

Further along at my usual bus stop on Leicester Street all was quiet. The town was closed down for the night. Bill was not there. The last bus had gone some fifteen minutes ago. I was in for a long walk home. Midnight was approaching and downtown was almost deserted. The night took on a winter like chill. I turned up my coat collar, thrust my hands deep into the pockets and broadened my stride towards home.

My mind rambled through a maze of thoughts as I walked along, but a consistent theme kept repeating itself. Phyllis Oakley, Phyllis Oakley. Try as I might, I just couldn't get her out of my mind. Over and over again I reviewed the events of the evening. No wonder she looked vaguely familiar when we first met. But then, you see, we hadn't seen each other since we were both small children.

The cousin that she spoke of, the one who died in an RAF plane crash, was my cousin, too, Frank Oakley. I told myself that I must put this embarrassing affair behind me right now. Nothing could ever come of it anyway. Never had I fallen in love and out again so quickly. It was too painful a subject to dwell on now. As I turned the corner at the top of our street by the little triangular park with the public air-raid shelter in the middle of it, I honestly wished Phyllis and I were not related at all, so that we could continue our close friendship.

The Hudsons' house was dark and quiet like all the other houses on Parkfield Crescent, except for ours. Mother was still up when I arrived home well after midnight, sitting in her favorite chair beside the fireplace, reading a book. The fire was down to its last embers.

"You're late. Where have you been 'til this hour? I suppose you missed the last bus. Did Billy come home with you?"

"No, we met two girls and walked them home. Bill wasn't at the bus stop in town. He either caught the bus or is still walking home."

"Would you like something to eat?"

"No thanks, Mom."

"A cup of tea?"

"No, thanks anyway. I'm tired. I think I'll go straight up to bed."

"Who was she and where did she live?"

"Too many questions, Mom," I answered, along with a sleepy yawn. "Her name was Phyllis. She lived down by Christ Church somewhere."

"Phyllis who?" she insisted.

"Do you know, I didn't even ask her. She was really nice, a good dancer, too, but I don't think I'll be seeing her again."

"That's a shame. You should bring one of your girl friends over to tea some time."

"Do you think so? Would it be all right then?"

"Of course it would. I would rather have liked to meet this Phyllis what's-er-name."

"Oh yes, I'm sure you two would get along fine. You could quite possibly have a close relationship with her."

I hung up my coat, took off my shoes, kissed my mother on her cheek, smiled, and said "Goodnight, Mom, you're still my best girl."

Danny Boy

The beautiful and haunting "Londonderry Air," best known as "Danny Boy," has been played and revered since the earliest of times when traveling minstrels were common entertainers in Ireland. The melody's origins are unknown but generally attributed to ancient Celtic culture. The words, however, were set to this melody by an English gentleman, a barrister by the name of Fred Weatherly, in the latter part of the nineteenth century and are recognized as perhaps the best loved of a long list of sentimental Irish ballads.

I recently had the pleasure of renewing my love and admiration for this old melodic treasure after hearing several renditions of it on last St. Patrick's Day. As I listened to all the words, I was impressed as never before by the precious and poignant lyrics. Although I have hummed, whistled and attempted to sing "Oh Danny Boy" on countless occasions since early childhood (most often in the shower) I had not until now fully appreciated the eloquence of those emotion filled verses and how appropriate and fitting they are to certain events that occurred in my own experience.

> Oh Danny boy, the pipes the pipes are calling
> From glen to glen and down the mountain side.
> The summer's gone and all the roses falling
> 'Tis you, 'tis you must go and I must bide . . .

The words would have fitted the occasion of a mother saying goodbye to a son going off to war or a wife or sweetheart bidding farewell to a loved one leaving to establish a new life in America or Australia, when sailing ships were still the most common means of transport overseas, so it would likely be many years (or possibly never) before the emigrant would return home. The parallel in my personal experience would be the occasion of my leaving home and my widowed mother in January, 1951, to establish a new life and seek better opportunities in America.

> But come ye back when summer's in the meadow
> Or when the valley's hushed and white with snow
> 'Tis I'll be here in sunshine or in shadow.
> Oh Danny boy, oh Danny boy, I love you so."

It was a cold mid-January morning. My belongings were packed in an old cabin trunk and a suit case, ready by the front door. A taxi was waiting in the street to take me to the railway station. Mother was suppressing tears as I put on my raincoat.

"Now write to me as soon as you get settled. Let me know how things are going."

"Of course I will, Mom, don't worry. Everything will be all right. If things go well I'll be back to see you soon and maybe you could join us if you'd like to."

"I think I'm too old to start all over again in a strange place. You *will* come back, though?"

"Of course I will."

I hugged her and kissed her goodbye. "I have to go now. The taxi is waiting."

"You won't forget me, will you?'

"Of course not. I'll write often, so don't worry about me. Goodbye Mom!"

I joined my fiancée, Rebecca, in the taxi. We rode to the main railway station, bought one-way tickets to Liverpool, then made our way onto the platform, burdened with our heavy luggage, to await the arrival of the express train. We were pleasantly surprised when my former employer came on the scene to bid us farewell and wish us good luck in our venture. We thought it to be very generous of him, so early in the morning, too. Mr. Barbour handed me an envelope, said it was a character reference, might be useful in obtaining employment "on the other side of the pond." He requested me not to open it until later. Probably didn't want me to be embarrassed by what turned out to be a glowing tribute to my personal integrity and skill as a qualified craftsman, etc. etc., all typed out perfectly on the best company letterhead and bearing his flowing signature.

By early afternoon we had arrived at dockside in Liverpool by way of taxi from the train station and boarded the proud Cunard passenger liner *Britannic*. The weather was bone chilling cold, drizzling wet, and a stiff breeze blew from seaward. Getting into the warmth of our assigned quarters was a welcome relief. I was to share a cabin with a Mr. Roberts and Rebecca was lodged with another lady in a similarly appointed cabin on the same deck but on the port side.

After stowing our luggage, freshening up, changing clothes and becoming acquainted with some of our fellow voyagers, Rebecca and I set out to explore the many facilities on this well appointed ship. There is a certain shipboard routine that passengers are expected to follow so that life proceeds in an orderly and enjoyable manner, such as being assigned a set lifeboat station, taking part in fire and lifeboat drills, choosing early or late sittings in the dining room, table seating, and so on. We soon got into the routine and began to intermingle with many of the three hundred or so fellow passengers.

The *Britannic* was not among the biggest of the trans-Atlantic liners. She was of intermediate size, displacing about 24,000 tons compared to the gigantic Queens *Mary* and *Elizabeth* at 85,000 tons, but *Britannic* was the biggest motor powered vessel at that time. We were bound for New York by way of Queenstown in Ireland and Hamilton, the capitol city and principal seaport of Bermuda. Our departure from Liverpool was delayed because of heavy weather, but we got underway the next morning in spite of the wind and foul weather. The following morning dawned clear with only a slight swell on the sea's surface. I went out onto the boat deck for a morning walk-about in the fresh air and discovered that we were approaching the harbor of Queenstown, the port nearest the city of Cork, to take on the passengers from Ireland. *Britannic* hove to just off shore and took aboard the newcomers from a small transfer vessel by way of a stairway rigged outboard. In little more than an hour we were again underway and soon rounding the southern tip of Ireland heading out to the broad Atlantic.

The ship was quite crowded now but everything was well organized. There were games, movie theater, gymnasium, a swimming pool, and a constant round of food and drink served in the dining room and several other cafes and bars about the ship. The dining room was only lightly patronized on the first day out. Many passengers had not yet got their sea-legs—the sea was kicking up and causing widespread *mal-de-mer*—but by the third day, almost everyone aboard had become qualified sailors.

My cabin mate turned out to be a prince of a fellow. He was of middle age, a bespectacled scholarly looking man, probably in his early fifties, while I was just 23. Mr. Roberts was returning from England back to his position as headmaster of a grammar school on the island of Barbados. He had traveled widely in the States, including Michigan, where we were to settle, and was able to describe the geography and environment and assure us that we were going to a highly desirable place in which to establish our new lives.

I don't remember exactly where I was on the ship or what I was doing the third or fourth day out from Liverpool, when I heard my name called over the intercom, requesting me to report to the telegraph office.

"There is a radiogram for you, Mr. Hammonds. It came over just minutes ago." The radio officer handed me a small brown envelope. "Sign here please and note the time and date. Thank you, sir."

I opened it immediately and read the terse message: "Mother passed away January 22nd. Ken." I stood there in disbelief, paralyzed, mind and body frozen for what seemed to be a very long time.

"What's wrong, Bob?" Rebecca's voice refocused my befuddled mind. Without a word I handed her the radiogram and watched the color drain from her face. " 'Oh God, no!" she said. "Bob, I'm so sorry." She put her hand on my shoulder and we walked away from the busy ship's office to find a quiet place. My first feelings were those of grief and self pity, eventually changing to a deep sense of guilt and helplessness. I certainly had no power to turn around and go back. I was haunted by the last vision of my mother holding back her tears and pleading with me to come back some day and not forget her. That was just a few short days ago. I was to learn later that she died from heart failure two days after I left home. She had had a history of heart disease but nothing could persuade me, even to this day, that my going away, the youngest and last of her five sons to leave home, had not contributed to her sad demise, all too soon at age 62.

I tried desperately to suppress my sad feelings and to present a Spartan attitude. Mr. Roberts was very supportive and understanding and with his and Rebecca's cheerful presence I was able to put on a false front and to mask my true feelings of deep remorse while joining them in the busy shipboard life.

Seven days later *Britannic* cruised slowly into the harbor at Hamilton, Bermuda, under a cloudless blue sky attended by bright, warm, sunshine, a perfect day, which Rebe and I took full advantage of, exploring the narrow streets and steep lanes and flower bedecked sidewalks of the fascinating town. Every building was painted white or shades of pastel with most flaunting red tiled roofs to the bright blue sky that covered those sun-drenched islands. About forty fellow voyagers ended their journey in Bermuda. We had come to know some of them as good friends and we were reluctant to say goodbye, knowing it to be a final farewell. In the morning *Britannic* let go her mooring lines and eased away from the dock. Several blasts from her sirens echoed from the tiers of stucco buildings that surrounded Hamilton harbor; then she made slow passage through a hazardous channel to the open sea. The pilot was dismissed and he boarded his launch by way of a rope ladder which had been deployed over the lee side of our vessel. Heading north by west we began to encounter heavy weather. The further north we traveled the worse it became with chilling winds, driving rain and high waves on the ocean curtailing all recreational activity on the open decks.

Early on the morning of the tenth day of our voyage we came upon the Ambrose lightship which, in those days, marked the approach channel to the port of New York and the Hudson River. *Britannic* took on the harbor pilot, an expert navigator in those waters, who would direct the ship to its designated pier at the Cunard Line terminal. The temperature was near freezing. Light rain was falling through a heavy mist as we glided slowly through the narrows in the river estuary. In spite of the forbidding weather there was much enthusiasm among the passengers at the prospect of being greeted by "Lady Liberty," that monumental Statue of Liberty that embodies powerful significance for all immigrants coming to America for its promise of freedom and a welcome to their new homeland. Our ship took on a slight list to port as everyone, except those members of the ship's company on duty, crowded the side railings on the open upper decks. Alas, the huge statue was only a giant, fog-shrouded apparition, silent, but echoing the mournful blasts of fog horns from several unseen vessels navigating in the vast harbor.

The full significance of the Statue of Liberty, what it stands for, why it was placed in that particular location, and why it is revered by so many thousands, yea millions of people, myself included, made my spine tingle. But why, I asked myself, was I so moved by the experience?. I wasn't fleeing from tyranny or oppression, nor was I particularly poor, although that point could be legitimately argued. I wasn't hungry or yearning to breathe free; I was here by my own choice, coming from a free, democratic society; and yet I felt deep emotion and was moved by the rare experience of seeing the impressive monument raising high the torch of liberty that calls out loud and clear . . . "Welcome to America."

The towers of lower Manhattan appeared in clearer outline as we approached, the fog now thinning to a mist over the city, the tops of the tallest buildings disappearing in the low clouds. Rebecca and I were tense with anticipation and a slight fear of the unknown as *Britannic*, pushed and nudged by a pair of tug boats, eased her way into her mooring alongside the Cunard pier. After disembarking we claimed our luggage in the cavernous terminal building and proceeded through customs and immigration. Names were processed in alphabetical order and Rebecca's name beginning with B (for Brackstone) was called well ahead of mine beginning with H. All of her documents being in order she had her passport stamped and was free to go. My turn eventually came up and I was assigned to a rather stern and unsympathetic INS officer who discovered that I was missing a required document, a medical health report which I had mislaid somewhere along the way—probably somewhere in my luggage.

"You will be sent to Ellis for further processing," the officer declared icily.

"But I can't, we're together," I pleaded anxiously, pointing to Rebecca who was beginning to take on a worried look as she waited on the far side of the barrier. He led me to a fenced off holding area where several other unfortunates had also been confined. After a short period of apprehension a different INS officer approached me and asked why I was there. I explained about the missing medical report and that my fiancee had already been processed and was anxiously waiting for me. He looked over in her direction and sensed her concern. The fact that she happened to be a very attractive number at that time could have had some influence on his decision to pass me through and stamp my passport.

"You look healthy enough to me, young feller, best o' luck to yer," he said, in a lovely Brooklyn accent.

Rebe and I stepped ashore into the U. S. of A. on January 30th, 1951.

Sharing a cab ride with a fellow *Britannic* passenger, I asked the driver to take us to a middle class hotel in mid-town Manhattan which he did, dropping us off in the area of Broadway and 45th street. After resting for a while we freshened up and headed out into the crowded streets on our first exploration of New York City. The top of the Empire State building, the tallest building in the whole world at that time, was our first priority, and what a thrill it was to look down on the city and surrounding water-ways as if from a hovering balloon! Particularly intriguing was the fact that we could look down on the extensive docks and see among many of the well known ocean liners of that era, the very ship that had brought us here making ready for her return voyage to England. Times Square and the fabulous lights and neon signs on Broadway were also high on our list of things to see and do on that memorable day.

Our next order of business was to visit a brother of Ken's wife Norah, by the name of John Muldoon, who lived at 177 East 66th Street, a convenient subway ride from where we were staying. He, along with a younger brother, had come from Galway, Ireland, in the late twenties and was a New York City policeman. John and his wife Ann had two teen-age children, Gary, 16, and Mary, 18. The Muldoons were absolutely charming people and treated us like family. They all welcomed us warmly and were most interested to learn all the latest news from home and what our plans might be. We stayed with them for two days and were reluctant to leave their company. When we left, they saw us safely to Grand Central Station and the train that would take us to Michigan.

"If things don't work out for you out there in the wild west of Michigan, you can come back and we'll help you get settled here in New York," John said, half jokingly I suppose, but he was the kind of man who could be held to his word.

The train followed the Hudson River closely for the first hour or so. It was dark now, light from the moon reflecting off the bright steel tracks ahead and dancing on the black waters of the river. It would be a long night; we must try to sleep. Tomorrow we would be in Michigan. But that's the beginning of a whole new and different story.

> But when you come and all the flowers are dying
> If I am dead, as dead I may well be
> You'll come and find the place where I am lying
> And kneel and say an Ave there for me.

Four decades and a few more years have slipped by over a busy life of hard work and simple pleasures, the anxiety and blessings of raising four children, and now the delight of watching five lovely grandchildren mature, not to forget now the aches and pains that are inevitable with our advancing years. On a recent visit back to England, while staying with my brother Ken we decided to visit the country churchyard at Bushbury and the graves of our parents and maternal grandparents. Our grandparents' burial places were completely overgrown by a dense holly bush, undisturbed for many a year. I located the gravestone on my parents' burial place which was covered with tall grass and vines. The ground was somewhat sunken and the marble slab tipped at an angle. I worked to pull away the overgrowth and managed to straighten the stone which read in still legible lettering,

Frank Hammonds 1889~1938
Jane Elizabeth (Oakley) Hammonds 1889~1951
In Peace

And I shall hear 'though soft you tread above me
And all my grave shall warmer, sweeter be,
For you will bend and tell me that you love me
And I will sleep in peace until you come to me.

Now I am not a firm believer in life hereafter nor do I harbor any faith in the theological concepts of heaven and hell, but I did bend over my mother's grave and frame some words in silence, asking her to forgive me for all the things that I did and ought not to have done and for all the things that I failed to do and should have done. I told her that I had appreciated all the things that she had done for me; that I was grateful for my very existence; that I had given her four fine grandchildren, also five lovely great grandchildren and that we all loved her.

I left that hallowed place happier for having made the effort to visit, but the disconcerting question still lingers uneasily on my mind: "How much longer would my mother have lived and enjoyed life if I had not gone away from her just when I did?"

SHIRLEY HARDING

I was born in England, the second child in a family of four children. My father was a cricketer who played for Worcester. Two life-changing events occurred within several months of each other when I was almost four years old. My father was killed in an automobile accident and the Second World War started. At the time of my father's death, my mother had three children under six and was one month pregnant with my brother David.

In 1940 my sister Gillian and I were sent to a boarding school: The Royal Wanstead School. All the children in the school were fatherless, and the costs were underwritten by a philanthropic organization. When my brothers were old enough, they also attended the same school.

My mother remarried and in 1952 my family emigrated to the United States. Originally we lived in Connecticut but moved within two years to Annapolis, Maryland. This was the beginning of a life for me where moving from state to state became a constant. I married a Naval officer in Annapolis and lived in such disparate states as Hawaii and Idaho. In 1961 my daughter, Heather, was born.

I came to Ann Arbor in 1968 with my husband for him to attend graduate school. At that time I tentatively started taking classes at the University of Michigan. I only had one year of college before marriage and entered as what was politely called "a mature student." I was 32; the other sophomores were 18. This was an extraordinary experience, as those who remember the student demonstrations of the late '60s and early '70s may remember. I majored in English and went on to get a graduate degree in Journalism.

For several years I worked as a medical writer at the University of Michigan Medical Center, and again returned to college to get an advanced degree in Public Health. I worked for 17 years at the Michigan Department of Public Health in Lansing.

A few years ago I took an early retirement and am relishing being able to program my own time. I take classes when I choose. I still have a pile of books waiting to be read. I now have the time to travel and returned to

England last year for the first time in many years. I was reintroduced to my remaining relatives and went to a reunion of my boarding school. A classmate took me to see the wonderful old Elizabethan house where we were in school during the war. I hope to return every other year to be again with the women who shared those formative years with me.

Reminiscences
of Ingatestone Hall

During the Second World War I attended a boarding school in England called the Royal Wanstead School (RWS). The school was unusual, because all the children who attended it had lost their fathers, and their mothers had been left without sufficient money to support their children. My mother became a widow in 1939, just before the war started. She was left with three children under six and was one month pregnant with my brother David. The details of how money was collected to send us all to school were vague; we knew only that we had to receive a certain number of votes to be admitted to the school, and that these votes were purchased by wealthy patrons who advocated for the fatherless children.

My family emigrated to the United States in 1952, and it was not until 1999 that I started to research the circumstances of my schooling and to investigate whether the school was still in existence. It took several months of research via the computer and contacts I made in England to find that the school was no longer in existence. However, I did learn that there was an organization called Friends of the Royal Wanstead School which held periodic reunions, and that there was a reunion scheduled for July 8th, 2000, so I started planning my trip to England around the reunion with my exclassmates. The person who organized these reunions was Marianne Thorne (née Thackray), who had been in my form at boarding school. Marianne had become the self-appointed archivist for the school. She and her twin Annette had been good friends of mine, and I now had a contact who would be knowledgeable about the school, and who I hoped could answer the many questions I had.

The school had originated with the Royal Wanstead Foundation which was started by an influential philanthropist, the Reverend Andrew Reed, in 1813. He raised money for middle class fatherless children to attend boarding school. The school was originally called the Infant Orphan Asylum, and the children were admitted by election by the subscribers to the Foundation. The Charity was under royal patronage, and was a popular organization for wealthy people to support during that time. The name of the foundation was changed to Royal Wanstead School in 1938. I thought it odd that children attending the school were called orphans when they had lost only their fathers and not their mothers. But this really was a reflection of the status of women at the time. After all, women had no financial resources of their own, and if they became widows their children were as good as orphans without the income of their fathers. This reminded me of the constant preoccupation in novels by Jane Austen of the pursuit of suitable marriages for young women. Suitable marriages, of course, had little to do with love and a great deal to do with money.

I received a letter from Marianne, including a class picture with the names of the girls identified on a separate sheet of paper, a list of names and addresses of ex-scholars of RWS, and a couple of newsletters. She said that I was the only girl missing from the small group of senior girls who spent their first year together at Ingatestone Hall. Apparently there were only eight of us in the class, and it was therefore not surprising that the names I still remembered were of the girls in that class.

Looking at the picture, I would not have recognized myself, without the legend with my name on it. We looked so terribly British, standing or sitting in four rows with our teachers and nurses in the center. The youngest girls sat on the ground in the front row with their legs crossed, and their backs very straight. We all had on the traditional uniform of white blouse, navy skirt and school tie.

During the war, children at the Royal Wanstead School were evacuated from Wanstead in North London to Ingatestone Hall, the lovely home of Lord and Lady Petre in Essex which was less likely to be targeted by German bombers. The hall itself was U-shaped with a horizontal wing and two parallel wings with a large courtyard in the center. The hall was built of lovely mellow brick which was partially covered with vines and wisteria. The mullioned windows had large ledges on the inside which made wonderful window seats for little bottoms. The right wing was the dining hall, the staff room and the kitchen. The dining hall was paneled and had stags' heads on the surrounding walls. We ate at large refectory tables which I believe were original to the Hall. Outside the dining hall was a large fir tree which had branches that swept the ground, but there was enough room to stand up inside underneath the branches. This was my favorite place to read. When the weather was warm, we took a book and a ground cover and found a place to read. Lying there, protected from the outside by the fir branches, and journeying off to some other place or time is one of my favorite memories of this place. When the weather was warm, and it was a weekend we had no classes, and we played outside the whole weekend. I would lie in bed at night, thinking how wonderful it was going to be the following day. I would spend all day playing games with the other girls and I couldn't wait until the morning came. I thought that this was what life was going to be, and I could not imagine how different life was for adults.

Behind the right wing was a grassy area where we played, but we also performed plays there. Beyond the grassy area was a walled garden that I never went into, which is very surprising, because any place that was out of bounds was a magnet to us. Moving back, beyond the house there was a large lake bordered on one side by the Lime Walk, which was an avenue with lime trees on either side. On the side farthest away from the lake was a high wall which surrounded the Secret Garden. It was a rite of passage to be able to walk along the wall of the Secret Garden. I think when I first did this I had to have someone boost me up, because I was far too small to reach the top of the wall by myself. Looking into the Secret Garden was a bit disappointing. I don't know what I expected; it was rumored that someone had been killed in there. It was totally overgrown and the only thing there was a small stone bench. The name of the garden was infinitely more intriguing than the reality.

The lake was a wonderful place to get into mischief. We caught tadpoles and scooped up frog spawn, and watched the baby moorhens swim behind their mother in the spring. I also thought how interesting that William Wordsworth had been here and seen the profusion of daffodils growing all along the side of the lake, and then had written a poem about it.

One of the games we played around the lake was called "Blind Ladies." One day Shirley Bond and I tied scarves around our eyes, held hands and walked toward the lake. When we fell in, we had to go back to the nurse dripping wet; she scolded us, gave us dry pajamas and put us to bed. I'm not sure if being put to bed was a punishment, but for a child I suppose it was. I do remember that we missed supper in the dining room, but we were given a boiled egg and bread and butter and tea. This was a real treat during war time, because we almost never got fresh eggs, and I remember my mother getting them on the black market which I thought was a real place called the Black Market.

Another rite of passage which we all had to achieve, was climbing the great willow tree at the end of the garden. The tree had branches going in all directions and I believe that the head mistress said it had been planted in honor of Nelson, but that could be apocryphal. A special route had been devised on the tree so that one's various skills were tested. When we initially made the climb, another experienced climber went first to show you how to negotiate the different levels, rather like learning to climb mountains. I remember there was a long branch which sloped down toward the ground which one had to inch down toward ultimate safety. For me this was very frightening. I was frozen right in the middle of the branch not being able to move forward or backward. But after much coaxing and suggestions from the little group of conspirators, I eventually made it down.

One of the things I had remembered about Marianne was that she and several other girls had run away. I remember them standing near the end of the gardens asking me if I would like to go with them. I, of course, thought it was so much talk and didn't think any more about it until the headmistress called me into her room, asking if I knew where several missing girls had gone. I didn't. I would never have considered going with them because I didn't know how to get home. I lived a long way from the school and had to take several trains to get there. Apparently Marianne lived only about three miles away, and told the little band of runaways that she would take them to her mother's for tea. Marianne said their punishment was to be sent home for two weeks. I howled with laughter when I heard this and told her that it was a good thing the rest of the girls were unaware of this punishment or there would have been an epidemic of runaways.

These were halcyon days for us as children, but not all our days were happy. Being away from home we did not have the usual protection from our mothers and families when things went wrong. We learnt very early that we had to survive on our own, regardless of how we were being treated by the other girls. It was unheard of to go to one of the nurses or mistresses to complain that someone was teasing you unmercifully, or was being mean to you. By the end of the term, there was a list of hurts a mile long which had not been attended to.

The worst thing that happened was being "sent to Coventry." This was when someone decided that neither she nor any of her friends would speak to you. It was usually started by a girl who was part of "your group." I don't know how one person was able to convince all the other girls not to talk to you, but somehow she did. If you went to speak to someone, a girl would come up and say, "Don't speak to her, she's in Coventry." It is difficult to describe how cruel this practice was and how much children suffered. But the other children were your only companions, and there were no other people there who would listen, speak to, or play with you. The whole thing was very capricious, and would end as unexpectedly as it had begun. These actions revealed the vindictiveness of certain girls. It is amazing to me now how teachers would allow these girls to tyrannize the others without intervening. There was one girl who was particularly mean, her name was Jean Peak. She was one of those people who knew just which button to push to make you cry or to exasperate you. She had offended so many girls that they would yell after her, "Jean Peak is a sneak," and indeed she was. She was one of the few girls there who would run and tell her older sister, or a nurse, that girls were teasing her.

We slept in a large dormitory with metal bunk beds. The beds seemed somewhat unstable, because we could rock the bunks until they swayed. I don't ever remember them coming apart; maybe they swayed because of the constant abuse they took from us. At the end of our beds, we always kept our folded coats, which we would have to put on in the event of an air raid warning when we all had to get up and line up outside away from the building. Actually, it was very comforting to have my coat lying across the end of the bed over my feet, because it was bitterly cold in the dormitory and the coat acted as an extra blanket. There was no central heating, of course, because the building was so old. The only heating was from radiators placed around the side of the hall. I think there were only two or three radiators in this very large hall. Whenever we got a chance we would crowd around the radiators placing our hands and feet on them trying to get warm. Most of us had bed socks, knitted by our mothers, aunts or grandparents, which we would wear to bed as we inched our feet down between the icy sheets. The colder it was, the longer it would take to get my feet all the way down to the end of the bed. When we were at home, there was a little ritual mother went through every night, when she would fill the hot water bottles with boiling water and place the bottles in the bed to warm the sheets before we got into bed. It is interesting that even today when I live in a perfectly comfortable centrally heated house, I still have a folded mohair throw lying on the end of the bed over my feet.

When we went to bed at night, it was still light. I think we went to bed by 7:00 p.m. and the older girls and prefects would come to bed later. We were not supposed to talk or get out of bed, but as soon as the nurse said good night and left the room, there was a flurry of activity, as girls scurried over to other girls' beds to talk or get something they wanted from another girl. We would hide books under our pillows, and read until it got dark. Even after dark I would burrow down under the covers and read with a torch. First of all we would have someone sleeping next to us make sure that the light from the torch could not be seen through the blankets. As soon as the prefect came to bed, all our nightly wanderings stopped until it was dark, or we thought the prefect was asleep.

One night I was caught doing something, I don't remember what it was. The prefect's name was Mabel, and I think she was in line to be head girl the following term. She had a weak chin, and I never liked her. I don't know why. I think I thought I was stronger than she was, and I resented being told what to do by someone who I thought did not deserve to be in a position of authority. I think I made the mistake of arguing with her. This was unusual, because we learnt very early not to answer back or argue with people in authority, if we wanted to stay out of trouble. It is no wonder British people are not very open; our training assures that. Anyway, I must have argued a lot because I made her cry. I couldn't imagine a "big girl" crying over an argument with a "little girl." Anyway, she made me go and stand upstairs on the "Square." This was an area where there was a classroom to the right and a long corridor led from the Square to the Picture Gallery. To the left of the corridor was another corridor where all the mistresses had their bedrooms.

It was very dark up on the Square unless there was a moon out which would shine through the stained glass window over the stairway. I know I was seething as I stood up there in the cold and the dark ruminating over this latest injustice. I thought of getting revenge on everyone who had crossed me in any way. I'm not sure what that revenge would have been, but it was nice to think about it. I think I probably sat down with my back against the wall after awhile, because I was getting tired. Eventually one of the mistresses came along and asked me what I was doing there. I told her, but I think she made the mistake of telling me to apologize to Mabel. It is definitely a mistake to tell a rebellious child who has been standing in a dark hall to apologize to her tormentor. I responded in a most atypical way. I cried and screamed at the mistress saying I hated it at the school and I was going to tell my mother to take me home immediately. It was unheard of for any well brought up English schoolgirl to cry and scream and make a commotion, especially when a mistress was talking to her. I insisted that I wanted to write to my mother and tell her of all the hateful things we had to put up with. The mistress brought me some paper and a pencil, and I went into the classroom and wrote to my mother. In the letter I included the fact that Miss Willis had thrown a blackboard eraser at me in a fit of temper. I knew that this would scare the headmistress, if I told my Mother that a mistress had tried to hurt me. I think I included every grievance or slight I had suffered during that term. After I had finished I was told to go back downstairs to bed. I think I felt much better, but I didn't really know if the school would send the letter to my mother.

When Mother came to visit on the next visiting day, she said Miss Barkell, the headmistress, wanted to see her. I don't know if Miss Barkell let Mother read my letter before she spoke to her, or if I told Mother what had happened ahead of time. Mother didn't seem to be the least bit upset with me. She said that Miss Barkell said she was sure that Miss Willis would never throw anything at the pupils, "she was such a pleasant person." That showed me right then that grownups would always be believed over children, even though the grownups were not telling the truth. I think Mother believed me. Miss Barkell said that there were many girls who would love to come to this school. I don't think Mother believed that, but she did try to tell me how to deal with people when I was having trouble with them. This is really what we all needed, someone who loved us telling us how to handle people who upset us, and someone who would help us direct our own anger in such a way that it would not cause us further harm.

With the memory of those ancient torments in mind, I read with great fascination the reminiscences of several of the ex-scholars who had been making yearly visits to Ingatestone Hall since 1993. Their reminiscences were collected together and sent with a letter of thanks to the current owner of the home, the eighteenth Lord Petre, son of the seventeenth Lord Petre who was the owner of the home we lived in during the war years. Of course these written remembrances tended to be very positive, because they are an acknowledgement of gratitude for allowing the ex-scholars to explore the private grounds and rooms of this historic home.

Marianne, the organizer of these little reunions, wrote in the letter to Lord Petre, "For all our lives, Ingatestone Hall has seemed the epitome of the Elizabethan manor, with its warm friendly bricks and stepped gables and tantalizing towers. While there, we were almost entirely unaware of the rigours or privations of war. It was a place of extreme safety, beauty and excitement. It is a paradox that wartime to us represents such memories."

We all have selective memories, even of common experiences, and Marianne's is definitely atypical. It is true that Ingatestone Hall represented beauty and excitement, but I don't think many of the girls would say we were unaware of the rigours and privations of war. At one point during our stay, those children who lived in relatively safe areas of England were sent home, because the bombing raids around Ingatestone intensified. (I was one of the lucky people who were sent home, because I lived in Worcester which was not a target for German bombers.) For many children the experience of being at boarding school was one of fear, loneliness, and extreme anxiety because they had been sent away from their mothers. Actually, what does seem to be universal in our collective memories is the magical quality of Ingatestone Hall. When I think of it, I feel as if I had been living in a novel like *Jane Eyre*, or *My Cousin Rachel*.

My memories of boarding school are intimately tied to the physical beauty and romantic atmosphere of Ingatestone Hall. After reading the reminiscences of other women who had attended the school, I could tell that this Elizabethan Manor had affected us all in a similar way. Our lives, though sad in many ways, had been infused with the magic of sharing our childhood in this unique place.

⸎

Guests in a Country Home

When Gillian and I were home on holidays, Lady Cobham would invite us to stay with her. I don't remember feeling unduly excited but accepted, in that egocentric world of childhood, that everyone would want us as guests.

Sir Alan and Lady Cobham lived in what we called a "black and white" house in the country. The house was white and the dark timbers supporting the structure were visible on the exterior walls. The name of the home was "Pevensey". In England our homes had names which usually had some significance to the owner; our house was called the "Wicket". My father was a professional cricketer who played for Worcester. I believe that "Pevensey" was a place, maybe it had some particular significance to Sir Alan and Lady Cobham.

The home was rambling and comfortable; it was surrounded by fields, orchards with apples and peaches, vegetable and flower gardens. Sir Alan had his own horse in one of the fields. It apparently was very spirited. Mother told me that Lady Cobham frequently had to drive the country roads around the home looking for Sir Alan, when the horse arrived back at the house without its master.

One of the reasons I loved to visit "Pevensey" was for the animals. There were several white angora rabbits in hutches, three dogs, two spaniels, Flush and Dinah, and one boxer, Rex. There was also a large pig in a sty. I played with all the animals except the pig—although I spent quite a lot of time hanging over the wall of the sty watching the pig snuffling and snorting around in the muck.

One day when I was playing, Rex the boxer snapped at me. I don't know what I did to cause this, but Sir Alan got very angry and chased Rex with a broom stick, yelling at him. To my wonderment, Rex leapt all the way across the pig sty from one wall to another. I quite forgot my fear at this amazing sight and dissolved into giggles.

Sir Alan, or A. J. as he was called by his wife, was a short but imposing man. He had a devil-may-care confidence about himself, like so many men I knew who were pilots. He was an aviation pioneer and had been knighted for his achievement. He developed equipment which enabled aeroplanes to refuel in the air, and he owned a company called Flight Refueling. His aircraft and refueling technique contributed to the success of the Berlin Airlift in 1948. I, of course, only knew him as the man who gallantly chased his dog across the pig sty because Rex had grazed my hand. I remember him standing in front of a large open fireplace in the living room; he stood with his back to the fire, lifting the bottom of his jacket, warming his backside. He and other male friends did this while talking about business.

One time when we were staying at "Pevensey," one of the spaniels had a litter of puppies. I was in love with these little furry bundles and wanted to play with them. Lady Cobham had them brought into the living room where they tumbled and fell all over themselves. I went around picking them up, cuddling each in turn; they wriggled and squirmed, nipped my fingers and flailed away with their tiny paws. Periodically they would piddle on the carpet and Lady Cobham bustled around behind them wiping up the puddles. Mother told me later that it was a valuable Persian Carpet—

which didn't really mean anything to me. But the image of Lady Cobham cleaning up after the puppies made mother laugh.

There were always lots of flowers in the house, which contributed to the overall feeling of its being bright and sunny. The flowers came from the cutting garden. The maid was foreign and spoke very little English; her name was Ankara. She wore a babushka and smiled at you when you spoke, but I don't think she understood you. This became apparent when Lady Cobham asked her to pick some sweet peas for the house. Ankara picked all the sweet peas off the trellis, not leaving any. Lady Cobham and the butler were putting sweet peas everywhere, stuffing them in large metal buckets, trying to hide them from Sir Alan.

Gillian and I had a small, cozy room with sloping ceilings. Each of our beds was under one of the eaves. The butler, Owens, who was very tall, rather old, and quite solemn, would bring us our breakfast on trays in the morning. Gillian and I were feeling very self-important with this indulgence. Our breakfast was a soft-boiled egg in an egg cup with bread and butter and tea. We would cut the top off the egg, butter the bread and slice it into strips which we called soldiers, and then dip the strips into the egg yolk and eat them. This was my favorite way of eating soft-boiled eggs. One day we decided to play a trick on Owens. When we finished eating the inside of the egg, we turned the egg shells upside down so they looked as if they hadn't been touched. When Owens came to pick up the trays, he said, "Oh miss, you didn't eat your egg." Gillian and I dissolved in peals of laughter and then showed him what we had done. He smiled indulgently . I don't think he was used to the antics of silly young schoolgirls.

HELEN HILL

I was born in Brooklyn, New York, in 1915, but because of the death of my mother in the flu epidemic of 1918 I grew up in Taunton, Massachusetts, among the ghosts of my father's ancestors who had settled the town in 1637 and the Pilgrim ancestors of my mother. I was brought up by my father and various housekeepers until my father and his sisters combined households during the Depression. The happiest memories of my childhood are of summer days on Cape Cod.

The small WASP world I grew up in held itself aloof from the larger world of second generation Irish Catholics who had come to dominate city politics and education, and it frowned on our playing with the children of first generation immigrants—Portuguese, Italian, French Canadian. My years at Wheaton College, only eight miles away in Norton, were liberating. There I not only had friends of different faiths and backgrounds, but had stimulating teachers who encouraged me in my love of reading and writing and opened my mind to new ideas and attitudes.

Wheaton was followed by a year at Brown for a master's degree in English, two years of teaching in a small high school in New Hampshire, and then the great adventure of leaving New England for that strange unknown country, the Middle West, when I went to the University of Illinois to teach and study for a Ph.D. in English. There I met my future husband, Donald, who was studying for the same degree. In 1941 I followed him to Washington when he volunteered as a cryptographer for the Navy. (It didn't occur to me in those anxious days to stay behind and finish my graduate work first.) Our first child was born in Washington. After the war I taught at Illinois and had our second child while Don finished his Ph.D. We came to Ann Arbor in 1948, when Don joined the English department at the University of Michigan.

Although the war and four children put an end to my graduate work, I did return to teaching when my youngest child was eight and taught writing and Children's Literature at Eastern Michigan University for 20 years.

While there I co-edited and published three anthologies of poems for children and young adults and did much of the research for A Proud & Fiery Spirit, *a book based on my seafaring grandfather's journals, published by the Duxbury Rural and Historical Society in 1995.*

Ann Arbor has now been a good home to me for more than 50 years, but the imprint of New England is still on me and part of my heart will always be there near the salt water among the ghosts of my ancestors.

May Festival, 1919

Although I was born in Brooklyn, New York, my father removed me and my brothers to Taunton, Massachusetts, late in March, 1919. I celebrated my fourth birthday in Boston on the way. Our mother had died the previous October in the flu epidemic, and we had no roots in Brooklyn. Though my mother's younger sister, Aunt Molly, stayed to care for us those first six months after my mother's death, that arrangement was of necessity a temporary one. When her husband returned from France in the spring after the Armistice it was time for them to reestablish their own lives which the war had interrupted shortly after their marriage in 1917. With three small children in a city where he was a newcomer, with no family support or even old friends nearby, my father went home. He took us back to Taunton where his roots ran deep, where he had always lived except for the last five years when a new job had taken him to New York.

Taunton was where my father's family had lived since 1637 when one of our ancestors had been a First Settler. Taunton was where my father had gone to Bristol Academy, to Taunton High School, and to the Taunton Business School. He had worked there for 25 years, taking over the ice business when his father died, later becoming treasurer and a partner in the West Silver Co. He had belonged all his life to the Unitarian Church in Taunton, half of whose congregation was still named Williams, as we were.

Taunton was the place where he still had old friends and family and traditions. His mother and two unmarried sisters still lived there in the house where he was born. For him it was Taunton, not Brooklyn, that was home, "the place where, when you have to go there, / They have to take you in." Not that we moved in with Grandma and the aunts. Dad rented a house and hired a house-keeper to look after my baby brother and me, but there was fam-ily only half a mile away.

Though one of my mother's dying requests had been that Dad keep us three children together, Dad had been unable to find a housekeeper who was willing to care for three small children who were seven, four, and not yet one, so my older brother Edward was left with Grandma and the aunts, with whom he had been staying ever since Mother had died. I was left with no older brother to tease or be teased by and a younger one still too small to be a playmate. I knew no one and my father knew no one in the immediate neighborhood. It would be another year before I dis-covered a playmate my age down the road.

Since my father always went to church on Sunday I was proba-bly taken to Sunday School as soon as we were minimally un-packed, but I remember nothing of the first month beyond the day of our arrival. The introduction to social life that I do remember was the annual May Festival that my father took me to on the first Saturday in May. May Festival was a centuries-old English tradition still preserved at the Unitarian Church in Taunton in 1919 and all during my childhood. There were games for the children and a cake sale for the adults, but the main event was the traditional dance around the maypole performed by the children and enjoyed by everyone. I'm sure my father would not have gone to the Festi-val for his own sake, but he would have thought that May Festival was a tradition that I would enjoy and have wanted to share it with me. It would also give me a chance to get acquainted with other children. May Festival was a popular event with families not only from our church but from others in town.

The games, fish pond and grab bag, I remember happily from later years but not this one. Nor do I remember much about the cake sale which was always popular with the adults. What I do remember is the main event, the dance around the maypole which had been erected in the center of the Parish Hall and crowned with a garland of roses and colored streamers. The hall was crowded, not only with children, but with parents and grandparents who had come to watch their children dance and to remember nostalgically when they had danced around the maypole, too. I forgot about my father. Here were other children. The older ones, the eight or nine-year-olds who had practiced ahead of time, began to form a circle around the pole, couples facing each other, and then as the music played, they skipped around the pole in both directions, weaving the streamers in and out for several rounds until it was time to reverse direction and unwind. Again and again they wound and then unwound. I watched eagerly but with no understanding of how to braid. When they had finished, with much applause from their fond parents and the Sunday School teachers who were in charge, the younger children were given a turn and I was encouraged to join in. I was handed a streamer and set in place, but if I was given further directions, I did not absorb them. When the music began, some of the children, who had danced the maypole dance before, began to skip in and out, first to the left and then to the right around the children who were coming toward them. For the rest of us, and especially this four-year-old who had never heard of a maypole dance before, it was a scramble. The adults in charge kept pushing us in the right direction and stopping us frequently to untangle our streamers. I tried hard, but not knowing quite what I was supposed to do, I wound my streamer around two people instead of one. I turned before I was supposed to turn. Going the wrong way I bumped into people. Other children made mistakes, too, but I felt conspicuously inept. At last when we were thoroughly tangled, the music stopped, and the dance was over. There was some whispering among the adults who were in charge of the dancing. I knew I hadn't done it right.

Then I was being led by the hand, bewildered and apprehensive, to the stage at one end of the hall while the grown-ups clapped. What was happening, I wondered, as we walked up the steps? What were we going to do now? When we reached the center of the stage they sat me on a throne beside a little boy I had never seen before and never saw again, put a wreath of flowers on my head, and pronounced me Queen of the May. There was more applause and the ceremony was over.

Still bewildered, I was led off the stage and into the hubbub below. My father reappeared and, with a slightly self-conscious half laugh at our being the center of attention, took my hand and reassured me. It was all right to be crowned Queen of the May. We walked through the crowd, past the cakes he didn't buy, and out into the fresh air. By the time we got home I had accepted my royal status and was wearing my crown with some pleasure. But I think it meant more to him than it did to me that I had been singled out for such attention, the reasons for which I still did not understand.

I see now that the motive of those Sunday School teachers who made their whispered decision was in one respect a kindly one. It was their way of showing sympathy for Arthur Williams, an old member of their congregation who had just returned, a widower with three small children, and they wanted to make a motherless little girl feel welcome, but I understood nothing of that and neither did the other children. They understood that it was favoritism rather than justice, and Rowena Rhodes, a year older than I, protested angrily when they led me to the stage: I was new and didn't belong here and had been all mixed up. She had danced better than I had. I didn't deserve to be chosen Queen of the May. The grown-ups had shushed her, but she was right.

My father, however, saved the piece in The Taunton *Daily Gazette* for May 5th, 1919, which kindly overlooked my ineptitude and discomfort in its flowery report and confined its comments to praise for the dance by the older children.

"May Festival at Unitarian Great Success," proclaims the headline. "Merry May, queen of all the year, was given a royal welcome by scores of lads and lassies Saturday afternoon at the annual May festival in the Sunday school rooms at the Unitarian church. Little Miss Helen Williams was crowned Queen, and master James Knowles, king, at the merry party, which was attended by a large assembly of young folks. In an environment radiant with myriads of blossoms, the fair little sovereigns were crowned with pomp and ceremony, as many little ones joined in the merry dance around the Maypole. . . . .

"The Maypole was in the center of the hall, arranged in floral design, with the usual inner circle of ribbons for weaving and the outer circle of garlands of pink roses. The Maypole dance was very cleverly executed by the following: The Misses. . . . *[here the names of the eight and nine-year-old little misses are listed.]* Games and musical selections, fish pond and refreshments added to the very enjoyable program. There was also a cake sale for the adults."

The Grip of Tradition

I grew up among people who knew that there were only two ways of doing things: the New England way and the wrong way. The New England way embraced the whole spectrum of behavior from the right way to lead a virtuous life—"Straight is the path of duty/Curved is the line of beauty/ Follow the first and you shall see/The second ever follow thee."—to the right way to make clam chowder. (You NEVER put tomatoes in a clam chowder.) Thus, there was only one way, the New England way, to honor the Thanksgiving tradition established by our ancestors. One had dinner at home with the family, with stuffed turkey and cranberry sauce, mashed potatoes with giblet gravy, mashed turnips, Hubbard squash, and pumpkin pie. No sweet potatoes. One might go to a close relative's for dinner, but going to a restaurant was unheard of. Not until my junior year at college did I break from that tradition.

In my childhood in the Twenties we always went to "Aunt" Hattie's for Thanksgiving dinner. Aunt Hattie was really a first cousin of my father and his sisters, Edith and Mabel, whom we always called Aunt E. and Aunt May. My grandfather had owned an ice business. His brother, Aunt Hattie's father, had married the daughter of the owner of Staples Coal Co., had inherited the business, and—perhaps because winter was longer than summer, or perhaps because he was a better business man—he was the more prosperous of the two. Both brothers died in the 1890's. The two families lived diagonally across the street from each other in houses of post-Civil War vintage set far back from the road. Both were three story houses with Mansard roofs, fourteen or fifteen rooms, and an acre of more of ground. Grandma's house faced Weir Street, the road from the center of Taunton down to Weir Village where the Nemasket cotton mills had once flourished. Aunt Hattie's house faced White Street, but the side of the property ran for a long way down Weir Street. There was a porte cochère and another entrance on the Weir Street side. The distance between the two houses as the crow flew across Weir Street must have been the equivalent of a city block. Whether my grandfather had ever owned his house I don't know. I do know that after his death Aunt Hattie owned it and that every month for the next thirty years Grandma had walked over to Aunt Hattie's with the rent and that Aunt Hattie, a devoted niece, had always refused to accept it.

Not only had Aunt Hattie's father been more prosperous than my grandfather, Aunt Hattie had "married well,"—a man from Oyster Bay, Long Island. Her husband, whom we called Uncle Fred, had now inherited the coal business which was still doing very well in my childhood. They had no children. They had a cook, Nora; a maid, Katy; another servant, "the second girl," who did the mending and sewing; and Hugh, the chauffeur, who was charming and lovable and very respectful. When they let him go during the Depression, they found him a job as teller in the Taunton Savings Bank. The cook and the maids lived on the third floor. Hugh lived at home with his family.

We lived in a different world from that of Aunt Hattie and Uncle Fred—theirs one of affluence, ours one of what Aunt May called genteel poverty. They traveled to exotic places like Egypt and Romania. We traveled the 35 miles to Boston or to Cape Cod.

Nevertheless, Aunt Hattie had always remained close to Grandma and Aunt E. and Aunt May, who still lived together across the street, and as long as Grandma lived, we all went to Aunt Hattie's house for Thanksgiving dinner.

My older brother Edward who, ever since our mother's death, had lived with Grandma and the aunts, would usually be there before my younger brother Bradley and I and Dad arrived. We three would walk through the chill November air from our house half a mile away. On the way I sang "Over the river and through the woods. . . ," until Dad could bear it no longer. I was filled with gleeful anticipation, especially in the two or three years when I carried with me the pie I had made in school. The pie had a papier-mâché crust, a popcorn filling, and a top crust of orange crepe paper glued to the bottom crust. Uncle Fred, a big man with a Theodore Roosevelt moustache and a hearty laugh, never failed to act completely surprised when he greeted us at the door and as delighted as he might have been had the pie been a real one.

In the time of bustle and talk before dinner we children would be taken in to the library to see Aunt Addie, Aunt Hattie's mother, a sweet old lady in a wheel chair, who was attended by a nurse, Miss Cosgrove, known affectionately to the adults in the family as "Cozzie." Aunt Addie was "feeble-minded." The aunts would hover around to make sure we minded our manners and did or said nothing to embarrass them. We would quickly be led away and into the dining room for dinner.

It was a large dining room with waist high walnut paneling, a built-in walnut sideboard at one end of the room and a fireplace at the other. The wallpaper above the paneling was dark green, thickly textured, with a metallic glint. On the wall was a large grim painting of a hunting dog, a black and white setter, with a bird in his mouth, and on either side of it two sconces with carbon filaments that gave a dim light. A chandelier that gave more light hung over the center of the massive walnut dining table. The matching chairs were large and heavy, with high black horsehair cushioned seats. Even when I was an adult my legs almost dangled when I sat in one. On the floor a turquoise and rose Oriental rug stretched under the table from sideboard to fireplace. Near Aunt Hattie's foot was a button to step on to ring for the maid.

The adults sat at the table. Sometimes Mrs. Dudgeon, Uncle Fred's sister who still lived in Oyster Bay, was visiting. We three children sat at a separate table under the stained glass window beside the fireplace. I felt ostracized, especially as I grew older and Edward graduated to the big table, but I was kept at the smaller one because Bradley was still too young to be included. Once Bradley spilled his milk. Aunt May was upset and flustered; Aunt E. was upset and disapproving; but Aunt Hattie was gracious, made light of the accident, soothed the aunts, and asked the maid to clean up the mess. Dinner, of course, was roast turkey with giblet gravy, cranberry sauce, Hubbard squash, mashed potatoes, mashed turnips, and pumpkin pie. We ended the orgy with clusters of dried Muscat raisins and a great bowl of mixed nuts to crack in their shells, and much joking about needing to run around the block after dinner.

After Grandma died, Aunt E. and Aunt May and Edward moved to my father's house and we stopped going to Aunt Hattie's for Thanksgiving. I don't know why—perhaps because Uncle Fred had died. Aunt Hattie would send Hugh to our house the day before Thanksgiving with a turkey. I would help Aunt May pluck the pin feathers from the bird before roasting it. Aunt E. and Aunt May would cook the dinner. The dinner was just the same as it had always been, right down to the nuts and the clustered raisins, but the mood was different. We were performing the ritual that it would be unthinkable to change, but it was no longer the festive occasion it had been in my childhood. It was a glum time for every one, the time of the Great Depression. We were not nearly so badly off as many were. We lived frugally of necessity, though also as a matter of principle—"Waste not, want not"—but we had a warm house, well furnished with hand-me-down furniture, some of it truly antique. The antiques were more valued by the aunts than by me and my younger brother. "Don't sit in that chair," we were admonished. "It's fragile." "Be careful of that table. It was your great-grandmother's." We always had plenty of good food on the table and though we didn't have much spending money or often have new clothes, we did always have something we could wear for "Sunday best," and were decently clothed the rest of the time. By being frugal and by drawing on savings from better times they managed in the depths of the Great Depression to send Bradley to boarding school and to send Edward and me to college.

We were thankful for what we had, but ours was not a household to laugh at trouble, nor was it a happy family. The aunts and my father did not get along well with each other. Because they were my aunts, I thought I loved them and dutifully kissed them goodnight, but the kiss was accepted rather than returned. Aunt May once complained that I treated her like a housekeeper, and I suppose I did. I was about fourteen when the merger took place and until then had lived with housekeepers who were clearly not family. Those three should never have joined households. Every one had advised them against it, but a sense of duty and obligation on both sides made them deaf to all objections; and I don't know even now what else they could or should have done, given their strong sense of the right and moral way to do things. With Grandma gone, the aunts did not want to be beholden to Aunt Hattie. My father had bought our nine-room house a couple of years before the stock market crash of 1929, but he was in the life insurance business and now had very little income. He also needed a housekeeper and there was some feeling that it would be better for Bradley and me to be in the care of relatives rather than of some stranger from an employment agency as we had been for the last ten years. Aunt E., who was Supervisor of Art in the public schools, had a steady income of $2000 a year. They decided that Aunt May should give up her job in the Probate Office and stay at home to keep house for all of us. But instead of our moving into the large house where the aunts had been born and where they had lived for nearly sixty years, the aunts exiled themselves to our smaller one. They followed the straight line of duty, but the curved line of beauty failed to follow them. Resentments smouldered and flared constantly. Aunt E. had always resented my father's freedom to leave home and to marry, and though she would do anything for Edward who had lived with her since he was seven, she resented having to live with and help support my father and his other two children now. For a while my father was still the nominal head of the house and Aunt E. resented that. He resented her having usurped his authority with Edward, even though he had consented to the living arrangement by which he had lost him. Dad tried to keep the peace, but he was hot-tempered and explosive. Aunt E., when crossed, was icy and disapproving. She was a master of the Silent Treatment, a powerful weapon that spread a cloud of gloom over the whole house when she used it, as she often did, to express her disapproval. Aunt May, anxious and easily flustered, was so much under Aunt E.'s thumb that she could not serve as peacemaker. Nor, given my partisanship, could I. Breakfast and dinner, which we always ate together, were times for quarreling and tears rather than times of family companionship and fun. On Thanksgiving, though, respect for tradition overcame the hostilities. Dad and Aunt E. buried the hatchet and we all pretended to be happier than we were as we observed the secular ritual.

Had I lived on campus away from the tensions, instead of commuting to Wheaton from this dysfunctional household, I might have been less tempted when, in my junior year, a college friend invited me to spend Thanksgiving week-end with her in New York. Her uncle had an apartment there where we could stay. Adele came from a Jewish family in Nashville, was more sophisticated than I, and not bound by New England traditions.

"It will do you good to get away," she said. "You don't have to be home every Thanksgiving."

I accepted her dare and asked my father for permission. I think he rather enjoyed the idea of my having an adventure. The overnight boat trip from Fall River was one he had often made; it held no horrors for him. Glimpses of freedom perhaps and memories of happier times. He didn't even ask much about the uncle before giving me his blessing. But he thought it would be politic to ask the aunts for their approval, too.

Not so! Not for one moment did Aunt E. approve of two twenty-year-old women's traveling to New York alone on the night boat. There was no telling what might happen to them there or when they got to New York. She didn't feel so apprehensive about my roaming around Boston alone. Boston she knew. But the New York she didn't know was certainly not a safe place to go. I said I had Dad's permission and I was going. It was a rare triumph for me and a rare defeat for Aunt E. Her last words to me before giving me the Silent Treatment, which lasted for three days after I got back, were, "Well, you must certainly not take a taxi while you're in New York. Mrs. Dudgeon says it just isn't safe to take a taxi there. You never know what sort of person is driving it."

On Wednesday evening, the day before Thanksgiving, Dad put Adele and me on the train from Taunton to Fall River with his own words of caution. He would have liked to see us safely onto the boat, but we refused. The trip was exciting and uneventful. We watched the lights on shore as we sailed down the bay. Then we climbed into our narrow berths and let the noisy rumble of the ship's engines lull us to sleep. When we woke in the morning we were there.

As we disembarked, Adele said, "We'll have to take a taxi to my uncle's apartment.

"Oh," said I, now a little apprehensive myself after Aunt E.'s dire warning. "Aunt E. said it wasn't safe to take a taxi in New York."

"Nonsense," said Adele. "How else are we going to get to East 65th Street? We can't walk that far with our suitcases!" We hailed a taxi. We were not robbed or kidnaped.

There was no sign of the uncle when we arrived, nor at any time during our brief visit, but he had left a key where Adele could find it and we made ourselves at home. When it was time for dinner, we went to a restaurant, a good one with linens, but not too expensive. The waiter brought the menus. Until then I had felt that I was having a slightly daring escapade, but it was a lark. Now as I faced the question of whether to order a traditional Thanksgiving dinner, a sense of disapproval hovered over me. I wasn't homesick. I didn't miss the family. But I knew that the right way to celebrate Thanksgiving was with a turkey dinner. As I studied the menu and waffled back and forth, Adele grew impatient.

"Helen," she said. "You *don't* have to eat turkey just because it's Thanksgiving."

It felt like treason, but I finally ordered lobster.

Chasing the Dream

The place that we have called "The Farm" for the past 23 years—
ever since 1976—was the last three acres of a 100-acre dream.
For years we had dreamed of having 100 acres in New England with
an old farmhouse where we could spend the summers and where
perhaps, if that unimaginable time ever came, we could retire. Don,
my husband, having grown up in central New York state, longed for
the hills. I, having lived near Cape Cod, longed for the ocean. His
roots, though, as well as mine, were in New England and, as Aunt
Molly used to say after living more than half her life in California,
"Once a New Englander, always a New Englander." The landscape
of childhood is always home. We were recent transplants to the Middle
West. We both dreamed about going back.

When the children were small we spent summers or parts of
summers in the east, in rented or borrowed houses or camping on
some friend's land. We had a 9′ × 12′ canvas tent that slept six
comfortably. When our fourth child Alan was a year old and still in
diapers, we camped in New Hampshire where friends had a hundred
acres with the requisite farmhouse, an outdoor privy attached
to the house, and water that ran downhill from a spring and
was then diverted to the pump in the kitchen. The next summer
we pitched our tent on the sands of the Outer Banks where the
wind blew the tent down in the middle of the first night. While
Don and Becky, then thirteen, struggled to hold up the tent poles,

I hauled the three small boys out from under the canvas and we spent the rest of the night—all six of us—in our old Ford while the wind howled around us. One summer we camped less dramatically for a couple of weeks in Rhode Island, in the back yard of a friend of my brother's not far from the ocean, and once again satisfied our longing for sand and salt water. We also tried camping in Michigan, but we found state campsites so crowded that we ended up in a national forest with no facilities. (When we woke in the morning and went to walk the dog, three-year-old Alan asked, "Mummy, why do we have to have a dog *and* a sister?") The next year we drove east again, rented a friend's farmhouse in northern Vermont, and dreamed about finding a place near the wilderness of the Lost Kingdom. A year or two later, friends who were going abroad for the summer lent us their cottage at the tip of Chappaquiddick Island out by the Cape Pogue lighthouse. There was no road to the house. It was three miles across the sand beyond the Chappaquiddick Bridge and one could get there only by Jeep or Bronco with 4-wheel drive. The cottage was on the edge of an eroding bluff overlooking the ocean. The wild roses all around it were luxuriant. The poison ivy, tangled in the wild rose bushes, was equally luxuriant and unavoidable and, except for Don, we all suffered. Yet we returned the next year for part of the summer, drawn by love of the ocean and a sense, for me at least, of returning home. Wherever we were those summers, we drove around and dreamed about buying our own place; but in those days we had more children than money so we just kept dreaming.

After I had gone back to teaching, and a colleague offered to sell us 100 acres he owned in New Hampshire for $1000, we thought for a little while that we might realize our fantasy. On one of those trips east we drove through his woods during a thunderstorm, restless children in the back seat and tried, without success, to imagine how any one could build a house on that rocky wooded hillside. We couldn't even have pitched a tent. As the children grew older and less interested in family expeditions, we went east less often and spent several summers in Ann Arbor. Then there was a final summer with just Alan, now a reluctant thirteen-year-old who didn't want to leave his friends or his baseball league, when we house sat in the Berkshires for a friend's twelve cats and a hundred million fleas while the cats' owners happily went to France. Don worked happily in the library at Amherst; I was happy because Aunt Molly spent much of the summer with us; but though we took along a friend for Alan, it was not a happy summer for him.

Some years later, after all the children had left home, I spent a couple of weeks in Duxbury, Massachusetts, doing research on my grandfather's seafaring journals. Duxbury is right on the coast, just a few miles north of Plymouth. Though I had never lived there, Duxbury is where my mother and her father and all his ancestors back to the Pilgrims had been born. This would be the perfect place, I thought: history, family associations, the ocean, one of the most beautiful towns in New England. We could spend our summers there now and retire to Duxbury later. But when I went to see a real estate agent in Duxbury I discovered with dismay that houses, even old decrepit ones, were just as expensive there as they were in Ann Arbor. It was only then that we began to come to our senses and realize that we couldn't afford such an expensive fantasy. By then, too, it was becoming clear from the experience of friends, that New England was too far away for people of our means to own a house while living in Ann Arbor. The old days when you could leave your house in the woods or at the beach closed up during the winter and find it unharmed when you went back in the summer were gone.

But old dreams don't always die. Don still had a hankering for a place in the country and he began to imagine having a farm in Michigan. A farm in Michigan with no access to salt water was not the answer to my dream at the time, but I agreed that a farm within reach was better than no farm at all. When I married Don I had no idea that he had a secret desire to be a farmer. Neither had he. The first inkling I had came in the early fifties after Don visited Bennett Weaver one afternoon. Bennet Weaver was an English professor who had recently retired to a farm out in Dexter. When Don went to see him he was happily gardening and mowing with his tractor instead of grading papers, and Don came home wishing that he could be a farmer, too. At the time, though I could imagine living in the country, I couldn't imagine giving up the life of a university professor for that of a farmer, but to Don the life looked idyllic. After that, Don's desire to get away from the tensions of university life made the thought of living in the country not only appealing but something to aim for—not just in the summer but all year round. He read Wendell Berry, a contemporary poet who wrote about living the simple life on a farm in Kentucky. We met other poets who came through Ann Arbor, who seemed to thrive on poverty and country living while they wrote, whether in Alaska or Montana or the Berkshires.

In the mid-fifties we seriously considered living outside of town before we bought our house on Olivia, and were strongly tempted by a house on Joy Road, a mile beyond Stein Road, but the thought of driving four children to school and Little League and to their playmates' homes had been too daunting for me. For me, living in the country was a dream for summer vacations and retirement. So we stayed in town and confined our dreams to talk and trips in the summer. All this was still some years before my visit to Duxbury, but once we faced the realities of trying to manage two houses a thousand miles apart, buying a farm in Michigan began to look like a good compromise.

I don't remember whose cocktail party brought the right forces together, but it was a fortuitous one. In a conversation with Anne Knott, Don discovered an accomplice as enthusiastic about our buying a farm as Don was. Not just because she sold real estate, but because she, too, dreamed of living in the country. She understood that we would not be put off by an old house that needed work, that it had to be a place that was run down. We still couldn't afford much, but we had paid off the mortgage on our house on Olivia; the children were grown, if not entirely independent; and with two incomes we had begun to save a little money. Anne promised to let Don know if she heard of anything suitable.

Once in a while after that, at rather long intervals, she would call and tell Don about a house that he might look at. He would drive by and come home without much enthusiasm for what he had seen. Not an attractive house. No trees. Or too far away. Nothing to catch his imagination and make him want to take me back to see it. Then one day Anne called and said, "I have another farm for Don to drive by," and since Don wasn't home she told me about it. It was nearby, in a very good location just beyond Barton Hills. It was rented, she said, and that might make it easier to pay for. It hadn't occurred to us to buy a house and rent it, but suddenly that idea made buying another house seem more possible. We could rent it now and live in it ourselves later. The next day, I remember, was rainy, not a good day for seeing an old farmhouse, but the following day, a bright and sunny one, we drove out with Anne to look at the house on Stein Road. It was the 7th of May, 1976. As soon as we crossed the Main Street bridge and turned onto the old Whitmore Lake Road we felt that we were in the country. The leaves were just bursting out in their spring green and the branches were feathery overhead. As we drove past Washtenong Memorial Park, Anne pointed across the cemetery and said to Don, "There's your barn!"

At the far corner of the cemetery we turned west onto a dirt road, the cemetery on one side, open fields on the other, and a vista of a slightly curving country road lined with trees ahead. Not a car or a house in sight except, a quarter of a mile up Whitmore

Lake Road, Charlie Braun's fertilizer farm. Beyond the cemetery on our left was an old orchard, the apple and cherry trees just coming into bloom. Just past the orchard was the house, set well back from the road, facing north. There was a large silver maple near the road, a large catalpa in the center of the front yard, and another large tree, an old mulberry, near the corner of the driveway. At one corner of the house an enormous lilac and a mock orange crowded together and reached above the porch, well beyond the eaves of the roof. The house had a pleasing shape but it was painted an ugly pumpkin color, not bright orange, but the color of a dirty pumpkin stem with a little orange added to the mix. We turned left into the driveway lined with lilacs on one side and a thicket of trees and bushes on the other and saw ahead of us an open field with trees beyond. It was very peaceful. Beyond the lilacs the driveway curved to the left. Straight ahead it became a road to the barn. It went past an old well house and windmill covered with a tangle of grape vines and a cedar tree crowded against it; then it curved left over the barn bridge to a large red barn. On the right side of the road was a shambling old carriage house. Farther west and back there was also a corn crib.

Where the driveway branched off from the road to the barn it curved left around a turnaround—a large island with grass in the middle and old-fashioned lilacs, some lavender, some white, all around the outside. It went past what was called the Old House, now used only for storage, toward a magnificent lilac bush just coming into bloom, then curved past another dilapidated building that had been a tinsmith's shop to the New House which had been built in 1900. The New House had two porches on this, the south side, both falling down, and an unattractive outside stairway leading to the second story. Beyond the tinsmith's shop to the west was the old privy surrounded by lilacs and beyond that a thicket with a chicken coop hidden among the briars. At the south end of the thicket, built into the hillside and facing the barn, stood another old building, known as the Horse Barn. An overgrown, rutted dirt road between the Horse Barn and the big barn led to the cemetery which had once been part of this homestead. Only the roof of the Horse Barn showed from the back yard. Many years ago there had been a fire in the Horse Barn and a roof had been brought in from somewhere else. It didn't quite fit at one corner; there was a large gap where it didn't meet the wall.

We went through the tumbledown porches, undaunted, and into the kitchen, narrow and dark, but the rest of the rooms were pleasant and generous enough so that we could imagine living there. The living room was cool and shady, the dining room and two others bright and sunny. The upstairs rooms were sunny, too. One room upstairs had been made into a kitchen, so that the house now had two apartments.

We learned that the house would soon need a new roof. We went down cellar and found a muddy dirt floor with a stream running through it. This was more disconcerting than the porches had been, or even the roof, but we thought, "Maybe one just has to put up with wet cellars, living in the country." We went out into the sunshine and across the yard to the barn. It was a big barn with a high arched roof, an empty hay loft, spacious, full of old farm equipment, still smelling of hay. On the lower level, reached by some very steep stairs with no railings, the stanchions for cows were still in place.

When we came out we looked around us at the cemetery— "Quiet neighbors," some one inevitably remarked—and at the 80-acre field next door just being ploughed for wheat. We smelled the lilacs, listened to the birds singing their spring chorus, and thought, "This is what we have been dreaming of." There was no ocean, and no hills, but it was only five miles from home. We were enchanted. We bought the place that night.

⌥

On Facing Mortality

When I was five I said I wanted to live to be 85 so that I could see the year 2000. Well, 2000 is here and I'll be 85 in March. What I didn't think about 80 years ago was that now I would have to start facing the end of my life. It's not that I *feel* old, or have any unusual health problems, though each year I take more pills. There are other signs. My hip joints complain now when I go for a walk. I'm a little less steady on my feet. A fifteen pound box of books weighs a good deal more than it did fifteen years ago. Impatient drivers sometimes honk at me. There are also the dreams. Dreams about packing my bags to go somewhere when I have no immediate plans for travel. Dreams about trains. In the last six months before he died my husband had dreams of being on a train, hurtling through the dark to an unknown destination, sometimes alone, sometimes with silent hooded passengers, then with amazement and relief finding me at the end of the dream. "How did you know where I was?" he wondered.

When I retired from teaching at the age of 68, I made two resolutions. One was to clean out the attic; the other was to finish a book I'd been working on sporadically for years. It took me five years to get around to the attic job. A new roof which required taking off old roofs down to the rafters showered coal soot and scraps of shingle everywhere, prompting a massive cleanup. I threw some stuff away then, but left much, including the books on shelves that line the room Don had built up there for his study when the children were small. It took me fifteen years to finish, and publish, the first volume of the book based on my grandfather's journals. The second volume is still not done. I *want* to finish it. I *must* finish it or I won't be able to die with dignity when the time comes. I'm no longer sure, though, that I can count on another fifteen years of clearheaded energy. I'm also beginning to feel an urgency about housekeeping matters that I've been able to ignore for most of my life. Perhaps it's because my husband showed me that dying was a real possibility, that I must face it, too. He was only nine months older than I. It's been almost three years since he died.

Or perhaps it's living alone that gives me this sense of urgency, the knowledge that I'm now the only one responsible for leaving things in order for the children. I have lived in this house for 45 years and am infamous in my children's eyes for not throwing things away. I was early indoctrinated with a sense of thrift, not just because of the Depression; in my family it was a way of life. I re-use; I recycle; I save the things that might come in handy some time, though I don't go quite so far as the old New Englander who had a box in the attic for string too short to be saved. My children laugh at me for my saving ways; yet they are grateful when I can produce an old bookcase or chest of drawers that has been retired to the attic.

Selling the farm a year ago taught me that I needed to put this house in order, too, and seeing the farm through the eyes of a real estate agent opened mine to what needed to be done here, starting with the kitchen. Don and I had talked about bringing the kitchen up to date, but in his declining years neither of us had been willing to face the disruption. With only myself to consider last year I found it easy to rationalize: remodeling would make it easier for the children to sell the house when I die and in the meantime I could enjoy having a new and beautiful kitchen. I managed to weed out a few pots and pans and dishes then, but others went to the cellar. The ability to store things has one dubious advantage. When I finally get to clearing out the cellar, perhaps I'll be able to say "I haven't missed that in the last five years. If I can't find a taker now I'll just chuck it."

My resolution this year to have the inside of the house re-painted room by room is spurring me slowly onward. When my bedroom and the south bedroom upstairs were painted I got rid of a few old clothes, but it was too easy to move still wearable old fa-vorites from one closet to another and postpone the hard deci-sions. The north bedroom is a different problem. I cleared the closet shelves of games and baseball cards and cowboy paraphernalia and gave away the last of Don's clothes without too much re-gret. The problem is the three bookcases full of children's books. For sixty years I have collected children's books and am still much attached to many of them. I've already taken several boxes of chil-dren's books from my downstairs study to the attic to make room for office supplies and computer stuff. When I packed those books up several years ago, my two granddaughters wailed, "Oh, Grandma, don't give away any children's books. We may want them someday." They're still saying that, though they're both thirty and taking their time about needing them. But since I still have more storage space than they do, it seems heartless not to save them a little longer. I have managed to make a stack of books so worn and ragged that *no one* will want them, beloved though they were. I haven't yet put them in the recycle bin, but they're on the floor ready to go. The best books have gone back into the book-cases. There are still dozens on the bed, each one waiting for a thoughtful, time-consuming decision—perhaps even a rereading?

For the first year or so after Don died I didn't want to go through his papers. So much of his life was invested in them and, vicariously, mine too. I was his sounding board. Since then it's been inertia. I might not have pushed myself out of the inertia yet if the painter hadn't been ready to do Don's more recent study – a bedroom on the second floor which he appropriated after the children had left home. Getting ready for the painter meant not only taking books off the bookshelves, deciding which to keep and which to give away, but emptying and removing Don's four-drawer file cabinet. The way to do it, I decided, was to offer the file cabinet to one of my sons and insist that if he wanted it, he had to come and take it. Then I would *have* to deal with the files of papers on the floor. It took two weeks to reread the correspondence, decide which letters and articles to save, and make lists of books and articles that might come in handy for some other scholar interested in Walter Pater. I've filled two or three recycle bins; and I have found takers for some of the books. It gave me great satisfaction this morning to send off that fifteen pound box of books and newsletters to an acquaintance in Texas! The rest of the papers are not disposed of but at least they are now tidily organized in storage bins made for holding files, one of which now sits in the north bedroom closet. The other takes up floor space in my small study.

It will take longer to clean up my study where I need to weed out more precious books in order to get things off the floor. But they're not weeds! When I gave my oversized desk with its seven precious drawers to one of my sons, I had to take several boxes of children's books from here to the attic. Must I put the poetry up there, too? What pleasure is there in looking at shelves with reams of computer paper, pens and pencils, scotch tape, and paper clips instead of *The Wind in the Willows* and *Charlotte's Web*. or Shelley and Shakespeare, Robert Frost and Seamus Heaney?

Here, too, there are letters, in boxes, in files. Two old-fashioned file boxes 3½ inches thick and a foot tall, stuffed so full that the clasps can hardly keep them shut, have sat on the top shelf for decades. The other day I got them down to look for some family history for Don's nieces; Don's sister is dying and can no longer remember. There I found letters from Don's great-uncle Will Taylor, a curator for Henry Ford's museum, with information about Don's family and the Taylor name. "The name Taylor had nothing to do with cutting cloth, or clothes," he wrote, "but means 'To wield' or to Taylor anything, as an axe or sword." (I don't know where he got that idea. The *OED* does not agree.) There are letters from Louise Boas, my favorite professor at Wheaton, who not only "adopted" me when I was in college, inspiring me to do my best, but became a life-long friend and adoptive grandmother to my first two children; letters from my older brother from Europe during World War II; a batch of letters from an unexpected suitor and a much larger batch from Don. On the back of one of the letters from the man I didn't marry are notes that Don and I scribbled to each other one heavenly afternoon in late May 1940. It was one of those warm sunny spring afternoons when students long to abandon their books and cavort outdoors. We were studying together in the English Room in the University of Illinois library. It was almost time for finals.

"Je suis très amoureux," Don wrote. "C'est le printemps et toi." My reply was a hasty bit of doggerel.

> Le printemps has got you
> And ~~possibly~~ moi.*
> There's only one dictum.
> Il faut aller au bois.

---

* (*Possibly* put in for the rhythm but then crossed out.)

In his reply Don reverted to earthier English. "If you wish you may be kissed hell out of on floor 10 of the stacks way down at the left as you get out of the elevator. I leave first." Ten minutes later we were engaged to be married.

I haven't reread those letters in sixty years. I knew they were there on the top shelf, but too many other things have insisted on coming first—children, teaching, meals to cook three times a day, vacations, books or articles to write, the farm, grandchildren, founding the local AMI and Trailblazers—but I certainly can't die before I do reread them and rediscover my youth. Do I have the time? I haven't cleared out my study or the cellar yet and the attic needs it again! I haven't finished my book. I haven't finished writing my memoirs, either.

I'm banking on another fifteen years.

JANE KULPINSKI

The setting for my childhood and young adulthood was the city of Detroit where I attended St. Hyacinth Elementary School and experienced the meaning of the word limitations; Girls' Catholic Central High School where I learned the relationship between independence and responsibility; and Sapho Academy of Dress Design and Neron Millinery School where my creativity unfurled into a full-blown career.

I designed wedding veils and worked as a bridal consultant at the Detroit branch of Saks Fifth Avenue for a year and a half before I married John. Two years later we moved to Ann Arbor where I designed clothing until I decided to return to school.

After I earned a Bachelor of Science degree from Eastern Michigan University and a Master of Arts degree from Michigan State University, I embarked on a career in education which lasted for nineteen years until I retired. I taught at Roosevelt Laboratory School at Eastern Michigan University and at Ypsilanti High School. Both careers—teaching and fashion design—although quite different from each other, were equally gratifying. I truly feel I have achieved my career goals.

Now, during my retirement, I am pursuing my life-long interest in art and writing which evolved from my childhood experiences and, on occasion, precipitated disciplinary action by my second grade teacher, Sister Antonia. Drawing was not only my preoccupation but a passion in which I indulged when I became bored with a class assignment. When Sister discovered that I had been drawing figures and flowers in my arithmetic notebook, she enlisted mother's aid to correct the problem. My budding artistic career came to an abrupt halt.

I became interested in writing at the encouragement of my third grade teacher, Sister Cecilia, who often asked me to read little poems and vignettes that I had written. My concentration now is on completing my memoirs and on painting that one elusive masterpiece I feel I have within me.

He Never Said "Will You?"

Little snatches of romance have drifted in and out of my life ever since I was a child. My first great love was my father who showered me with affection and support at every opportunity. By the time I was three, Father and I had become team mates, conspirators, and mutual ego boosters.

I recall the times when the city bus dropped Father off at the far end of Lyman Street where we lived. When I spied my Tatuś (Daddy), I ran pell-mell into his arms as he scooped me up, kissed me and rubbed his stubby chin on my face, causing me to giggle and scream. Then he hoisted me to his shoulders and trotted home. It was our little routine until I started going to school. Only once afterwards did he repeat that ritual, and that was on my wedding day. After I had dressed for the wedding he nuzzled my face and, in a moment of déjà vu, I reacted by squealing as I had years before.

Of course, he thought I was the catch of the century, and it had taken some time and effort on my part to bring home a young man who met his standards. Did he plan to pursue an education? Who were his friends? Was he a man of his word? These qualities were merely the tip of the iceberg. I don't know if Father ever considered himself to possess all the qualities he wanted in a son-in-law, but I do know that he was one of the most totally honest, industrious, and charitable people I have known. Mother, on the other hand, made her assessment based on my date's potential to be a devoted husband, a caring father, and a good provider.

After a series of brief Platonic relationships, I met my life partner at a wedding reception. I noticed a tall, tan, "older" man walk in while I was dancing, and in my preoccupation with watching his moves, I completely blocked my dancing partner's conversation. When my friend Clare walked toward the visitor and placed her arm around his shoulders, I sighed with disappointment. My dancing partner, thinking my sigh was meant for him, gave my hand a little squeeze.

When the set ended, Clare led John over to me and introduced him as her brother who had just returned home from three years in the service. As we shook bands, it seemed that he held my hand for an uncommonly long time, and a warm flush traveled up my neck to my face. I was not as sophisticated as I thought. We danced and talked the rest of the evening. Our conversation seemed quite normal but, in retrospect, it was quite extraordinary. In a short time we knew each other's views on marriage, religion and children.

During our courtship John and I developed an understanding of each other's views and aspirations, and it was an unspoken expectation that we would support each other in achieving our goals. We had so much in common—the same ethnic roots, the same religious beliefs, the same socio-economic class, and we were madly, passionately in love. What's more, both sets of parents blessed our courtship. We had everything going for us, but our main focus was on our individual careers which we had been preparing for and anticipating for years.

Since his education at the University of Michigan was interrupted when he was called into the service during World War II, John's first priority was to work on his degree. We saw each other whenever he was able to come home, and after he earned his degree, we started dating in earnest. Our courtship was a sweet one, filled with promise.

Upon completing my studies at the Sapho Academy of Dress Design, I was hired as a bridal consultant at Saks Fifth Avenue in Detroit. Part of my responsibility was to help with the fashion shows when designers like Oleg Cassini and Sophie brought their collections to be shown in the Regency room at the store. I enjoyed this task because it gave me an opportunity to become acquainted with some of the most popular contemporary designers and eventually led to what I considered to be a springboard to the upper echelon of the fashion business.

As we worked on the preliminary details of the show, one of the designers became interested in my background preparation, and after considerable discussion, told me there would be an opening for an assistant designer in her New York establishment in a couple of months and asked if I would be interested in filling that position. I flew home that evening to tell my parents about this unexpected offer. Mother rejected the idea with her characteristic stamp of overprotective motherhood. New York to her was the other side of the world, but her spontaneous response did not surprise me, even though at age sixteen, she had crossed the ocean by herself to seek freedom and prosperity in the United States. Father, on the other hand, discussed the pros and cons of living away from home, but he didn't say "No." He didn't have to. The negative aspects far outnumbered the positive ones. I decided not to voice a few advantages that he omitted for fear of sounding argumentative.

I looked forward to my date with John that evening, and planned to surprise him with my exciting news. My words tumbled over each other in my eagerness to win his approval. He agreed that the prospect certainly had its merits, but there were many factors to consider before taking such an important step, such as finding a place to live, my ability to support myself, the permanency of the position, and my feelings about leaving my family and friends. He dropped the subject when we joined our friends for the evening and I suppressed my urge to share my good news with them until John and I had had a chance to discuss it further.

On the way home he opened the subject of my career again, but I didn't anticipate what came next. He asked me if I would have a lifetime of regrets if I stayed in Detroit and married instead. I didn't know how to respond. Was he asking me to marry him? I must have sounded rather naive when I asked him what he meant. He pointed out that distance would create a barrier to our developing relationship, and that he was in no position to interrupt his own career at this point.

That evening I lay awake reviewing our conversation and giving serious thought to my impending decision, even though I knew it was no contest between the two alternatives. The following evening I told John that I had decided to keep my position here at Saks, and that I felt that marriage takes priority over a career Given my upbringing of modesty in affairs of the heart, this was a rather bold statement.

"Well, then, why don't we set a date?" he responded.

We decided to marry on Thanksgiving Day since it is my favorite holiday, and because Father could not close the store on a Saturday to give me away. We joined my parents to share our happy news. John wanted some private time with Father to ask for my hand in marriage. How archaic, and how charming, I thought! Mother and I retreated to the kitchen for a cup of tea and second-guessed their conversation. She was happy about my decision to stay at home, and our plan to marry soon.

It took no encouragement on my part to activate her plans for the wedding. She spoke at length about the guest list, and I realized I was not going to have the small, intimate wedding I had always wanted, but that Mother was going to have the large wedding she had never had. I didn't protest too much because I understood that young people of her era who left their families and friends in Europe had neither the financial resources, nor a wide circle of friends, and few, if any, relatives to be able to plan a large celebration. The wedding would dominate our conversation until we married four months hence.

Looking very pleased, John and Father joined us in the kitchen, and, after fond embraces, settled down at the table for tea and animated conversation about our great venture. I thought, "How in the world did we get to this point when he never said, "Will you?" But then, I never said "I will."

Our wedding plans dominated the following four months. In addition to the usual arrangements of booking a Mass, a place for the reception, and musicians, decisions about food, flowers and invitations had to be made. In the meantime, I spent evenings and weekends sewing my wedding gown and the bridesmaids' dresses.

When we arrived at the church on our wedding day, the whirlwind of the past four months settled into a peaceful calm when I took Father's arm as the sound of the wedding march prompted our walk down the aisle. John and I took our vows at the High Mass at Saint Hyacinth Church and afterwards enjoyed a lovely reception for nearly two hundred people, then left on our honeymoon in Florida.

Upon our return, I learned that despite his strong, athletic image, John possessed a poetic quality that was to bring me pleasure and solace for the rest of my life. Like the way he hummed, "The Sweetheart of Sigma Chi" while we were dressing to go out for the evening, or the white rose he brought home on special occasions, and the poems he left in my drawers, on my pillow, even taped to the refrigerator door.

I was still starry-eyed and full of preconceived expectations of spending every waking moment together. Disillusionment set in when John told me that his card group was meeting the following week-end. My disappointment prompted feelings of rejection which translated into a pouting binge. When I narrowed it down to a choice of his friends or me, he rose to the challenge. He explained that he didn't think it was necessary for either of us to give up our friends now that we were. married because good friends are hard to come by. He pointed out that occasional separate interests would make us both more interesting people and that playing cards once a month would never change his feelings toward me. I liked hearing the last part, but could not reconcile my thinking to being apart for the evening. After all was said, he went anyway. That evening I set the breakfast table, filled the coffee pot, ready to plug in, and left a note with instructions for the remainder of the breakfast. I feigned sleep when he left in the morning, so I did not see him until dinner.

That evening at dinner John shared bits of news that he had picked up the previous evening, carefully avoiding the mention of breakfast. My coolness did not go unnoticed. The following morning when I went into the kitchen I found a short poem on my place mat. It said:

> Build no roof over my head,
> No walls to keep me in.
> I will stay by love and kiss
> Within.

I had not heard of its author, Ruby Zagoren, before or since that incident, but I bless her to this day for helping me to re-think my priorities. It was the first of a collection of poems John gave me throughout our twenty-eight years together. Now, whenever I need a little reassurance of my worth, or want a communion with my memories, I take out my little book of poems and re-create the moments of love, inspiration, and humor that we once shared.

⸙

The Royals and I

Ever since my first trip to Europe in 1969 I have been inundated with travel brochures from various companies and institutions. Acting upon a childhood dream that I would sail on the Mediterranean Sea some day, I signed on for a tour sponsored by the University of Michigan Alumni Association. I felt it was a great opportunity to explore the cultural and historical sites of Greece and Turkey with several people whom I knew. The vessel we sailed on was the tall ship, *Sea Cloud*, a four-masted square rigger with twenty-nine sails which were unfurled on the days when the wind was right. During the night it was powered by a newly installed diesel engine to facilitate greater speed in reaching our destination in the morning.

E. F. Hutton commissioned the ship to be built in Germany for his bride, Marjorie Merriweather Post. Together they enjoyed sailing to exotic places, entertaining their friends and business associates, and when their daughter, actress Dina Merrill, was a little girl, she was accompanied by a tutor to insure that her education was not neglected.

No expense or artistic talent was spared in creating this work of art. The dining room on the main deck is paneled and furnished with mahogany, and the massive fireplace surround is hand carved. A large oil painting of a seascape dominates the wall above it. Two elaborate master suites are located on the lower level and guest cabins are on the upper level.

The Huttons eventually divorced and Marjorie married Joseph Davies, the United States ambassador to Great Britain, who did not share Marjorie's love of the sea. In time, she sold the ship and it changed hands several times—most notably to President Trujillo of Mexico, whose body was transported on the *Sea Cloud* when he was assassinated. The ship was then docked in the Cayman Islands for a couple of years before it was sold to a commercial travel company which built additional cabins and refurbished the rest. It is now run by an international crew of seventy, and accommodates about the same number of guests.

The *Sea Cloud* is now well known among the ports of the Greek islands, and warmly welcomed by the residents there, including a friendly pelican named George who welcomed us to the island of Patmos and followed at our heels until he was given a treat.

I was realizing my dream as I stood on the teakwood deck, leaning on a highly polished solid mahogany railing which surrounded the ship, my eyes skimming over the azure blue ripples of the Mediterranean Sea. The gentle breeze wafted over the droplets of moisture on my skin and swept them away. Pristine air filled my lungs and I let my senses ramble from one serene view to another, from the softly rushing sound of the sea to the dull slaps of the waves against the sides of the ship, from the flap of the sails as they rode the wind, to the fragrance of the shampoo I had used on my hair that morning. An idyllic day, indeed.

I was jarred into reality by a voice chanting, "Skeet-shooting on the foredeck." Never having watched skeet-shooting, I moved to the foredeck with the others. As a clay pigeon was released from a trap, the marksman aimed his shotgun and pulled the trigger in the hope of hitting the target before the pigeon dropped into the sea.

It seemed like a simple procedure, but it required skill and co-ordination. When the shotgun was handed to me, I asked for instructions, as I had never held a firearm before and felt totally ignorant about its use. "Hold it snugly against your right shoulder. Squeeze the trigger, do not pull it. Fire while the target is ascending," were bits of advice called out to me by the experts.

I planted my feet firmly on the deck, raised the shotgun to my shoulder and shouted, "Pull!" The clay pigeon was ejected into the air and I trained my sight on it as it soared. A hush fell upon the group, and I held my breath until someone called out, "Shoot! Shoot!" But I continued to track its climb.

"Hurry before it starts coming down!"

It reached its pinnacle, then started to descend and I heard someone say, "Too late." I stood immobilized, following its descent with the barrel of my gun until my intuition screamed, "Now!"

I squeezed the trigger, then felt a mule-like kick against my shoulder, and heard shouts of astonishment when the target shattered and the pieces drifted downward to be swallowed by the sea. I had broken all the rules, but gained the admiration of the group for the duration of the trip. I handed the shotgun to the next participant with a flourish. By the time I returned home, the bruise on my shoulder had blossomed into a rainbow of colors and, for several days, I displayed it like a badge of honor.

That evening we assembled in the beautiful oak-paneled dining room for the Captain's dinner. The Captain, a red-bearded Scandinavian, greeted each guest individually, summoned the wait-staff, then proceeded to enthrall the group with sea stories as we savored the gourmet feast of fish, served in a pool of delicate wine sauce, and filet mignon with European dried mushrooms.

After dinner, the captain invited us to sign our names in the guest register which was displayed on a small mahogany table along the side of the dining room. Several of us enjoyed reading the names of previous guests who had sailed on the *Sea Cloud* at the invitation of its original owners. The list read like the *Who's Who* of the financial, social, and entertainment world. The names which intrigued me most were those of the Duke and Duchess of Windsor. I turned to a blank page, signed my name and thought, "Imagine! Jane Kulpinski in the same guest register with British Royalty!"

Sautéed Liver and Spinach, Please

From the time of the first EKG at a local hospital, until my discharge, I was poked, punctured, prodded, and pushed by a team of injectors, extractors, sticker-oners of nitro patches, and shuttlers who carted me from my room to the lab for various tests. Lovely as they may have been personally, I began to cringe like the cowardly lion when one walked into my room. I was especially impressed with the extractors because they came to visit me most often and I was able to evaluate their styles. They fell into four categories: the aggressive extractors, the jovial ones, the serious ones, and the timid ones.

The aggressive extractor strides confidently into the room, pulls himself up to an imposing height, gives you a "Don't you dare hide your arm" look and, with one fell swoop, punctures your skin and quickly extracts a vial or two of blood. Sometimes he misses and has to try again. The second time he takes a running start and plunges again. Wait a minute. I'll teach him a lesson. As he descends with what looks like a spike in the syringe, I pull away my arm and the mattress takes the full brunt of the spike, and I swear it cries "Ouch!" To be outwitted by a patient who was supposed to be lying passively, anticipating his next move, is a blow to his ego. He approaches with greater respect and humility on the third try.

Then there is the jovial extractor who smiles and asks you how you feel and makes small talk, throwing in a joke here and there, her eyes gleaming like cold steel, as if to say, "I vant your blood . . . all of it." You want to hide from this type because the eyes are a dead giveaway of her intention to extract FOUR vials of blood.

The serious one goes through the routine of scrubbing the site of extraction with alcohol until your skin takes on a fine patina like antique silver. This type positions himself deliberately at the most strategic distance from your arm, then adjusts his stance two inches one way, half an inch the other, bends over to scrutinize your arm, gently taps your vein below the tourniquet to bring it to full bloom, slips the syringe into it like a slippery little eel, and quickly extracts his pint of blood before you can say "Ouch!" These are the best kind and you want to compliment them frequently to keep them coming back. If you must give YOUR blood to THEIR project, it may as well be as painless as possible.

Ah, the timid ones. So dear to my heart as a teacher and lover of students. A sweet young thing, holding a syringe, following a veteran nurse who turns to me and says, "You don't mind if the student nurse takes your blood today, do you?" It is more like a predetermined statement than a question because she does not wait for an answer, but proceeds to instruct the student nurse in how to draw blood. I'm really in for it now, I think. I put on my confident, trusting expression in order to elicit her best effort We teachers have cultivated a myriad of expressions to accommodate any situation.

She ties on the tourniquet, disinfects a patch of skin directly over the martyr vein, and proceeds to push in the needle. That little push couldn't tickle a butterfly's wing. She looks up apologetically as I try to reassure her saying, "You have to learn sometime."

She pushes a little harder and, still smiling, I think, "Saints in heaven, let her get on with it." But what I say is "Push!", like a coach at a baby's delivery. She looks again, and in a little voice, says, "I did."

The veteran nurse and I zero in on my vein which has swelled with pride and given without a whimper. Our eyes meet and exchange the message that this student nurse is a keeper. "Give this girl an "A", I say. "She can take my blood anytime—if I have any left to give."

When I returned home I made a concentrated effort to consume a diet of red meat and dark green vegetables to replenish my blood supply for my next visit to the hospital.

Raise High
the Blue and White

Some of my fondest memories were formed during the years I spent at Girls Catholic Central High School which was located on Parsons Street near Woodward Avenue in Detroit. It was once a prized location, flanked by Orchestra Hall on one side, and the Detroit Women's League on the other, but it has deteriorated into what is now known as the Cass Corridor where poverty and crime proliferate. The area hosts a large number of street people, and local housing is occupied by the indigent and elderly population who are prisoners within their own walls after dark. It is no wonder that the focus of their social life is the former Catholic Central High School which now serves as a community center, open every day to serve a hot meal and provide recreational activities, as well as volunteer and learning opportunities, for those seniors who wish to participate.

I was full of anticipation as we boarded the chartered bus at the Pontchartrain Hotel to be transported through dense traffic along Woodward Avenue to Catholic Central High for my fiftieth high school reunion. In spite of the many changes which have occurred since I last traveled this route, I was glad to see the main landmarks still intact, and could identify what stood behind the barriers that concealed the boarded up or demolished buildings.

I hastened off the bus when we arrived fifteen minutes later and walked through the same front entrance that I had used fifty years ago. Neither the heavy oak door nor the worn brass handles had been replaced, and when I entered the building I noticed that the floors gleamed as they had in the past. A familiar scent of antiseptic permeated the air and mingled with the aroma of food cooking in the lower level kitchen. The piano at the far end of the hall caught my eye and, to my delight, I recognized it as the same piano we used during lunch time to thump out current tunes in order to practice new dance steps.

We toured the classrooms, some of which had been converted into office space. Each room brought back unique memories, not the least of which were the nuns who taught in those rooms. These nuns were the backbone of CCH, the teachers who made it their business to know each individual student well. We idolized the nuns for their intelligence, kindness, and personal interest in the girls.

One of my favorites was Sister Mary Christine, a diminutive, gentle person whose inner beauty matched her classic good looks. She never turned away a student who sought her attention, or who was troubled and needed her counsel and moral support. Although I did not appreciate it at the time, she possessed extraordinary administrative abilities which were recognized by her superiors, and some time after I graduated, she became Mother Superior of CCH, and subsequently headed Marygrove College.

A frequent subject of discussion among the girls was our French teacher, Sister Henrietta—tall, extremely slender, and very erect. She carried herself like a spire of Gothic architecture. On the rare occasions when she smiled in class, she revealed a pronounced overbite which some of the bolder girls sometimes mimicked. Her strict demeanor concealed her fun-loving nature which surfaced during the lunch period, partially spent in the playground area behind the school. She pulled the skirt of her habit up to just below her knees, and bloused it over the rope around her waist, then played field hockey with the girls, her habit and the veil attached to her wimple flying every which way. Not a ladylike pursuit, and certainly not included in the physical education program, but fun for students and nun alike.

During one play, her wimple was knocked askew and she needed to take it off to re-position it, thus solving the great mystery of our lives at the time, "What exactly did nuns do with their hair?" We stood agape when she revealed a blaze of very short cropped, straight hair that glimmered in the sunlight like a new copper penny, and tousled by the wind like an unruly mop. Our Sister Henrietta a carrot top! Amazing! This revelation opened a whole new topic of conversation among the students after school that day.

Before returning to the classroom, Sister dusted off her habit, resumed her formal posture and, once again, became the classic teacher and quoter of verse which she plucked from her memory to suit every occasion and transgression. I remember the one she quoted whenever a student dared to apply lipstick during class behind the shield of a raised desk lid: "Vanity, thy name is woman." Once when a student parried with a quote of her own, "If one has no vanity in life, there is not sufficient reason for living," she was invited to stay after school to engage in a dialogue with Sister. We never could pry the nature of the discussion from her, but we guessed it probably had to do with Christian reasons for living and humility.

My memories were interrupted by a voice announcing that lunch was ready to be served. As we moved to the cafeteria, I glanced out the window at St. Patrick Church where we attended daily Mass, and thought of Father Hardy, the pastor and religion education teacher. He was a tall man of stalwart build, black wavy hair, and straight black eyebrows over expressive blue eyes which could be as soft as the spring sky, or as electrifying as a storm cloud when he was angered by a provocative situation. He impressed me as a formidable man who would not tolerate any nonsense. In time, he proved my first impression. to be correct when a piece of malicious gossip regarding one of the students came to his attention. He stormed into the classroom like Moses coming down from the mountain to behold frenzied dancing, debauchery, and worship of false idols. His baritone voice rose an octave as he denounced the story as a "damnable lie."

Then there were times when he used his Irish wit to make a point, or showed great compassion and understanding in dealing with delicate or serious problems. By the end of the semester, many of the girls had developed a crush on him. I was especially grateful for his handling of one of the few transgressions I committed during my high school tenure. I belonged to the goody-two-shoes set who did what was expected of us. However, this status did not preclude a daring escapade my classmate Beth and I embarked upon on sheer impulse. We traveled to school on the same bus each day, and as we neared our destination one beautiful spring day, we spoke of how much fun it would be to go downtown instead of to school, never considering the possibility that we could be found out. When the bus driver called Parsons Street, Orchestra Hall, we neglected to pull the cord and turned our faces away from the school. We smiled at each other nervously and discussed what we would do when we reached our destination. We decided we would shop, lunch at Sanders, which was famous for its cream puff hot fudge, then return home at the usual time.

Since the retail shops did not open until nine thirty, and it was only eight o'clock, we looked at the store windows along both sides of Woodward Avenue, then took the diagonal walk across Grand Circus Park to the shops on Washington Blvd. By this time our nervousness had turned into a sense of adventure. Then it changed to panic, when we saw Father Hardy walking toward us from the other end of the park. He was returning from the Chancery office and, apparently, heading for the school. "Dear God, Sweet Mother Mary", we muttered under our breaths, our hearts pounding as we made a hasty detour behind some tall shrubbery. Father Hardy passed the shrubs, apparently unaware that two of his students were holding their breaths with a "Thank you, Lord."

After that narrow escape we wandered around aimlessly until lunch time. We ate a sandwich at Sanders, but found that we did not have enough money for a cream puff hot fudge if we were going to see a movie. We couldn't browse through the shops all day, so we opted for the movie. I don't recall the name of the film, or the story, but I do remember that Jean Arthur played the leading role of a woman from Kansas who, at one point, consumed a large steak with great gusto. After we got home, we called our classmates to get our assignments for the following day.

We arrived in school to be greeted by a warmly smiling Father Hardy. "Good morning Beth and Jane." During his lecture he consistently directed his questions to us. "What are your views on this, Jane?" "Do you agree with that statement, Beth?' Our classmates noticed that we were being singled out and began to fidget and glance at each other. He knew! He *had* seen us! It was the longest hour I ever spent in a classroom. When the bell signaled the end of the period, Father stood at the door as usual, and as Beth and I tried to blend into the group, he called out to us, "Have a nice day, Beth and Jane."

That evening I called Beth to find out if her mother had been notified of her absence, because my mother certainly seemed unaware of our caper. Father Hardy never referred to the incident, knowing that we had been punished enough. I doubt that he told Mother Superior, because she would have followed the rules of discipline as stated in her black book, and mother would have had to come to school for a conference, and who knows what kind of punishment would have followed at home? Our escapade was a disaster, not the carefree, enjoyable day we had anticipated, and hardly worth the purgatory we had suffered at the turn of events. I much preferred being a goody-two-shoes.

The memory of Father Hardy faded as our reunion group passed the window and St. Patrick church was no longer in view, and we proceeded to the cafeteria for lunch consisting of a salad, entree, and lemon pie. I sampled each dish, trying to savor the flavors I remembered from fifty years ago. Somehow it didn't taste the same. Perhaps too many different and more exotic foods had desensitized me to simply seasoned fare.

My eyes locked with those of several of the local residents while we were having lunch, and I could read in them shyness, despair, or gratitude to be able to spend time with their friends and enjoy this meal in a comfortable, pleasant place. No class or racial distinction here. Simply all kinds of people, interacting, glad to be alive and have a place to which they could come and expect to be treated with dignity. A few sat by themselves and quietly left after they ate, to go about their business of survival.

After lunch we moved to the auditorium for an informational meeting and a songfest. All the old familiar songs brought back memories of my senior prom. I thought of the hours Mother and I spent in stitching and fitting a gown worthy of a princess which I wore to the senior prom. I shared my interest in clothes and the joy of creating something beautiful with my mother, and as we worked on the gown, she would suddenly become a girl again while we talked and laughed about the events of the day.

When I was at CCH the girls had limited opportunities to meet boys, so a couple of months before the prom the nuns arranged an afternoon reception for students from a local Catholic boys' school. We all attended with the same purpose in mind—to find a suitable prom partner. From the moment the boys stepped off the bus, the girls became the most charming of hostesses, and the boys the most chivalrous of guests. After a couple of hours of making small talk, circulating around to meet as many boys as possible, drinking the punch bowl dry, and eating the snack trays bare, most girls decided whom they would invite to escort them to the prom. The nuns pointed out that the boys had to have some choice in the matter; therefore it was permissible to exchange telephone numbers with two or three of them and wait for them to call. The girls handed cards to the boys of their choice, who could be seen furtively writing brief notes on the cards. Oh, what we wouldn't have given to read those comments!

I was taught that beauty is not the most important attribute in choosing friends, so I looked for sincerity, neatness, and, of course, the ability to do the Lambeth Walk. I accepted an invitation from a boy named Anthony because we seemed to be attuned to the same interests. Father suggested that I invite him to our home, to be scrutinized, no doubt. Anthony came over the following week, looking very neat, hair slicked down, except for a little cowlick on the left side of his part that I hadn't noticed before. Then the interrogation began. Father drew him into a conversation which included his recreational preferences, his feelings about his teachers, and plans for his future. I don't think Anthony anticipated the drill, and I noticed that by the end of the evening, little beads of perspiration had formed on his upper lip. He laughed at father's jokes and told a few of his own, and when it was time to leave, he shook father's hand. Later, as my parents discussed his attributes, father made the comment that he had a grip like a man. I felt relieved that Anthony had passed the acid test of parental scrutiny. We exchanged a few phone calls to become better acquainted and to discuss the color of my gown, my preference of flowers, and the time he would call for me.

A week before the prom, seniors were assembled in the auditorium, which seemed much larger then, to receive instructions regarding etiquette, particularly when dancing. Most of the girls danced well, as we were taught by a professional dance couple as part of our physical education program which also included fencing and archery. The main concern of the nuns was impropriety which, in their view, meant the girl's bosom could not touch the boy's chest while they were dancing. Mother Superior demonstrated the proper distance by holding her hands, palms down, parallel to each other, in front of her chest. This distance was to be observed at all times.

On the night of the prom Anthony and I floated euphorically into the ballroom at the Women's League, he in his tuxedo, with hair slicked down, and I, in my off-shoulder pink tulle gown, the corsage Anthony had given me tied around my wrist. The sweet scent of the gardenias blended with all the other flowers as we moved about the room. The band started to play "Sophisticated Swing" and, when Anthony asked me if he might have the dance, I remember thinking, "Isn't that why we're here?" The lights dimmed—but only slightly—and we glided onto the floor, trying our best to emulate Ginger Rogers and Fred Astaire. Apparently the good Jesuits provided dancing teachers for their students as well because Anthony was, indeed, a good dancer, and we were in. perfect sync when executing some fairly sophisticated moves.

Mother Superior stood near the entrance in all her girth, hundreds of tiny creases wrinkling her angelic face into a benevolent smile, eager that "her girls" have a memorable experience. All the teaching nuns were there observing the activities. As one of my classmates aptly described the scene, "There were nuns lining the walls on all four fronts." As the evening wore on and the couples became better acquainted, they occasionally snuggled too close, and their chests touched. More than once, when the nuns observed "The Rule" being broken, they would signal their disapproval by holding their hands palms down, parallel to each other in front of their chests, and the offending couple would draw apart. By the end of the evening they resembled a group of umpires signaling penalties for offenses made.

The supervision did not deter us from having a grand time. Anthony was a perfect gentleman and always held me at a respectable distance. Have you ever tried to dance cheek-to-cheek like Ginger and Fred while maintaining a two-hand space between your chests? It isn't easy.

In his nervous attempt to kiss me goodnight when he brought me home, Anthony missed the mark by an inch and I walked into my home feeling the wetness of his lips on the corner of my mouth. On the way to my room, I noticed a light under my parents' door, and a few minutes later, as I lay in bed reviewing the events of the evening, Mother opened my door and said, "Sweet dreams." That was all—no questions. The discussion would have to wait until the following morning.

The melody of our school song nudged me into the present, and I joined in singing,

> CCH we're all behind you!
> Raise high the blue and white.
> For there's nothing half so glorious
> As to see our school victorious.
> We've got the pep girls,
> Let's get in step girls,
> Come on, don't give in
> C-E-N-T-R-A-L,
> Oh, Central High will win.

We prepared to leave and, as we boarded the bus, we bid a wistful farewell with a single backward glance. A nostalgic silence prevailed for several minutes as we each became lost in our own private thoughts of the days we spent there.

The dinner that evening was held at the Pontchartrain Hotel and was attended by a surprisingly small number of former students. Several of our classmates had passed away, the most tragic of whom was Mary Louise who became a nun and died in a fire at the convent. Some moved to other areas and could not be located since many of their surnames had changed when they married.

As much as I loved the school when I attended classes there, after a tour of the center during the fiftieth anniversary of my graduation. I love it all the more for the function it serves at the present time, still useful in providing a link to civility to the residents of that community—people who by a quirk of fate or lack of responsibility, are not able to provide for their basic needs. My earlier disappointment at seeing the devastation in that area was replaced by satisfaction and pride that good old CCH continues to serve where the need is greatest. Some of us decided that this is a charity worth embracing.

JOSEPH T. A. LEE

I was born in 1918 in the coal mining town of Nanaimo, on Vancouver Island on the Canadian-Pacific coast, the youngest of four siblings of immigrant Chinese parents living in Chinatown, an ethnically segregated community, mainly of contracted laborers in mines, lumber camps or sawmills with little outside intercourse due to language. Admittance of Chinese in public schools was in dispute until after the first World War. By the time the four of us were ready for school, this question had abated. I learned English at age eight. I enjoyed high school, represented grades 10 and 11 in student council, and became its president in my senior year.

My parents wanted me to join in our family business selling fruits and vegetables. My sight was toward the unknown—to go to college, the first Chinese from Nanaimo, in 1937. After three hard-earned engineering degrees with factory and corporate training, the threat of Communism in '48 shattered a promised bright future in China. The disaster was a blessing. It awakened a boyhood dream to go into architecture.

My life-partner, Elsie—we married in 1945—was an American citizen. I became one in 1950. After four years in architectural night school at Columbia University, working during the day in downtown offices, I joined the architecture faculty at the University of Michigan in 1952, and completed requirements for an architectural degree in 1955. After settling down in Ann Arbor with family and raising three children, I participated in community activities. I chaired the Ann Arbor Area Goals Conference in 1966 with the entire community involved. But community attention was soon diverted by the student uprising. Its turbulence was at its height when I was on School Board from 1967 to 1970. Environmental quality continued as a community concern. With the late Doug Fulton and others we had the canoe livery in Gallup Park repositioned to its present location. I chaired the Mayor's Committee to design the Huron Parkway Bridge, and took part in other issues in the city, Ann Arbor Township, and Washtenaw County.

After partnership with the late George Brigham until his retirement in 1960, I continued architectural practise until recent years. I did Kerrytown, the small-shop complex, next to the Farmers' Market developed by Arbor-A, Inc. of which I was one of the founders and vice president. I did a number of remodelings and residences in town over the years. Outside the city I did work in Chicago, Madison, and Seattle, and served as housing consultant for the U. S. Operations Mission in South Korea in 1962 and the International Consultants Corps in Sierra Leone in 1976. In addition, Elsie and I, with six other families, established in 1959 the ongoing Midwest Chinese Family Camp that meets a week each year, with headquarters in Chicago.

After 32 fulfilling years of teaching, I became Professor Emeritus in 1984. Meanwhile, artist wife, Elsie, became an author, and I began learning how to put words together under the baton of Helen Hill. We are moving in slower pace with symptoms of advancing years. Our baby boomers with offsprings are on their own. With modern technology flourishing in an age of information, Elsie and I are challenged for a simpler life.*

---

*EDITOR'S NOTE: It saddens us to report that Elsie Choy Lee died May 25, 2001, just as this book went to press.

We Met, Read, and Wed

Elsie and I met in 1941 when she and her sister, Catherine, transferred from the University of Hawaii to study at Michigan. I had transferred two years earlier from the University of British Columbia. Jimmy and another fellow student and I shared a rented apartment. One day Jimmy received a letter from his uncle in California. He wanted Jimmy to look up two new arrivals on campus, daughters of his former associate in China, J. K. Choy. His uncle suggested that Jimmy offer whatever assistance he could, being familiar with the campus and the city. Jimmy told me about his uncle's letter. He wanted me to accompany him to make the call. He said he felt somewhat uneasy to face two young ladies, especially ones from China, when his Chinese wasn't so fluent. Neither was mine. But hearing his plight, I consented to join him on his adventure.

It was a Friday evening. The night before the Saturday Varsity game. After downing our bowls of noodles, all we could afford for breakfast, lunch and supper, we started for their apartment. It was in the corner house where East Jefferson and Maynard meet. We got onto the porch. Jimmy walked over and knocked on their front door. We waited. No answer. He knocked, again. Again, no answer.

Almost skipping off the porch, we decided we needed a breather before heading for Yost Field to join in the celebration around a bonfire before the Saturday game, an old Michigan tradition. We decided on a long stroll around campus. Heading toward State Street down E. Jefferson, (this was before the University Administration Building blocked the way), we turned right, crossed State, and got onto South U. Looking some distance ahead, along the sidewalk, under dim streetlights, we noticed the silhouettes of two young females dressed in Chinese gowns, one taller than the other. Before we reached them, because of their difference in stature, I suggested that if those were the Choys, that he, Jimmy, take care of the tall one and I the other. He agreed. When we caught up with them in front of the President's house, Jimmy introduced himself and found they were the Choys! We spent the rest of that Friday together enjoying the bonfire at Yost Field. The next day at the stadium!

Who played in that Saturday's game? Who knows? What was the score? Don't remember.

A year later, in the Fall of 1942, we were engaged. Elsie was in her senior year and I in my Master's program. Together, we started planning for our future: what to do next after Michigan? With little understanding of life and the world at large, we thought for a secure future, adding business to our learning might be the right thing to do. The cost of another two years of college would not be easy for me. I felt the monthly checks of $100 from my family, the maximum amount allowed by Canadian law during the Second War, could not be asked to continue. The years at Michigan, even supplementing family support with work as student assistant at 35 cents an hour, made it necessary to skimp on basic needs, such as food and clothing, to carry on. As I had mentioned, my friends and I ate noodles for breakfast, lunch and dinner, at 10 cents a pack, condiment flavoured. Not knowing it, I grew pudgy.

I applied for admission with requests for scholarships in the business colleges of two Eastern Universities: M.I.T. and Columbia. I was admitted by both with promises of scholarships upon enrollment.

The question for us was then: which to accept for us to enroll? After mulling it over, our decision was Columbia. It was not on academic standing, for both ranked near the top. It was place, where each was located. Aside from learning business, we decided New York City would provide greater challenges to broaden our perspectives of the world and the people around us. That crossroad of the world seemed to be the right choice. Elsie's application to Columbia was accepted, and I was admitted with a scholarship.

In the summer of 1943, we left Ann Arbor by train and arrived in Metropolitan New York a month ahead of the fall semester. The day we arrived, Elsie checked-in at Whittier Hall on Broadway, the women's dorm for Teachers College at Columbia. She had earlier applied at the International House, but there wasn't an opening in the women's dorm available for that fall semester. There was one available in the men's section for me to move in the day we arrived.

That month of freedom, we put on wings. We learned to use the subway for five cents a ride, with transfer, if needed, to reach our destinations. We went sight-seeing in Times Square, Central Park, the Brooklyn Bridge, Chinatown, the Italian East Market, museums, art galleries, shows, especially the Radio City Rockettes, and the Rockefeller Center sunken plaza. We called on friends living in the city whom we had got to know while students at Michigan. We took long walks along Fifth, Park and other avenues, taking in their store fronts and displays. On leisurely walks in Riverside Park we enjoyed the views along the Hudson River and the Palisades beyond. We sat on too tall toe-touching high stools snacking at Chock-Full-O'Nuts, and ate luncheon in Horn and Hardarts on 42nd Street. We covered as many high spots as we could, leaving others for later, including the Statue of Liberty. Mixed in with the many adventures was an occurrence that changed the direction of my life for the next four years.

It was the morning we took the subway at the 110th street station. After the long ride, we exited at the Wall Street station. I was accompanying Elsie to call on a Mr. Hunt on an upper floor of the Chase Bank Building. Mr. Hunt, who had been a member of the American Consular Service in North China and a shipping agent in Shanghai, was the founder and president of William Hunt & Co., Inc. that represented over 40 American manufacturers in the Far East. The floor in the Bank building was their headquarters. Elsie had met Mr. Hunt with her family in Hongkong before she and her sister left for the University of Honolulu to study. That was before the Japanese invaded the island of Hongkong. The year before, her father had managed covertly to have his family escape to Hongkong after the Japanese invasion of Shanghai. He stayed behind to complete his mission to negotiate the protection of government properties from enemy hands before escaping himself to the island. Mr. Hunt was one of the entrusted protectors . After Mr. Hunt transferred his own operations to Hongkong, the two families met and came to know each other.

After their greetings, and inquiries of each other's family, Elsie told Mr. Hunt the reason for our being in New York. After probing into my background and person, he said to me, "You don't want to learn business from Columbia. I can teach you all the business you want. What I would like you to do is to study electrical engineering. After your degree, I can send you to factories of one of the manufacturers we represent, for some practical experience. Then after a year in our headquarters here, you can go to Shanghai as part of our operation there."

It was breath taking. His offer, I told him, was hard to refuse. But I could not accept, for coming to New York with Elsie, to enroll in the Business School at Columbia was possible only because of their offer of scholarship. His answer was direct.

"Tell Columbia you don't need their scholarship. I'll pay your way."

After talking it over with Elsie, I accepted his offer the next day. Elsie remained enrolled in the Business School, while I changed colleges and became a student in Columbia's Electrical Department in their Engineering College.

The next two years were busy ones for us both. My first day in class, I found myself sitting among students all dressed in white. They were students of the Navy studying under the V12 program. Despite my nonconformity in class attire, we got along well. Our Professor-Advisor, a small, kind gentleman, was the inventor of the wet cell battery, versions of which we are using today.

A year in college during the war years meant three semesters cramped into one year, with only breaks of a few weeks in between. But it was that unimaginable offer of a dream that kept me going, with subliminal guidance from parental admonishment to work and study hard—the future will be bright. With credits from courses at Michigan, I received my degree in Electrical Engineering in the spring of 1945. Elsie got hers in Business Administration.

We found our balance outside the classroom as we involved ourselves in a number of extracurricular activities. The first week in class we received notice from the Chinese Students Club on campus of a meeting the following Sunday at 2:00. We arrived on time, and found the president and secretary with two other students present. An hour later the meeting began, with a handful more of students coming in.

An opening in the women's dorm allowed Elsie to move into the International House. Being together in the same building, Elsie proposed we start a newsletter for the Club. She named it the *New*

Horizon. She was the editor and I became its manager. We spent evenings working on the newsletter in the second floor lounge. The janitors often reminded us to switch off the lights before leaving.

The second year at Columbia, I was president of the Club. We put on dances, planned picnics, and organized Friday evening language-exchange classes for Chinese students from China to improve their spoken English, and Chinese students born in America to learn Mandarin. By year's end, two cases of exchange turned out to be exchanges of vows.

Right after we received our degrees, Elsie and I married in the University Chapel. That was on June 30th, 1945. Elsie's father, who left China early that Spring, gave the bride away. Dan, her brother, a medical student, was present, with their sister Catherine as bridesmaid. Fredrick Kuh, a former fellow student at Michigan and a fraternity brother from Shanghai was my best man.

The Chapel was filled with fellow students, teachers and friends. The ceremony started on schedule with a slight glitch. Our friend, once head of a conservatory in China, began with an extensive song of joy with the accompaniment of the organ. Finally he finished and took his seat. Waited, the congregation in silence. No procession. A few moments later, our friend was asked to give another song. He finished the second. Sat down. Congregation waited. Again, no movement down the aisle. Our friend was about to be called for another time. At that moment, father and daughter appeared following bridesmaid down the aisle.

It was on arriving in their car at the back entrance of the Chapel, that Elsie found she had forgotten the marriage license for the minister to witness. It was that hectic journey back and forth over long blocks crossing Broadway that gave time for the congregation to enjoy our friend's voice for a second time.

The rest of the wedding went smoothly that sunny June day. The reception was in the campus Faculty Club. The three layer wedding cake, ordered from Schrafts' Bakery, was thickly covered with white butter -cream icing, decorated with flowers, colored, of the same thick cream. Just as we laid down our knife after the cutting, our minister stepped forward and thrust his hand toward me for a shake. I grabbed his with gusto, and squeezed it with all my might with all fingers and thumb. Small white splatterings began to appear over his black suit sleeve!

Lesson for grooms: never touch the icing, no matter how delicious—especially, the thumb.

When we returned to our room in the Hotel Paris on 97th Street, completely exhausted, we flopped down on the bed, wedding clothes and all, and fell fast asleep. We woke ten hours later at four o'clock in that early morning. We showered and changed. After a snack in a nearby restaurant, we strolled into Central Park under the bright moonlight. Took rests along the way, enjoyed the peace and quiet of the night, without a single soul passing or in sight. Reaching the restaurant in the park, closed for the night, we turned back, and retraced our trail and exited through the same gate, back to our hotel.

The peaceful beauty of pure youthful innocence!

(Written for Joe on our 34ᵗʰ anniversary, June 30, 1979)

Do You Remember?

We went to a concert, you and I
We came away, and what did we hear?
We heard each other's heart beat,
Drowning out the orchestra's feat,
Wishing we were somewhere else,
Wishing we had not pretended
To be crazy music lovers.

We sat through a course in logic, you and I
That A is equal to B, and B is to C,
Therefore A is equal to C,
B being the key to all concerned,
Bringing together A and C
Inescapably for each other.

To you on this day,
Elsie

Ping Pong Diplomacy

First Serve

In 1972 I stepped foot on our ancestral soil for the first time when the world witnessed an historic change in Sino-American relations after nearly a quarter century gulf. As Dr. C. K. Jen, who was with me on the trip, wrote, "The ping-pong diplomacy between the People's Republic of China and the United States", and the subsequent visit by President Nixon in 1972, "unlocked a door that was closed for nearly a quarter of a century, thus allowing direct communication between the two peoples."[1] Dr. Jen, now retired, was then Vice-Chairman of Johns Hopkins' APL Research Center. After the successful ping-pong diplomacy, and during the overtures by President Nixon to establish better relations between the two countries, Dr. Jen, through his long-standing contacts in academia and government in his former homeland, began exploring ways and means for Chinese-American educators and scientists here in America to contribute their share toward improvement of that relationship. It was Dr. Jen's vision and tenacity, that brought about an official invitation for our delegation of twelve scholars to visit China in 1972.

---

1. "Mao's 'Serve the People' Ethic." *Science and Public Affairs*.March, 1974.

Our group consisted of scientists and educators in many fields: meteorology, biology, fluid dynamics, physics, architecture, mathematics, history, electrical engineering, and philosophy. Institutions represented were Catholic University, Cornell, the Worcester Foundation, Johns Hopkins, University of Michigan, M.I.T., Princeton, and the University of California, Berkeley.

Of the twelve scholars, only I was born outside of China. I was born in Canada, of immigrant parents from South China. I was brought up speaking Chinese, the Cantonese dialect, standard for the southern Province of Guangdong, and learned English when I reached the age of eight or seven. The others, who left China in the early '40s during the Chiang regime, came to the United States to pursue research and higher learning with intentions of returning, but thwarted by the 1949 communist take over, they'd remained in the United States, and established themselves in professions, raised families, and become citizens.

The academic and government wheels were putting together our invitation the week when President Nixon was in China, in February, 1972. That historic event remains vivid in my memory to this day, because of an unexpected phone call one afternoon that week from Paul T. K. Lin, someone I hadn't seen or heard from for years. He was both a former school mate and house mate at the University of British Columbia before we both transferred to Michigan in 1939. I thought he was calling from Canada, or maybe from China. But no, he was calling from Lane Hall, here at the University.

Delighted, and no less surprised, I was puzzled when he said he was calling from Ann Arbor: How did he get across those borders when he was supposed to be expelled?

"When did you get in?" I'd asked. "And what are you doing in Ann Arbor?"

"I came in early this morning," he said, "on my way to New York. Right now I am having a meeting at the Center for Chinese Studies. I'm free this evening. Can we get together?"

My question was soon dissolved, when he answered my next question: "I'll be on CBS television, a panel, when President Nixon, who's in China now, comes on."

For such an historic occasion between China and the United States, there were good reasons for Paul 'to be chosen. After our transfer to Michigan, he continued for a year in engineering, but switched into political science the next. After graduation he continued on to The Wharton School for International Studies where he earned his Ph. D. Following that, he became Executive Secretary of the Chinese Students Christian Association, headquartered in New York City, with responsibilities to look after the welfare of Chinese students studying at universities throughout the United States. After the second or third year, because of his rather left leanings in the performance of his duties, the United States government expelled him from her borders, sometime in the late '40s or early '50s.

After his expulsion, I'd heard nothing more from or of him for some time, until I'd found that he was heading the National English broadcast in China. In that position for five years, he then became English secretary to Premier Chou En-Lai for another five. His health, however, brought him back to Canada. Following his recovery, he became Professor of Political Science, and Director of the Center for Asian Studies at McGill University. Pierre Trudeau's visit to China, when he was Prime Minister of Canada, was one of Paul's diplomatic handiworks.

That evening at our home, gathering a few friends on short notice to meet Paul, I'd learnt that application for permission to enter China had to go through Ottawa, the Chinese Embassy in Canada. There was no China representation in the United States at the time. The person at that evening's get-together, to whom I am most grateful for the opportunity to visit China, is Dr. C. T. Tai, Professor Emeritus in Electrical Engineering and Computer Science of the University of Michigan, a renowned specialist in electromagnetic theory. He was one of Dr. Jen's associates at the Radio Research Institute, in Kunming, at the time of the Japanese invasion in the late 1930's, when Tzinghua University moved inland.

While we were waiting for our visas from the Chinese Embassy in Ottawa, the President of Peking University asked each of our members to prepare lectures and papers to be given in various universities when we got there. Since China was just recovering from the Cultural Revolution of 1966–69, and in the midst of reconstruction, I felt the art of architecture was not exactly a timely subject to present. I chose instead a topic that I felt was of importance to them at that moment of industrialization, as it was to us, and still is: "Pollution: The Impact of Industry and Technology on the Living Environment."

Meanwhile, a warning was issued from the mainland that "Taiwanese agents intended to thwart (our) trip by terrorists measures." Apparently it was too much for Taiwan to learn that a few members of their National Academia Sinica had accepted their arch enemy's invitation to visit the land from which they were ousted. Among a number of the distinguished members of the Taiwan Academy in our delegation was Dr. Jen. Membership in that island's Academy is equivalent to membership in our U. S. Academy of Sciences, an honour for the individuals chosen, and a pride to the nation to have such representation in the world of sciences. Acting on their warning, our delegation divided ourselves into four subgroups: ours, one of three that booked independent flights across the Pacific for Hongkong, and the fourth, across the Atlantic through Europe.

I found packing for the trip was a challenge: not knowing where we would be; where we would stay; the means for getting around; the weather to expect; the functions and meetings to attend; people to meet, etc. etc. With all the unknowns, I decided to take the simplest route: to take along only absolute necessities in one suitcase, and one shoulder bag. The shoulder bag I'd carry the whole way, with on-the-spot needs. One decision I made was not to skimp on film. I wanted to take a lot of slides so I could bring home a good record of my experiences. Taking no chances of not having films when I needed them, I'd bought 20 rolls of Kodak 35 mm slide film, and squeezed them into my shoulder bag before I left. Should I be so lucky, I'd have 720 slides to show when I got home.

Finally, the much waited envelope from Ottawa arrived. Opening it, I found no official seal stamped on my passport as expected. Instead, there was a small slip of paper clipped inside its cover. On it was stamped China's official seal: the visa. Later, I learnt that that procedure was taken by them to help us avoid future difficulties upon visits to Taiwan. A stamped passport with a Mainland seal would find rejection in Taiwan. A thoughtful consideration.

Hong Kong and Kowloon

Finally, on June 23rd, our contingent took off from the San Francisco International Airport, arriving in Hongkong three days before our scheduled entry into China. A van from the Jingmen (Golden Gate) Hotel picked us up after a long wait at the crowded airport and brought us to their modest Mainland operated hotel in Kowloon. The members of the other two subgroups had already arrived. During the three days' stay at the hotel, the eleven expatriates, to quote from Dr. Jen's memoir, "had several sometimes agitated meetings, at which we discussed what should we do and how we should behave once in China." Their quandary, it seemed, had arisen from being expatriates, returning to the land of their birth after a quarter century's absence, albeit invited. As Dr. Jen wrote, " . . . many in the Chinese academic community in this country *[i.e., the U.S.]* were still fearful of the uncertainties and risks of such an undertaking. . . . many were either uneasy about, or negatively disposed toward, the Communist regime. In addition, there was concern as to possible repercussions on relatives in Taiwan." I sat in on those meetings, but did not participate.

During those three days in Kowloon, our delegation had two formal meetings with the head of the China Travel Bureau, outside of China, in Kowloon: a Mr. Yang Chi-Ming—a gentleman with a head of white hair. The first meeting took place the second day after our arrival. He reviewed for us a preliminary draft of our itinerary, subject to changes on our way, and expectations and regulations after crossing the border. Aside from these scheduled meetings, we were left on our own for the following two days.

I looked up William Choy, one of three heirs of the owner of the largest department store in Shanghai before the Communist takeover. I hadn't seen him since my sabbatical in 1962, when Elsie and I stayed with his sister in her second story flat of their three-storied family building up the hill on Caine Road. After lunch, William called his friend, the owner of a camera store in Kowloon. He introduced me, and said I was looking for a good camera. Should I come over? Could he help? I took the Star Ferry to Kowloon, and had a good walk on the way to the store, while reacquainting myself and noting changes that had taken place since my last visit. It was a well-stocked store with cameras and photo equipment of endless choices. The Leicaflex I have today was from there. I bought it at a good price. When the store owner learned of my bringing rolls of Kodak film into China, he expressed doubt. He told me that in China, at that time, they could develop only German made films. Having been told that, to be on the safe side, I bought 20 additional rolls of film from him, this time the German brand, Agfa, building up a modest cargo in my shoulder bag.

I thanked him, and rushed to our second late afternoon meeting with Mr. Yang at the China Travel office. After giving us more information and instructions for our trip, Mr. Yang asked if any of us had questions. With the camera store owner's remarks still fresh in my mind, I asked, "I'd heard that in China, only German film could be processed. Can that be true?" "Yes," was his reply. "Furthermore," he continued, confirming what the store owner had said, "All films are required to be developed, before they are allowed to be taken out. One other regulation," he went on. "Only two rolls of film are allowed to be taken in." Hearing that, my jaw must have fallen open. There I was: after careful planning to bring 20 rolls of Kodak, and now adding another 20 of Agfa, I should be told that only two rolls were to be brought in. Ending the meeting, Mr. Yang said he would be at the Kowloon Station to be with us the next morning.

We hurried back to our hotel to have supper, and then a last meeting before the morning's departure. Mr. Yang's comment was unsettling. Should I leave my rolls of film with friends in Hongkong? Leave them with this hotel? Hand them in at the border customs? Not certain of any of the answers, I stuffed them into my shoulder bag and lugged them to the station the next morning.

The morning was bright and sunny. Mr. Yang had not yet arrived. Strips of sun rays streamed through beautifully designed iron-grilled arches over the open-air station platform. While enjoying the morning quietness in a usually noisy Kowloon, I saw Mr. Yang appear at a distance. He walked straight toward me, and pressed into my hand two plastic calling-card-sized calendars, with images of China's National symbol on their backs, the Tiananmen, or the Gate of Heavenly Peace. Without the expected greeting, he asked,

"Are you Joe Lee who was at Columbia? Your wife named Elsie?"

"Yes," I said, "My name is Joe Lee. My wife's name is Elsie. How do you know?"

He broke into a smile. "I thought so," he replied. "I wasn't sure at our meetings with the use of your Chinese name. I see you don't remember me. Do you remember those days at Columbia, when we visited each other, in our apartments?"

When he reminded me of that, his features began to become familiar. Looking at him, I kept asking myself: Could he be another victim of the Cultural Revolution? Ten years younger than I, yet his hair was completely white. It brought to my mind someone I knew at age 30. She found her hair had turned white over night, after the trauma that was administered to her and her two companions by the revolutionary Red Guards in the region of China's scenic spot, West Lake in Hangzhou.

I lamented that we hadn't discovered each other's identity earlier. If we had, I said to him, we could have spent some time in the last two days together to reminisce, and bring each other up to date since New York.

"We still can on the train,'" he said, "I'm coming along."

We had a pleasant hour's ride north to the Chinese border. We did have a little chance to talk while moving through the New Territories of the British colony, occupied by Britain after the Opium War, together with Hongkong. While we were bringing back old times, I didn't broach the subject of the film; it would have been inappropriate, for he, too, must follow the rules.

When we reached the last stop at the end of the Kowloon line, the late morning remained sunny and beautiful. Mr. Yang escorted us off, as he did afterwards, on foot, across the famous international bridge. The bridge, although famous in itself, was of ordinary trestled steel, of no particular character; and no more than 100 feet long. However, it could be proud to be guardian of the invisible international fine line defining the invisible boundary between two different Chinese worlds. I wonder today what difference it would have made to that bridge's thinking, had it known then what we know now, that in another quarter century, in 1997, with its duty relieved, it could return to a life enjoying peace and comfort with its neighbour, the brook below, that flows forever on.

Approaching the bridge, we saw beyond, framed by its trestled length, two green-uniformed PLA (People's Liberation Army) sentries with red stars on their caps, who stood with guns at attention by their sides. With Mr. Yang leading, we walked across noisy planks, over the invisible line, and stepped off onto Red soil—the then frontier village of Shun Zhen—now, today, the burgeoning metropolis of sprouting high rises and high production factories, competing with its neighbor to the south, Hongkong.

In Mao's China

Leading the way to the government building inside China's border, and seeing us settled in its visitor lounge, Mr. Yang bid us farewell, and took the return train back to Kowloon. Getting comfortably settled in too-well-padded chairs and sofas, with crocheted doilies on their arms, we were served hot tea poured from half-gallon, colorfully decorated thermoses, into porcelain cups with covers—a welcome reprieve after the long journey. No sooner had we begun to relax than a customs officer entered with forms in hand. Giving each of us a copy, he told us we must enter every item we carried on our persons and in our luggage, which would be later inspected, with signatures when complete. He said he would be back to collect the completed forms in the next quarter hour and left. Putting my head down, I conscientiously entered one item after the next while leaving the stockpile of film to the last. Not without reluctance, I decided to do what seemed right: to turn in the excess 38 rolls with the request that I pick them up on our way out.

At that very moment, the unexpected happened. The door into the lounge crashed open. A messenger dashed in, saying the process was waived. The messenger was no other than the same customs officer who earlier handed us the forms to fill out. But this time, when he appeared, it was with a big smile. In a loud voice, almost a shout, he announced that our group need not fill out the forms. Neither would our luggage be inspected. We were taken to an elegant reception room where we were served a luncheon banquet and were told that Mr. Li Guang Tzer, the Head of the Chinese Travel Administration, was taking off from the Beijing airport at the time of the announcement. He was flying down to meet us at the City of Guangdong railway station, where we would arrive early that afternoon.

The simultaneous announcement of our exemption from customs regulations and the upcoming greeting at the Guangdong Station by a top government official was the harbinger of the welcome mat laid before us, as honoured guests of the government and her academic institutions, the first official ethnic Chinese group of educators and scientists from abroad to set foot on her land since opening her door no more than four months before.

Among our delegation, the emotions ran deep: sparkled glows among moist eyes, and controlled smiles from happy souls. It was a celebration, especially for our eleven expatriates, like the replay of the Biblical scene, the homecoming of the prodigal son, after the separation of a quarter century, to be received with opened arms by the motherland, whose ideology among some might not have been comfortable, but whose openheartedness and hospitality, they could not but appreciate with inexpressible joy. These were prodigal sons with a difference. They bore good tidings to their motherland: gifts of new knowledge in fresh lights from a distant adopted land. They'd returned with enrichments for their beloved, deeply rooted, ever evolving culture, from which they'd once drawn sustenance.

Relaxed, after a short rest following the sumptuous luncheon, we were escorted to the railroad station and put onto the City of Guangzhou bound train on our first leg of an eventful month. Every detail was taken care of far beyond what any of us could have anticipated. Each day our schedule was filled. Every request from group or individual was satisfied. Transportation was always at the door. Every surprise was a revelation. Every meal was a feast. Each accommodation was of comfort. And the most thoughtful was the two hour break after each lunch for rejuvenation, before the second half of always eventful days.

Our itinerary for the month included the following: three days in Guangzhou, the capital city of the southern province of Guangdong after a 31 hour train ride to Hangzhou, the city made famous by Marco Polo, where we stayed for two days; then three more hours on train to Shanghai for four days; and finally, by plane to Beijing for ten. Then to wind up the busy formal portion of our month long schedule, a visit to the 196th Division PLA army base near Tianjin.

After that, the last week was left open to our own devices. We could plan our own agendas: either as small groups or as individuals; to visit relatives anywhere in the country; to call on former colleagues at far away institutions; or to journey to significant places of ancient or recent times. Many places would not be ready to receive visitors, because of the brief period since the country's door was opened. Whatever might be our needs, the government would try to respond to our every request, be it transportation, lodging, meals or whatever. They would provide guides to pave our ways.

I found one requirement upon entry unusual. We had to hand in our passports and have them given back to us upon leaving. Having traveled in many countries, that experience of not having my passport in my waist belt was like being without security blanket, for a while, at least.

But the more pleasant request that came afterwards was for us to submit names of persons we would like to see while in the country. They would make the contacts and arrange for one-on-one meetings at appropriate locations along the way.

That was good news. Before leaving the States, I was asked by a Chicago friend, who came to the United States as a student in the early 40's, if I could find some way to give a message to her 80-year-old father in Beijing. She had tried to get a visa, but to no avail. It was possible that her difficulty had to do with the fact that her father was an intellectual, Professor Chou, a holdover perhaps from the Proletarian Revolution when intellectuals were suspected and ostracized. Another person I had wanted to see was Dr. C. S. Huang, who was at the time the Head of the China Academy of Medicine, a fraternity brother who was at Michigan for a few years doing lung surgical research. With his expertise in both Eastern and Western medicine I had wanted to have his opinion on Elsie's chronic condition, the reason why she was not with us.

I saw Professor Chou on the fourth day of our stay in Beijing. The youthful 80-year old came by bike for our meeting that morning at the Peking University administrative building! Our group was having a meeting with the president of the University at the time. Two days after that meeting, I was told at dinner that Dr. Huang was coming in from the countryside, probably a commune, and would be in the meeting room waiting for me that evening at our hotel. We had a pleasant hour together. I took a number of snapshots of him. Of the thousand odd slides I took on that month's journey, those I took that night were the only blanks. It could have been the wrong type of film for the lights the hotel had in that room. I would never know.

As for our itinerary the first three weeks, we visited universities, people's communes, hospitals, factories, and historic and scenic spots; and for some members research institutions of particular specialties. We each gave lectures and held seminars at universities, especially in the two large cities: Beijing and Shanghai.

The most unforgettable experience in those three weeks was witnessing at close range the lung operation of a 40-year-old lady in the Beijing Hospital. For two long hours with cloth screening her view, using the ancient art of acupuncture for anesthesia, an application discovered in 1956, with one needle on her ankle and another on her wrist, she chatted with the attending nurse, sitting by her side, twirling needle on her wrist while giving her an occasional fruit or juice to eat or drink.

One episode in my lecture experience at Tungzhi University in Shanghai, I will always remember. It was an extremely hot sweltering afternoon on July 6th. After meeting with the architectural faculty, I was escorted to the auditorium where I was to speak. An audience had already assembled. Every double-hung window on both the rear and side walls was pushed wide open to let in whatever cool air there might be from the outside.

While I was loading the carousel, the blinds were being pulled down over the opened windows to darken the room for my slides. Finishing loading and looking up in the darkened room, I noticed the poor condition of the blinds; shredded and splattered with holes, letting in daylight; almost washing out the images of my slides when I later showed them on the screen. Apparently, the maintenance of that facility in Tungzhi, not unlike buildings in universities throughout the country, had not caught up with its neglect since the beginning of the Cultural Revolution in 1966. Not unlike other universities in China, Tungzhi was closed down. It was only a year before our visit that efforts were being made to revive the campuses and to resuscitate higher education in the country. Ironically, for that hot day, the poor conditions of those blinds could have been just what we might have ordered: to let in some cooling air.

I was introduced to the waiting audience and was walking toward the speaker's stand, when the door to my left into the auditorium came open. Outside the lobby, framed by the door opening, I saw four men, each carrying a large laundry tub brimming full with blocks of ice. Without a sound they entered the auditorium, one following the other, the audience in complete silence. Dumbfounded, with arms resting on the speaker's stand, I watched; they came up onto the stage; circled me; the first let his load down in front of me; the second, his load to the right of me; the third behind me; and the last to the left of me; and left.

The law of nature says cold air drops. And it works the same way in China. It was not the ice that kept me cool; it was the thoughtfulness that saw me through the rest of that sweltering day.

The last event on our formal agenda was a long morning bus ride to Yang Tsun, on the outskirt of Tianjin, where we spent a full day on the base of the 196th Division headquarters of the People's Liberation Army, the PLA. Of historic interest was that many of China's past warlords were graduates of its top-notch cadet training school.

It was on that visit that we learned of the self-sufficiency of the People's Liberation Army; that they were not just a fighting force.

"Perhaps to emphasize, to us, the non-military aspects of their operations," as one member observed, they showed us first upon arrival that morning, their "various production units, besides those tilling the fields: *[facilities for making]* soy-sauce, bean curds, *[army uniforms and]* sewing." At that point, after the word *sewing,* he recorded within brackets an insertion that reads, "where one friend had his slightly torn shirt immediately repaired by a soldier, while other friends clicked their cameras." Then he went on: "shoe-repairing, hog raising, and . . . a small-sized pharmaceutical factory . . . where workers, mostly soldiers' wives, *[were putting]* . . . herbal medicines into modern forms."

The shirt that was repaired was mine. I had no idea that I had made such a scene. After I removed my shirt to have its torn pocket restitched by the soldier running the sewing machine, a PLA soldier standing nearby, noticing my discomfort in bareback, despite the hot July weather, handed me a PLA army jacket to put on; and I did. For an American visiting that country for the first time, it was an experience. Especially, since the PLA uses no insignia to identify rank, the one I had on could have been a barefoot rookie's or even a general's.

After touring the production units, we had an elaborate luncheon with dishes prepared from produce raised in their barns and grown in their fields. From the dining room, we were escorted to a theatre to be treated by in-house talents, the soldiers and their wives: solo performances, choral singing, native dances, skits, and the playing of Western and Chinese musical instruments. The most interesting was the playing of a percussion instrument made out of cannon shells.

News of the highlight of our visit came while we were in the Peking Hotel dining room having our evening meal. Premier Chou En-lai would meet with us that evening in the Great Hall of the People. We rode in a motorcade of curtained sedans from the

hotel to cross the half-mile-wide Tiananmen Square. That hot summer night it appeared that the entire population was out cooling
themselves. Our motorcade had to plow through the rowdy mass
in order to get to the other side of the square.

After welcoming handshakes through the reception line, our
host escorted us into the meeting hall and sat down with us in
chairs arranged in a comfortable circle. In the audience were
members of the China Academy of Science and a small group of
Chinese-American scientists who came on their own. The opening
question the Premier asked was "What was our American attitude
in that presidential election year?" He gave his views on the rights
of women in his country in which infant mortality stayed high,
while preference for boys kept their reproduction rate strong. He
turned to contraception for discussion, for a member of our delegation was the scientist at the Worcester Foundation in Shrews-
bury, Mass., who co-founded the pill. Every topic he raised was far
ranging. Rebuttals and contradictions were invited. Every topic he
brought to its conclusion with a touch of humor.

In politics, he said the 20-odd years since his country's liberation was but a moment in history. China would never sit back, but
would continue to be alert, and work hard to transform her society. He then plunged into a long review leading to the 1980 ending of China's relation with the USSR, and to the death of his
country's defected General Lin Bao in his escaped-plane crash over
Inner Mongolia. While he was introducing subjects for general discussion he also asked for suggestions that would help his country
and people.

I made no contribution that evening. I did make a few at a sem-
inar held earlier that week at the Peking University. They were 1)
Keep their use of bicycles; 2) Within the ancient walls of Peking
build buildings no taller than four or five stories in height; and 3)

Do not borrow Russian architectural styles for future public buildings in China.

Before we all reassembled for a group picture four and a half hours later, the Premier closed the meeting with the reminder that President Nixon was the one who had made our meeting that evening possible. Followed with smile, he added: "However, neither had Peking turned right, nor Mr. Nixon turned left!" As for us, our delegation, after the group picture we went straight back to our hotel for another good night's sleep.

CECILY LEGG

Born in 1915, my first eight years were spent in northeast England. We then moved to the southeast coast. I remained steadfastly loyal to the north— often quoting Tennyson: '. . . bright, fierce, and fickle is the South / And dark, true, and tender is the North.'

My first career—lasting eight years—was as a Nursery Nurse (Nannie) to families stationed overseas. I enjoyed three winters in South Iran. World War II abruptly ended that and I decided to become a hospital trained nurse. However, the nurse training school for which I was accepted had to suddenly cancel their student intake because of a direct enemy hit on the hospital. It was only a very few weeks before the call-up date for my age group, just time to volunteer for military service. I chose the Women's Auxiliary Air Force, asking to be attached to the medical section. As the war trailed on, civilian hospitals faced seriously depleted staffs, at which time I received discharge "to civilian service of greater priority need," and so began my nursing training.

The war over, and now a State Registered Nurse, I made my final career change when Anna Freud accepted me for training in Child / Adolescent Psychoanalysis at the Hampstead Clinic. After the four year training I stayed there on staff for eight years before moving to the States—first to Case Western Reserve University, then south to Tulane, and then back north to the University of Michigan.

In retirement, as in childhood, I remain loyal to the North and continue to make my home in Ann Arbor.

A Yorkshire Childhood:
Early Memories

Dalton Hall

A Yorkshire morning in early May in the second year of World War I. Clear and sunny with a tang in the air as a strong breeze coming inland from the North Sea swept over the wolds, the open upland country of East Yorkshire—"blowing the cobwebs away," as the country folk said. Small patches of snow, reminders of the winter's heavy drifts, still lingered under some hedgerows. Several degrees of frost the night before had left occasional slippery patches on the driveway from the head gardener's cottage at Dalton Hall to the stables that belonged to the kitchen garden. Father's own stallion Bob was stabled alongside the two heavy cart horses. As he ran down the driveway in a hurry to harness up Bob to the governess cart to fetch the doctor to supervise my arrival, he slipped and fell. It had not been a bad fall, but as I grew, my father—always a tease—used to remind me that my being in such a hurry to get born had caused him a bruised derrière. By the time I was old enough to express concern and apologise, I knew that in fact my arrival had not been unduly hasty—just that Father had not been given much advance news of it. One day Mother quietly added other information. The monthly nurse/midwife was already staying in the house. There was no need for Father's haste. In fact, Mother and Nurse Honey had managed quite nicely. By the time Daddy got back with Dr. Clements I was all washed and snuggled up in my cradle. Everything was tidy, even a freshly brewed pot of tea on the kitchen hob waiting for them.

We left Dalton Hall when I was a year and half old. Dalton Hall Gardens was my Father's second headship. Newstead Abbey, once the home of Lord Byron, had been his first where he had taken Mother as a new bride. In between Newstead and Dalton he had returned to Walton Hall Gardens, his boyhood home in Warwickshire, for six months to take charge until his father was sufficiently recovered from a stroke to resume responsibility. As I grew up I heard many stories and reminiscences about the garden, the villages, and the people of Newstead, Walton, and Dalton. The village belonging to Walton Hall was Walton d'Evil—an intriguing name for a child. What, I used to wonder, was the devil doing at Walton? Although I was never at Walton except *in utero,* I amassed a great deal of information about it and the interesting people in my father's childhood. Strangely enough Walton seemed more alive than Woburn, my mother's home where I actually stayed sometimes.

Walton was foxhunting country. When he could slip off undetected, my father, at ten and eleven years old, had played hookey from school to follow hounds on an old donkey. The hunting group admired his determination, but the escapade had its downside. My grandparents spent what little money they could scrape together for further education on my aunt, who never played hookey. My father never got to grammar school. My aunt became a teacher—but my father married one, and with her help continued his own education. In the years at Warter Priory, Father's third headship, I remember many lamplit evenings when my parents worked together on the estimates for the gardens. Mother was a whiz at anything to do with figures.

But the two years at Dalton seemed always to have had some hidden magic for them—to have been especially carefree and happy—though they were by no means well off. In fact, what decided the move was not only that Warter Priory was a more prestigious position, but that the salary was much better. My own memories of Dalton are very limited. Just of Mother finding me sitting up in my cot one sunny afternoon when I was supposed to be quietly sleeping, and of one dark day sitting in my high chair in the kitchen watching what was going on. The more important memory is of one day during the week long visit of my grandparents. Dressed in a clean white dress, I was led out onto the lawn with its enclosing high hedges. As Mother let go my hand, Father called me to come to Grandfather. They were sitting in the summer house. I went to Father but wouldn't leave his side to go to Grandpa. This I later heard surprised every one and hurt Grandpa's feelings. He was such a gentle, kind man, how could I be afraid of him? It seems not much was known about the "stranger anxiety" of childhood in those days. Later on I was sad about it, because there was no second chance. Grandpa died in 1918.

The move from Dalton on the lower wold to Warter on the upper wold left clearer memories, as I proved to Mother when I was five years old. My father drove mother and me over to Warter in his governess cart. It snowed all the way across from one wold to the other. Wrapped in an old black and white shepherd's plaid, I was held on Mother's lap. When I was five I watched as Mother spring cleaned her store room.

"Look, there's my rug," I said. She assured me it was her rug, not mine, her traveling rug which she had been given a long time ago. I insisted, "But I did have it, with Bob" (Father's ex-army charger) "when it snowed and snowed all the way."

Then she understood. But there was more. I remembered arriving at Warter and being taken to one of two cottages just past the back way into the high walled kitchen garden. It was where an under game keeper and his wife, Tom and Eva England, lived. We stayed the night with them; the horse-drawn moving van bringing our furniture could not arrive in time to get it unpacked before dark.

It was all very strange and new, quite puzzling to a small child. But it was the beginning of a very lovely six and a half years, the best time of my childhood. It was long over before I understood how wonderful it had been and started to treasure my many memories of it.

Warter Priory

At Warter Priory the gardener's house was not old and cosily surrounded by the kitchen garden as at Dalton. Our new home stood proudly four square to the keen east winds, apart from the extensive kitchen gardens and on the main road to Pocklington, the market town and nearest railway station. Across from our house was the grassy treed park separating the kitchen gardens from the pleasure grounds which extended for several acres around the Priory. Our house had been built for Frank Jordan, a well-known horticulturalist, who was head gardener when, during his training days, my father was an under gardener at Warter. The plans for the new house had been passed by the estate office and the foundations dug when Lady Nunburnholme went to inspect progress. She declared the rooms much too small for the size of Jordan's family and ordered the walls to be thrown out further. Thus we had a very roomy farmhouse style kitchen that could be furnished so that it was also a comfortable family room and very much the center of social life for the gardens.

Sometimes on Sunday evenings in winter the young gardeners who lived in the bothy—not unlike the old apprentice model—were asked up to our house for a sing-song, followed by home baked cake and rich creamy cocoa. My bedroom door would be left open so that I could listen to the singing in lieu of the usual bedtime story. This was all very well for a few years, but once it was discovered that I was tone deaf and couldn't sing in tune, I protested the open door, declaring it made me jealous to listen to singing I couldn't do myself. Such sentiments were not acceptable to Mother, but she did let me have my door shut.

At teatime during the week Father often brought one or other of his foremen in to tea. Mark Moore, the outdoor foreman, was my favorite—an older man very tolerant of young children, always good for some anecdotal tale and the latest weather forecast. But I was very suspicions of Bill, the indoor foreman, who let it be known he was looking for a new pollenating brush and that my two pet rabbits had just the right kind of bushy tails. In pollenating time the grown-ups used to be very amused by my quick dash up the yard to check on my rabbits whenever Bill came near the house.

The large old mahogany table had so many uses. I can remember plans for new landscaping in the gardens being unrolled on it. Or Mother cutting out dressmaking projects; while at fruit bottling time a large number of glass Kilner jars stood on it waiting to be filled. Then, on winter evenings, the extra leaves would be put in for the ping-pong Mother and Father sometimes played. On summer evenings it was badminton on the lawn. Mother regretted that our lawn was a tad short of being usable for lawn tennis. Likewise, of course, it hadn't the dimensions for cricket. Nevertheless, once I was big enough to handle a small specially made cricket bat, Father tried to teach me the rudiments of his own favorite game. I remember my unholy glee, his chagrin, and Mother's annoyance when he sent a ball through a pane of the kitchen window.

I have only a few scrappy memories that I can authentically place as belonging to the first two years at Warter—wartime years. One is having my crayons requisitioned once when Father was making a large brown paper chart to use for one of his lectures on food production for the East Riding of Yorkshire Agricultural Advisory Service. Warter Priory kitchen gardens provided Hull Naval Hospital with fruit and vegetables during the war. This, together with his services as lecturer and his warden's duties, accounted for my father's not being called up for military duty. It was no small feat to achieve what he did with his wartime skeleton staff. I still remember overhearing some then not understood talk between Father and Mother about the use of a land army girl. Father had no use for wimpish girls for sure, but neither did he think they should be expected to do heavy manual labor. Mother tried to give him guidelines on appropriate employment of this new category of staff.

Scraps of memories from early childhood puzzle and tantalise. Their context is lost and the years may have distorted what I remember. Like the precious fragments uncovered in an archeological dig, early memories are intriguing and treasured. Not the archeologist's tools but evocative sounds, sensations, sights, or scents may uncover memories for which we often need the equivalent to the archeologist's carbon dating process. But two of my favorite memories can be placed when I was about three, since both concern World War I.

Mother and Grandmother were about to go indoors. It was a rather gray but pleasant day. We had all three probably just returned from an afternoon walk. But something bothered them. They didn't go in; they just stood looking across the wolds to something I couldn't see. It may have been Grandma who asked,

"Where are they going?" and Mother who answered, "Up the Humber, they're not coming this way." I wanted to know who was going up the Humber and was told, "Two Zeppelins belonging to the Germans." Mother pointed, but I couldn't see. I was told to stand on Daddy's office doorsteps; they were higher than the one into the house. But still I couldn't see. I just didn't know the Zeppelins were airships. Mother told me to look at the two black things like big birds in the sky. Then I saw them. I knew the Germans were the bad people our soldiers were fighting and that it was worrying Grandma and Mother that their Zeppelins were coming up the Humber. It was a little scary—not because I understood the danger, but because Mother and Grandma seemed upset. How differently I would feel years later about enemy air activity in World War II!

The first time I remember Daddy being away for several days and nights was at the end of the war. Lady Nunburnholme gave a large house party at her London house in Grosvenor Square to celebrate peace. The Princess Royal had accepted an invitation. The floral decorations could not be trusted to any one but Daddy. It couldn't have been easy to find enough plants and flowers to take up to town, since for four years the work had been on fruit and vegetable production. Some of these, too, had to be despatched to town without diminishing the regular supply to Hull Naval Hospital. How my father and his wartime skeleton staff of old men and very young boys did achieve it, I've often wondered.

My memory is of his return. As well as his portmanteau, he carried a sack of something into the kitchen. When the sack was untied, it fell open. There was a very special chair for a small person—me. On the seat of the chair were several London papers for Mother, with pictures of the peace celebrations. It was an old chair with a carved back and a rush seat. Many years later, when I had my first unfurnished bed-sitting room in London, it was sent to me from home and arrived done up in the same kind of sack it had arrived in at Warter thirty years earlier. It was with a pang that I left it behind when I came to the U.S.A.

First Companions

When I was old enough for lessons Mother—a kindergarten teacher—decided to teach me herself instead of sending me to the village school. Between the end of lesson time and our midday meal was outdoor playtime, often an opportunity to check on the latest happenings in the kitchen garden to find out more than I could from gazing out my spy window. Without a regular peer group to play with there was time to keep grown-ups and their sometimes puzzling behavior under strict surveillance. Only a few places in the kitchen gardens were out of bounds on my unaccompanied expeditions—the stables, the stokehole with the big furnace, and any greenhouse with shut doors unless there was a gardener working in it—but that out of bounds was lifted once I could be relied upon to carefully shut doors. There was more space to roam in than could be covered in one playtime, especially if I tarried too long talking to any one person. I had to be selective. My particular people to call on were the four Old Men—Ankers, Johnnie Dresser, Bob Smith, and Frankish, as well as the very young crock boy, a red-headed much freckled youngster called Ephraim.

As I left the house Mother always reminded me to listen for the Priory clock to chime. When the three-quarters sounded I had to hurry back from wherever I was to wash hands and brush hair ready for lunch. If the wind was in the wrong direction I could not always hear the chimes. Then Mother would say, "Today you must remember to ask the time." Once I could tell time myself, she would remind me, "Keep an eye on the packing room clock."

There were three ways the kitchen gardens could be entered. The way I was supposed to go ran past the bottom of the large orchard to some stone steps—about twelve, I think—that were at the end of the brick wall enclosing much but not all of the gardens. That was quite an important way in. You were right in the centre of things: the packing shed, the potting shed, and Ephraim's open sided little crock washing shed. But sometimes there would be a chance for a chat before the steps were negotiated. Mark Moore, the outdoor foreman might be in the orchard pruning or otherwise caring for the apple and pear trees. There were a few cherry trees, but most of the cherry trees were under glass if I remember rightly. Mark Moore was younger than the Old Men, but nevertheless a figure of authority whom I held in some awe until the day he teased me about my concern over time. Mark was amused by my worry about time. Afraid the wind wasn't blowing in the right direction, I had asked him if he heard the Priory clock that morning. He asked "What did it matter if I was late in? I could tell Mother I'd made 'a beef steak.'" Literal-minded little me was very puzzled. How could I possibly make a beef steak? That was the meat inside beefsteak and kidney pie. Mark explained he was teasing. Playing with the words "beef steak" meant "big mistake." One way and another I came in for quite a bit of playful teasing on my rounds of the gardens. It did nothing to prepare me, however, for the quite unkind teasing I got at age eight from my first peer group. When we moved away from the Priory to the town of Margate, my classmates were as bewildered by me as I was by them. But that time was still way off in the future.

Once down the steps and into the center of things it was necessary to find out what kinds of pots Ephraim was scrubbing that morning. I didn't stay long, partly because I had been warned not to waste his time and partly because I needed to check on the carpenter's shop and see if Ankers was there or elsewhere, in which case I'd need to search for him. His magical skill had provided some of my most treasured possessions: a doll's house, a wheelbarrow, a special stool that could be turned upside down to make a doll's bed. And of course I had him to thank for my swing and my cricket bat.

Ankers, like the others, came up to the house to see Mother if he was unwell, but whereas the others accepted cough medicine, aspirin, or what seemed needed, Ankers had his own countryman's cures. It was these he asked for. Some of Anker's requests worried Mother. I remember listening one teatime as she told Daddy that Ankers had come to ask for a lump of sugar and then wanted her to put a few drops of turpentine on it, saying he hadn't any turps in his shop that hadn't had paint brushes in it. Mother had reluctantly done so, figuring that at least clean turpentine would be safer than turpentine and paint. But then Ankers had got her really worried, saying, "Thank'ee Missus. This and five minutes standing on my head and I will be ow't job again." When he heard the story Daddy just chuckled and said, "The Old Boy's cure for a headache. He's been using it for years. He looked fine just now when I saw him setting out for home." I could picture him in his well worn boots, much worn corduroy pants and faded shirt, setting off to walk home to the neighboring village of Nunburnholme with Johnnie Dresser, who also lived in a cottage there, both of them carrying lunch tins and glad to be going home to their wives and a hot meal.

Johnnie Dresser, our stableman, was another grand old Yorkshireman. Whereas Ankers was tallish, somewhat lanky, Johnnie was square built and squat, looking grandfatherly with close cropped curly white hair. He was most often out ploughing, taking the dray to the railway station, or just across to the pleasure grounds, perhaps with a load of manure. If he was down at the stables, then it was OK for me to go and see the horses and give them carrots, with Johnnie carefully standing by.

Like all of the Old Men, Johnnie Dresser spoke the broad Yorkshire dialect of the wold. Once when my headmistress grandmother was staying with us, Johnnie drove Mother and Father in to Pocklington to catch an early morning train to York. The arrangement was that he would meet the train they planned to return on. That way Daddy's horse didn't have to spend the day at the Buck Inn. That afternoon Grandma was surprised to see Johnnie loading up the dray at a time she thought he should be setting off for the station. She hustled down to speak to him with me in tow; she asked if it wasn't time for him to go to the station. "Aye, aye, Missus, ane more load, yon side ower and I be awa."

"Really, Johnnie, I don't understand you," said Grandma.

But Johnnie's dialect was no foreign language to me. Quite unasked I promptly translated, "Johnnie says he has one more load to take to the other side, the pleasure grounds, and then he's going to the station."

"Aye, aye, that's it, Missy," said Johnnie. "I'll be off, Missus." He pulled his forelock, gathered the reins, and told Polly to giddyup. Grandma rather coldly suggested we go indoors.

Later I listened as she recounted this episode to my returned parents, ending with "The child understood him. Really, Susie (my mother), you shouldn't let the child hear talk like that." The measure of disapproval was to be judged by the fact that I was referred to as "the child." Silly Grandma. Didn't she know both Daddy and I talked broad Yorkshire outside the house? Mother understood that was the way it had to be. That was the language of the wold.

Playmates

Betty Rogers, whose father was the butler at Warter Priory, was the only other little girl living anywhere near us. But although she was only one year older than I, we seldom saw each other. Our mothers were friendly. If we met out walking; they always stood chattering for some while, but there were few house visits. My busy mother was occupied not only with running our home, but also with the life of the garden community. That she could still find time for the occasional painting says a lot for her organizational skills. Betty's mother, less energetic, often poorly, was a very different sort of mother. In retrospect, she was probably a very lonely woman. A butler's wife didn't have the every day contact with her spouse's work that my mother could enjoy and respond to. The Priory and the Servants' Hall over which Rogers presided were places apart from her family, whereas my mother and I were in the midst of my father's work. For instance, sick or hurt garden men were sent up to our house for Mother to care for, just as were any small creatures found in need of care. People wanting to see Father usually came first to our house, which served as the major gateway to the kitchen garden. Daddy kept Mother posted as to which side of the Park he could most likely be found, kitchen garden or pleasure grounds. Daddy came in to all our meals; it was very seldom he was away for a whole day. So different from Betty's father who left home every morning correctly attired in black pin-striped trousers, black tie, black jacket and bowler hat, carrying the inevitable carefully furled black umbrella. He walked off across the Park, and many days Betty never saw him again, for she was long in bed by the time he returned at night—in dark moonless nights needing a flashlight to find his way across the Park. Worse still, when Lady Nunburnholme went up to her London house each summer for the season, Rogers had to go, too—just as in the long winter months when he had to go to the south of France. Only once do I remember Betty and her mother going with him to France.

Yes, two little girls, close neighbors, but with such different experiences. By the time we were old enough to visit each other unescorted, I don't think the idea occurred to either of us. By five, Betty was going to the village school, a mile and a half walk each way, and probably was very content to stay close to home afterwards. Whereas I had lessons at home and my free time was spent in the kitchen gardens, of which I was allowed the freedom so long as none of the Priory folk were walking around them. It has to be admitted that I found the grownups who worked in the gardens more fun company than Betty. I wonder what she thought of my company, probably nothing very complimentary. It was a good few years later before I managed peer relationships with anything approaching graciousness, let alone real pleasure.

Early on I decided the trouble with Betty was not seeing enough of her father. Surely Betty would have learnt to be more spunky if she had both parents more often. If you had both parents right there expecting you to behave like a Big Girl, you knew it just wasn't done to whine or fuss over small things. You jolly well knew tears were only for real disasters. Then they were permissible and comfort and understanding would be given—but only then.

The time when Betty and I were most likely to meet up was in the summer when Lady Nunburnholme's three granddaughters came to stay at the Priory. We were often invited to join their afternoon picnics somewhere or other on the estate. Susan, Malice, and Ann Wilson were looked after by Nanny Frewin and May, the nursemaid, who was Nanny's young assistant. Nanny was an imposing personage. Her word was like the unalterable law of the Medes and Persians, but I suspect we five children were far less in awe of her than May, who seemed to have a knack for getting into difficulties, not entirely of her own manufacturing.

One of the picnics Betty and I went to gave substance to my suspicion. It was a rather warm sunny afternoon. Cream Cheese, a docile old pony more or less retired to pasture, had been requisitioned and harnessed to a small light buggy to carry the provisions and give rides to us smaller fry—i.e., Ann and myself. Once at the chosen picnic site Nanny had us collect brushwood so that May could light a campfire and bake potatoes and eggs. We all chose an egg and a potato and put some mark on each to make it ours. There was always competition to see whose potato cooked first. May was keeper of the fire and we had to keep our distance from it. The fire was looking very promising and we girls were practising for the obstacle race at the upcoming Priory fête, when Gavin, a teen-age cousin of the Wilsons', found us. He was all set to stage some disruption of our activities, but Nanny Frewin promptly headed off our would-be tormentor. Not to be completely vanquished, he turned his attention to May. How it began I didn't see, but I do remember looking up into a large old tree—an oak most likely—and seeing May high up, sprawled along one of the limbs. She was pleading with Nanny for help, saying she couldn't get down. Gavin was standing nearby, smiling. Nanny turned to him, sternly. "You got her up there, Master Gavin. Now get her down, this minute!" When May was on terra firma again, Nanny took one disgusted look at May's crumpled, grimy apron and said, "You better take that apron off—now." May was clearly in trouble, but I often wondered, and of course never knew, what had happened when May had her next encounter with Master Gavin a few days later.

It was one of those mornings that were much too sunny and pleasant to spend indoors. Besides, Betty and the girls were enjoying school holidays. I thought it unfair that I still did lessons. Mother's reasoning was that I had shorter school hours than the others all year, so I needed to work holiday time, too. I wasn't enjoying lessons. I could write easily with my left hand, but Mother was insistent that I learn to use my right hand. My rebellious heart rejoiced to hear the motor bike coming up the drive. It could be Father's friend, the Rev. Booty, vicar of the neighbouring village of Burnby. Reprieve was in sight. But it wasn't the Rev. Booty. The door was unceremoniously thrust open by Gavin with a cheery "Hey there, Mrs. Legg. Please take care of this baggage while I fetch the other two." He then pushed a somewhat bewildered-looking Susan into the kitchen. Mother wanted to know what this was all about and where was Nanny, but Gavin was already on his bike again and simply called out that he'd be back directly. Susan explained, "We were in the village with May and Gavin happened along and offered to give us each a ride back to the Priory, but May thought it would be safest if he just brought us to you." When Malice arrived she, like Susan, seemed to take this interruption of their morning's walk in her stride, but Ann was somewhat unhappy when dumped on our kitchen floor. The ride from the village included coming down Linney, a short but very steep hill, a funny enough feeling on a toboggan, let alone for a first pillion ride on a motorcycle driven by a tormenting big cousin. Ann told us, "I didn't like coming down and down Linney on that stupid motor-bike. I want May!" But her usual high spirits quickly recovered when Gavin returned with May. He didn't come in that time. Before the girls left to walk back across the park to the Priory, we all had milk and gingerbread for elevenses. When the others had left, I still had to go on with my lessons.

But just what did Nanny say to May for letting Gavin carry out that scenario?

The Vicar and Sydney

My other occasional playmate was the vicar's eldest son. The vicar, a tall gaunt man whose square, schoolmastery countenance hid a great sense of humor, was often in our kitchen in ice-cold weather enjoying a chat with my parents and a warming cup of tea laced with Scotch. On hot summer days it would be a glass of Mother's home made lemonade. Most often he cycled up to our house from the vicarage, but sometimes he walked. Then Sydney came, too. A year older than I, Sydney was an athletic boy who could do all sorts of things I was either a duffer at or too afraid to try. We were generally sent out to play. There were times I returned with a bloodied knee, a muddied dress, and very low spirits, because of my failure to match up to Sydney's expertise at tree climbing or walking along the tops of garden walls.

Sydney was also a great tease. I remember my delight when I found a way to tease back. He spelt his name the girls' way, *Syd*, instead of *Sid*. But I got into trouble over one of his teases. He told me his baby sister's name was Mary Magdalene. The vicar was amused when I politely inquired how Mary Magdalene was—but not Mother. It was some time before I understood why. It was one of the long list of things grown-ups never explained in those days. It was not until I was really grown up myself that a remembered scrap of a conversation between the vicar and my father from about that time made sense. My father had commented that the curate was getting another child, too.

"Yes," said the vicar. "I asked the young man, 'Isn't your family getting larger than your stipend can support?'"

"'Well, Vicar,'" the unctuous little fool replied, "'the Lord sends these little blessings you know.'"

"I told him, 'I've read the Bible too, but I've never found anywhere where the Lord forbids us to put an umbrella up against the rain.'"

In the days before radio and TV there was always grown up conservation to listen to—but what rubbish they talked sometimes—even in church. Sydney and I thought they were often difficult to understand. I used to get into trouble when I went to church with Grandma, the Grandma who was a headmistress and knew how little girls should behave.

I began to dislike Sunday matins mixed with Grandma. Something always went wrong. One Sunday as we passed by the lodge gates to the Priory, the Countess of Chesterfield walked out just as the last bell started chiming. Bidding a cheery "Good morning" to Grandma, the countess noted that we were late and invited me to race her to church to see if we could get there before the bell stopped ringing. It was in the days of hobble skirts. The countess gathered her skirt above her knees and off we ran. When we got to the church porch the countess said, "Now, what about you? I expect you'd better wait here for Grandma." Just as the bell stopped ringing Grandma caught up with me. I followed a very sedate unsmiling Grandma up the aisle to our pew and didn't dare even to grin at Sydney. At lunchtime my misbehavior was a topic of conversation: how I had left Grandma and raced off with the countess without asking Grandma's permission.

The most Sunday trouble I remember getting into with Grandma happened in conjunction with Sydney. We had walked sedately the mile and a quarter to church. Mrs. Vicar was home with the new baby. Sydney was all by himself in the vicarage pew. Had my mother been with us, he might have been invited to join us. The vicar's sermon was long and quite beyond the two of us.

We were bored. It was some relief to share our boredom by making faces at each other. Then Sydney hit on a wonderful idea. He'd send me a message down the heating duct which was covered by an openwork iron grill that ran down the aisle. This meant some slight disturbance. The vicar leant over the side of the pulpit and without altering his tone said, "and Sydney will behave himself, or else . . ." Turning back to the congregation he continued without pause, "and as I was saying, dearly beloved brethren . . ."

Grandma was coldly furious that I had been the cause of this little episode. The walk home to lunch was in icy silence. At lunch I heard that Grandma was also very critical of the vicar's unorthodox behavior. The Vicar of Woburn where she lived would never have done such a thing. Mother looked concerned; Daddy got his old age lines, the little crinkles at the corners of his eyes that meant he was amused. It wouldn't have done to tell Grandma that the vicar was used to boys' mischief; he'd been an assistant master at a prep school before being appointed to the living at Warter.

Oh, why wasn't I born a boy like Sydney?

A Yorkshire Childhood: Adventures with Ginger Pop

A Live Birthday Present

One mild but cloudy afternoon in mid-May 1922 Mother and I walked the short distance from our house to the young Englands' cottage. On our left was the long high wall of the kitchen gardens. On the road side of the wall was a deep border that in summer was a splash of color with the reds and pinks of California poppies. The other side of the road, the Park side, had cool shady patches where big old oak trees were near enough to the road to cast their shadows. It was the same way we started off when we walked the mile and a half to Warter Village. Today I was not skipping off on small side excursions of my own, like looking for hedgerow finds—late violets or early birds' nests. I didn't even delay to climb up on the five barred Park gate to ask to pat the old pony. Cream Cheese always trotted up to socialize if she heard footsteps. This particular afternoon we were on serious business—a time to walk sedately at Mother's side.

Two weeks before on my birthday there had been no birthday present from parents on the breakfast table, because my very extra special seventh birthday present was to be a puppy that had only been whelped the day before my birthday. So instead of the present, a promise had been given. "The puppy can be visited in two weeks but not brought home yet. Puppies stay with their mothers for at least six weeks." There was just a tiny bit of me that thought six years might have been better. I was not absolutely sure that a puppy was a top hole present. A puppy would inevitably become a dog, one of those creatures to be leery of. "Once bitten, twice shy" was my motto at that time. I had been bitten once when playing with a visiting dog. On the other hand, to have a little puppy all my very own was the most splendiferous idea. Perhaps when it became a dog some other arrangement could be made for it?

This proposition tentatively broached to Mother at a carefully chosen time when her attention was focused on the letter she was writing, met with "Of course not! Mothers don't give babies away when they grow up." Which just went to prove once again that grown-ups sometimes got very mixed up in the way they thought about things. It wasn't a case of babies, but puppies. Mother dogs most certainly had to give puppies away when the puppies were six weeks old, so there! Well, there was nothing to do but forget about the future dog and just think about the wonderful NOW puppy.

For quite some time Daddy had been looking for a suitable puppy for me. He wanted a thoroughbred sporting dog—preferably one of the terriers —since such a dog would be small enough to be portable by a seven-year-old. There were few terriers on the wolds. The farmers had sheep dogs. Other people had large hunting dogs, retrievers, and Labradors, and of course there were the hounds belonging to the local hunt. But not many pure bred terriers. When Eva said her Sealyham terrier would have puppies in May it had been just the thing. This was the afternoon of my first visit.

Eva was expecting us and had thoughtfully taken Scamp and her puppies out on the lawn where there was plenty of room to watch them playing without having to get too close too quickly. Eva was a kindly country woman who understood children and animals. She said it was important to talk to Scamp first and pat her, so she knew we would be kind to the puppies. If that was what had to be done, I'd manage. Those puppies were perfect, climbing all over each other and snuggling up to Scamp. I could not wait to find out which one was going to be mine. Daddy had already been to see them, so I knew he must have chosen one for me. But no. When I asked, Mother and Eva shook their heads. I was to choose my own! How simply super. But it was a difficult decision to make. Eva asked whether I would like a boy or a girl puppy; there were two of each. She told me which were which. I wanted a girl, but which one? In the end, the puppy itself helped in the choice by being so inquisitive about me. It seemed perhaps it liked me? Eva said maybe I'd like to hold it. When she picked it up and gave it to me Scamp didn't seem worried and that settled it, because I didn't want Scamp to be angry with me any time she met me walking one of her puppies. It was hard to leave the puppy behind when it was time to go home for tea, even though Eva invited me to visit it some more so that it was a little used to me before it had to leave Scamp. We had to hurry—it was almost time to get tea ready and Daddy would be in very soon—but we did stop to pat Cream Cheese. She couldn't be ignored twice in one afternoon.

That tea time I got to talk much more than was usually allowed at a meal time. Daddy wanted to hear about the afternoon's happenings and there was lots to tell. Mother had enjoyed the puppies too and liked the one I picked. She asked what I wanted to call it. That was even harder than choosing the puppy. It seems all the names I suggested were either ruled unsuitable for a dog or else too long. Daddy explained that when it was old enough my puppy could help him when he went rabbit hunting. (The wild rabbits were the perennial thieves of summer bedding plants.) A hunting dog needed a short name so that it could be called quickly. Oh bother! I didn't know the right kind.

"H'm," Daddy murmured. "What does she look like? What does she do that might give you an idea?"

"She's got a ginger patch under one ear and she pops all over the place," I said.

"Well, there you are," said Daddy. "You could call her Ginger Pop and I'll be able to call her Pop."

So that was how we settled it.

After lessons next morning I scampered off to look for Ankers to tell him about the puppy. He was most interested and said it would surely need a dog bed. He would see what he could do. Sure enough, a few mornings later when I went down to breakfast, alongside the hearth there was a new wooden box with a low place for a puppy to jump in. Daddy brought me a clean sack to make a bed pad. But when I wanted to take it up to my room Mother said puppies were never allowed upstairs, not even ones as special as Ginger Pop. It seemed that was another of the unalterable laws of the Medes and the Persians.

But one must protect one's very own puppy. Mother and I had had several chats about my responsibilities as a puppy owner. So reasonably enough I remarked, "Ginger Pop'll be awful lonely, left in the kitchen all by herself at night."

"*Awfully* lonely' I think you mean, girlie, not *awful* lonely."

Oh dear, more grown-up delaying tactics.

"Yes, I mean awfully lonely."

Mother now softened. Puppies, she said, were often comforted by the friendly tick of a clock. She would find an old one for Ginger Pop to have in her bed box. I must remember to wind it each night. A few days later when Mr. Todd came to get our grocery order, Mother inquired about puppy biscuits and ordered some. So she really did care about Ginger Pop. We were all ready for Ginger Pop days before she came to live with us. Daddy had even been to the saddler's in Pocklington and got a dog collar and lead for her.

Just one thing happened that puzzled me at the time, but made sense later on. Each week I had to write a short note to Grandma, the headmistress. It need be only one sentence long but it had to be something I thought of myself. Mother helped with the spelling. When I started to write about Ginger Pop Mother offered a clean piece of paper.

"Let's keep the puppy a surprise for Grandma's visit to us!"

Grandma came in August as usual. Daddy drove to meet her alone so that there would be room for her luggage in the buggy. As we heard them driving in, Mother told me to pick up Pop and come to show her to Grandma. Daddy helped Grandma out of the buggy. She hugged Mother and turned to look for me—but her smile faded.

"Good gracious me! What's the child got? A *live* puppy! I noticed it, of course, as we drove in, but thought it was just one of those nice stuffed toys!"

All this was said to Mother. I was ignored. We might be in for a troublesome time. Grandma didn't like puppies! Now the letter that couldn't be sent to Grandma made sense!

Grandma had arrived on a glorious afternoon. A cool breeze blew in through the wide open casement windows as we sat in the shade of the kitchen looking out onto the sun drenched lawn. Mother had baked fresh scones and gingerbread to welcome Grandma, who seemed to have forgotten her chilling response to my introduction of Ginger Pop. For my part, I was trying to remember to act on Mother's reminder, given just before Grandma's arrival.

"Remember, Cecily, Granny doesn't like children to talk at meal times. She likes them to be seen but not heard."

It wasn't easy to keep quiet; there were so many questions I wanted to ask. Once when I was much smaller, Mother and I had gone to visit Grandma and stayed a whole month at Woburn. There were a few things I hadn't liked about life with Grandma, but there had been some interesting things, and people too.

Now Grandma, good humor restored, was bringing Mother and Daddy up to date on the doings of their friends and acquaintances in Woburn, but she'd quite left out news of Miss Annie Neale, the interesting old lady who had once been headmistress of the tiny school in the little village of Sheeplane. One afternoon we'd walked the mile or so to have tea with her. Miss Neale's little cottage where she lived with her tabby cat was tiny, just a kitchen and living room downstairs and a bedroom and small store room upstairs. What made it so fascinating and special was the way it was joined onto the village church. You actually had to walk through the churchyard down a pathway between ancient grave stones, and round the side of the church to get to her door; or if you were good at climbing fences, you could go through the meadow at the side of the churchyard and climb over. The door opened into her kitchen; another door from the kitchen opened into her living room, but still another actually opened right into the church. On Sundays her kitchen became the church vestry once again where the vicar or one of his curates and the choirboys robed. After service the church warden counted the collection from the small congregation there, too. Miss Neale told me all about it and how for winter christenings she always made sure to have a little warm water ready so that the vicar didn't sprinkle the poor babies with icy cold water. Centuries ago, when the church had its own full time priest, Miss Neale's cottage had been his living quarters. It was a very primitive little cottage without gas, electricity, or running hot water. The one very black mark I had to give was because of its smelly outdoor earth closet. Grandma's house had only an outside loo, too, but hers was a proper w.c., always very spic and span—no creepy crawlies or unpleasant smells.

I now noticed a lull in the grownups' conversation. Dare I ask about Miss Neale and her tabby cat? Grandma also had a tabby cat. Maybe I'd better ask about hers first. Before I could, Grandma had become displeased again. Horrors! While I daydreamed and munched delicious scones and home made jam I'd not noticed that Ginger Pop had left her place under my chair. All uninvited she had gone to play with Grandma's shoe laces. Daddy moved to the rescue swiftly. With an apology to Grandma he scooped up Ginger Pop and removed her from the room. I was about to remove myself likewise, but a warning look from Mother reminded me I had not been excused and would not be even if I did ask.

However, despite the stupid beginning Ginger Pop and I had had to Grandma's month long August holiday, there was only one further bad happening in the Grandma and Ginger Pop story. Just inside our kitchen door was a peg for Daddy to hang his mackintosh on, when he came in to lunch on rainy days. Grandma appropriated this for her long summer dust coat. One night no one remembered to move Grandma's coat to the hall coat rack before leaving Ginger Pop in sole and lonely possession of the kitchen all night. In the morning Grandma discovered that "that child's puppy" had played at jumping up and catching a mouthful of her dust coat. She showed me the row of holes presumed to have been made by little puppy teeth. It was Mother's turn to come to the rescue. She told Grandma she would mend the little holes so that the damage would be almost invisible.

For the rest of Grandma's visit *my* puppy went out and about with Daddy an awful lot without my being consulted. He explained it was because she was three months old, just the best time to start training her to obey commands. But I knew he was really doing it to keep Ginger Pop and me out of Grandma's bad books, and so Mother wouldn't have to worry about us. I did get to feel a teeny bit jealous though, when Ginger Pop even got rides on Daddy's motor cycle, tightly buttoned inside his jacket with just her head poking out, looking so adorable.

After Grandma's visit was over and Ginger Pop's usual routine restored, I too was given a ride on the motor bike, but that's another story.

An Evening Adventure with Ginger Pop

Like its young mistress, Ginger Pop had a busy schedule; companion and playmate for me, she also took on the responsibilities of a good watch dog for the house. Then she too had lessons to learn— all those obedience commands a well behaved dog must know and respond to. On top of all this, my feisty little puppy was beginning to learn the skills of a hunting dog. Whenever my father went rabbit shooting, Ginger Pop accompanied him. Wild rabbits were a constant problem, especially in springtime. They nibbled tender young plants just bedded out in the pleasure grounds, with the same gusto and destructiveness that they expended on the cabbage patch in the kitchen gardens.

One evening Ginger Pop was called upon for help with yet another garden problem. It was just an ordinary evening in early spring. The curtains had been drawn across the kitchen windows; the large Aladdin hanging lamp lit to illumine the old mahogany table at which my parents sat working; mother sewing; my father busy with the paper work he had just fetched from his office. Ginger Pop and I were in possession of the hearth rug, toasting ourselves in front of the merrily burning fire in the kitchen range.

Ginger Pop had curled up contentedly by my side. Before settling to read my story book I watched the fire pictures and counted the sparks that flew up the chimney, remembering that on her last visit Grandma the Headmistress called such sparks "fire fairies." I never really bought that whimsey. At seven, going on eight, I was much too down to earth, trying to grow up a no-frills no-nonsense sort of girl. Since I could not be Tommy, the son my father had wished for (the boy I would have liked to be), then the next best thing was to be a sensible daughter for Daddy, while sometimes allowing myself to play pretend games. The fairy rings Mother and I found on walks in the woods were still fun; many of my favourite stories were in *The Blue Fairy Book*, though that would soon be given second place to *The Blue Book of Romance*, with the stories of Robin Hood and Maid Marion, my childhood heroes. I guess one might say fairies were still acceptable in the abstract; they just must not be given real representation. (Parenthetically—some ten years or more later an exasperated stepmother, puzzled by my plain Jane and no nonsense stance was to say, "The trouble with you is that there are no fairies at the bottom of your garden!")

While I was still counting sparks, not fairies, Ginger Pop suddenly went on alert, darting to the door barking, even before there was a knock. The night's duty gardener, carrying his lit lantern, was at the door; he and two of his fellow bothy lads had come to ask if they might borrow Ginger Pop. They were having no luck trying to catch a rat that had taken up its quarters in one of the greenhouses. (Ginger Pop's kennel mates had a terrific reputation as good ratters.) This conversation made me go on alert, too; there might just possibly be a chance for an evening adventure for *both* Ginger Pop and me, if I were careful. As politely as I could I reminded every one that Ginger Pop was my dog, my responsibility, so perhaps I should go along too? Daddy looked thoughtful, but not as though he altogether disapproved of the proposition. He turned to look questioningly at Moss, one of the trio, and my erst-while babysitter. Moss rose to the occasion nobly, saying, "I can look after the lassie and help her take care of Pop." Daddy turned round to see what Mother thought about it. She nodded; Mother always trusted Moss. I was made to wrap up warmly and given strict instructions to do everything Moss told me; Moss was re-minded that six-thirty was still my bedtime.

Off we went into the night—such a bright night that we could have found our way down the long path to the kitchen garden steps without the lantern, but we would need that in the green-house. Trees in the orchard to our left cast shadows across the path, while to the right the high brick wall of the kitchen gardens with its herbaceous border looked quite different than its daytime self. It was a wonderful, mysterious night world, suggesting a top-hole adventure. Once in the kitchen gardens we still had a little way to go. Mr. Rat had chosen one of the really large greenhouses at the far end for his residence. Crafty rat, that meant there were plenty of places to hide from its enemies, but it had not reckoned with the eager hunter now on the team. Ginger Pop quickly found its whereabouts in the drainage channel through the bottom of the stone steps leading up to the door at one end of the house. Moss lifted two of the tall plants off the staging nearby, then lifted me up into the empty space. A great grandstand, I would be able to watch everything. But suppose Ginger Pop went into the drainpipe and got stuck? Moss was quick to reassure me. "T'lads are much too careful to let that happen." Sure enough, he was right. One held onto Ginger Pop while the other smoked the rat out of its hidey hole. Ginger Pop, then promptly released, chased the rat in and out among the many plants lined up on the floor in the wide center space, upsetting only one pot. With such good teamwork, the poor rat was quickly cornered and despatched. The lads thanked Ginger Pop and me and hoped I would lend Ginger Pop next time they had a rat problem.

We set off back home with Moss and with plenty of time to do some star gazing on the way. The Plough and the North Star were easy to find; then Moss showed me Orion's belt and some others. An owl was flying around hooting, but wouldn't come close enough for us to see it. We did see the vanishing white scuts of night raiders in the herbaceous border; they didn't wait to see whether Ginger Pop was safely on her lead and duty bound to heel. Mother had hot cocoa and apple pie waiting for Moss, my usual bedtime milk and biscuits ready for me. Daddy rewarded Ginger Pop with the special dog biscuits kept for good hunting behavior.

Rat hunting was not all that much fun, though, so when Ginger Pop's services were requisitioned again I didn't ask to join the expedition—just said I would be pleased to lend Ginger Pop after explaining to Daddy that I had not bothered to go because I knew the lads would take very good care of Ginger Pop for me. Daddy gave me a quizzical look and murmured, "After all, rat hunting is no fun for the rat, eh?" He did not even tell me "Tommy Legg would have wanted to go"—nor did he ask the awkward sort of questions Mother would have asked.

A Yorkshire Childhood:
Leaving the Wolds

Changes in the Air

It was an unusual teatime. The grown-ups were so quiet! No telling each other about their day's doings; no bits of amusing local gossip; no serious considerations and lively discussion of things in the daily paper. Even the letter from Grandma was not mentioned and there had been one of her conspicuous grey envelopes among the post. I tried to cheer them up with chatter about what I had seen and done outside at playtime. No good. It barely captured their attention—not even evoking Mother's "All right, that will do, now finish your tea"; or worse, Daddy's "That would have been interesting had you not gone around and around the mulberry bush to tell us about it." That evening it seemed my would-be-cheering chatter was just some sort of background noise, tolerable, but not worthy of attention. I had given up and asked for another slice of cake. Wordlessly the plate had been passed to me. Nothing to do but eat the cake and try to ignore the strange change that had come over my parents. If I was very quiet—a nice little girl—surely they'd recover. It didn't work. I finished my tea, and before there had been time for me to ask, was promptly excused from the table, told to get my jacket and run and play outside. Goodness, gracious me! What ever was happening? They'd forgotten it was my responsibility to wash up the tea things for Mother! Mother had recently noticed that when I stood on the stool Ankers had made for me, I could perfectly reach to wash up tea things in the kitchen sink. Careful instructions had been given and the assignment made—"You are big enough now to wash up the tea things for us every day."—a responsibility that would in fact continue to be mine for many years to come. When I asked why not that evening, the answer was, "Daddy and I will see to it this time. We want to talk and have another cup of tea. Off you go. I'll call you when it's time to come in." Something odd and peculiar really was going on. What did they want to talk about that I mustn't listen to? Why couldn't it wait until I was in bed? I didn't think it was because some one had died; I had learnt how to intuit that kind of disaster. What on earth could it be? A seven-year-old sleuth was defeated, at least for the time being.

Out of doors it was a dreary evening, overcast and colourless, very quiet. The birds had not yet started their evensong and there was not enough breeze for the trees to nod toward each other in friendly tree talk. Sometimes I made up stories about the sort of things Mrs. Beechtree might tell old Lady Sycamore, or what the two young lilac children whispered about, but that evening it wasn't fun to pretend anything. I just wanted to know what was the matter. One of the kitchen windows, temptingly wide open, made the side lawn a No Play zone, so, off to our spinney; but I dawdled up the cinder path that was screened from house and lawn by the high privet hedge. Stopping first at the shed where Daddy's motor bike was kept, where there was also a place for my outdoor toys and where along one wall was neatly stacked a collection of packing cases, I looked around, but the place gave me no inspiration.

A little further up the pathway, sheltered by a clump of small bushes, stood the rabbit hutch. Another stop, this time to talk to

Moll and Poll. They didn't seem at all interested in my bothersome worry. The rule was they must not be taken out of prison unless a grown-up was there. Poor things. But at least they had each other for company. A little further along was my swing. As I was swinging, the Priory clock chimed the first quarter of an hour. Three more to go before it would chime six o'clock. Surely I wouldn't have to stay out much past six. I had to be in bed by half-past six. I got off the swing, trudged on.

Mother's drying ground was at the beginning of the spinney. Goodness! There were still some towels and things on one of the lines. She always fetched them in before tea time. This *was* a topsy-turvy day! I trailed on to inspect my garden patch. It didn't look any different than it had earlier in the day. Things grew so slowly—but at least I could improve it with some more stones for an edging. It took some time to find the kind I wanted, but still I had not been called. Nothing left to do but rearrange my pretend grocery store, a really good collection of discarded tins and jars carefully displayed around an old oak tree. The store stocked acorns for squirrels, crumbs for birds, sometimes a few wild flowers for the bees. The merchandise in the spinney grocery store varied with the seasons, of course. At last the clock chimed the first quarter past six. Any minute now I would be called in. But no! The clock actually chimed the half hour and still no call. They couldn't have heard the clock. I ought to tell them. I ran down to the side lawn and called through the window that it was bed time.

"Yes, we know," said Mother. "You can stay out a little longer. I'll fetch you presently."

This was awful. It was getting dusk and there was nothing left to do. I went down to the lower lawn to visit my drake and his three wives. No help. They were asleep, each with its head snuggled in its wing feathers. Back up the cinder path to have another try with the rabbits; they were sleepy, too. I'd have to find my favorite hen, Mrs.

Speckledy; she sometimes let me carry her around. Back into the spinney to the hen house. Not a hen in sight; they'd all gone in to roost. The cock must be as firm about bedtime as Mother usually was. How could Mrs. Speckledy be got out? The side door of the hen house had a latch too high to reach; the hens' own door was too small for me to squeeze through. Then I remembered the props for the clothes lines. Good idea! It was easy to drag one back to the hen house and push it through the little door, bump it up and down, and wake up the whole hen house. Just as I had succeeded with this ma-neuver in producing great noise and confusion inside the hen house, Mother appeared on the scene. To say she was displeased would have been the British understatement of that week. I listened to how dis-appointed she was in me, how selfish I was, and about my total lack of consideration for others, which she called quite appalling. The poor hens, etc., etc. And yet through it all she never sounded angry, just terribly upset.

The seven-year-old sleuth still did not catch on to a connection between that evening and an excited, happy morning a few days earlier when Daddy had come in and interrupted my lessons to share with Mother a letter he had just received offering him a very special job in New Zealand. Mother had been excited, too, about the idea of going to New Zealand, but also a little worried about what her own mother would say. Daddy had told her not to worry, Grandma could come with us. Mother should write and invite her to do so.

It was a few days later when things had settled down again after that funny peculiar afternoon that I remembered about going to New Zealand, so I asked Mother how soon we would go.

"We are not going," she said. "Grandma doesn't want to and we can't leave her here all alone."

But Grandma wouldn't have been all alone! Uncle Ted, Aunt May, and my Cousin Olga lived nearer Grandma than we did. Besides that, Grandma had a lot of friends in Woburn. She had lived in Woburn for years and years, ever since she had married Grandpa, in fact.

The pieces of the puzzle did not really fit together for several more years. Then one day I heard Daddy tell a friend how he and Mother had been so happy at the prospect of going to New Zealand. Why hadn't they gone? Because Grandma had written and refused the invitation to go with us, while at the same time adamantly refusing to be left alone in England. That letter must have been the one I had seen among the post that black afternoon long ago. All those things Mother had said about my waking up the hens and being selfish and inconsiderate of others—*phew!*—I had just been standing proxy for Grandma! But I never found out exactly why Grandma spoiled a wonderful opportunity for my parents or why they let her do it. It was not for nothing that Daddy's mother was my favorite grandmother. Children understand more than they can—or perhaps should—put into words.

Another Teatime Puzzle

Every day at teatime the grownups' conversation provided much information about all sorts of goings on and doings—here, there, and everywhere; but it was full of possibilities for misunderstanding on the part of a seven-year-old listener. Take, for instance, the matter of death duties. These I had learnt were things that gobbled up large gardens belonging to people like Lady Nunburnholme. It seemed that unlike the wild rabbits, always with us, or the occasional visiting deer who nibbled away at succulent young plants, these death duty creatures were only expected to appear at Warter when Her Ladyship died. They must be huge creatures, as big as grizzly bears and there must be lots of them, if they could gobble up all the Warter Priory Gardens. But how on earth would the creatures know when Lady Nunburnholme died? Why did they want to be so mean to her son, gobbling everything up so that he would have no gardens left?

A few days after I had tried to puzzle this out, the vicar came for a cup of tea and chat, Sydney tagging along, too. Before we were dismissed out of doors there was more about death duties. It seemed that there were public parks and gardens owned by towns and cities like York, and that these public gardens were quite safe from the death duty monsters. New Zealand, it appeared, would have been safe; however, there were places to be found in England, but it mustn't be put off; one had to start looking soon. As Sydney and I went out the door, the grown-ups were sounding worried about the old men who had spent their lives working in the gardens and saying something about Ankers and Dresser having to be provided for.

I found Sydney had a different notion than I about death duties. Not monsters, just money, he said, adding that it was all the fault of the Germans who had made the country spend all its money fighting the war. It seemed time to ask some grown-up to help straighten out the facts, but Mother was never very forthcoming on matters related to death. However, there was always my weekly letter to Grandma. I could ask her, even though it might mean rewriting the letter if Mother disapproved of the question; but at least then she would explain. The ruse worked. I found out that Sydney's theory was nearer the truth than mine. Also understood, but not put into words, was that though Grandma had jinxed the move to New Zealand, we still might leave Warter. The Dowager lady Nunburnholme was elderly and the startling increase in death duties made it unlikely that her son would be able to maintain Warter Priory after her death. Thus Daddy's livelihood was endangered, as were those of many other head gardeners on large estates. There would be a scramble to get positions in the public parks of large towns.

Leaving the Wolds

It was not long afterwards that the teatime conversation was about an interview my father was going to at Leeds. That was a cheerful teatime. But it was a dismal teatime when the letter of rejection came. Daddy was very disappointed when he was not the chosen applicant for the city of Leeds Parks Superintendent; he had been one of two finalists, but had lost to a man who had already had experience of public rather than private gardening. He next applied to Margate, a small seaside town whose recently elected chairman of the Parks Committee was spearheading an attempt to improve the town's parks and open spaces and playing fields as a means of attracting more tourists to the town. Hitherto, the parks and other spaces had been managed by the borough surveyor's office. The appointment of a Parks Superintendent and the setting up of an autonomous Parks Department was a new venture for the town. The possibilities intrigued my father and after some discussion with the vicar, who had been an assistant master at Margate college for boys and knew the town and surrounding area very well, Father applied for the position. When, summoned for an interview, he found himself once again challenged by a fellow applicant with experience of public gardening, Father suggested to the committee that it was difficult to gain an impression of a landscape gardener's capabilities without an on site visit to his work. He invited the committee to send representatives to Warter. The committee agreed and decided to visit both men's work.

The chosen delegates were the chairman and a fellow committee member who was a professional photographer. They came one early spring day. Daddy drove in to Pocklington to meet their train. After they had toured and photographed the gardens, they came in for lunch, all very formal in the dining room, with the best china and silverware.

There was one awful moment before lunch when I thought my Sealyham terrier, Ginger Pop, and I would be in the most terrible trouble. The grownups were having drinks in the living room. Ginger Pop and I were included; there was lemonade for me, but nothing for Ginger Pop. The chairman, Mr. Redman, a retired school teacher, had asked me where I went to school. When he learnt that Mother too was a teacher, he told her he had trained at Culver Teacher Training College. Mother said, why so had her father. I was so interested in listening to their conversation that I forgot my responsibility to make sure Ginger Pop behaved. Before I could stop her, she leapt up on Mr. Redman's lap and lapped up some of his Scotch. Instead of the trouble I expected, Mr. Redman laughed, said his dog was a teetotaler, how had I let Ginger Pop acquire a taste for alcohol? I had to explain about the cask of cider that Father always kept in his office in the summer. Ginger Pop had learnt to lap up the drops in the saucer that was placed under the spigot. The other visitor, Mr. Hoare, then told me his two children had a dog, too, and that his daughter and I were much of an age and would probably be good friends. Little did I know then how prophetic those words were. She is the one friend of my childhood with whom I am still in touch. I saw Una the last time I visited England, both of us then in our seventies. Anyhow, that long ago morning I decided that my father's visitors were very understanding grownups.

A few days later a letter came confirming my father's appointment to be the first Parks Superintendent of the Borough of Margate. The next few weeks were very busy. Besides all the farewell visits, there were two excursions to the coast. One weekend to Scarborough and the next weekend to Bridlington for Father to consult with their respective Park Superintendents. This was all very exciting. I had not seen the sea before. The idea of actually going to live at the sea-side became very attractive. I had no idea what I would be losing or how homesick I would become for the Yorkshire wolds. Neither did I foresee what the reality of going to school would really be like. I had long envied Betty Rogers her daily escape from home to the world of school, but would soon find out it was not a fun escape.

Kitchen, my father's assistant, had applied for the Headship of Warter and had been accepted on my father's recommendation. Kitchen was wanting to get married. His promotion made this possible; he would now have a house to bring his bride to. One Sunday Mother invited him to bring his fiancee, Elsie, to lunch and to see her future home. I liked her when she promised that she would take care of the ducks and drake I would have to leave behind, as well as the rabbits, whose tails she agreed to protect from people who were looking for pollenating brushes. Finally everything was ready to leave. Curiously, I have a less clear memory of the last day at Warter than I do of arriving there when I was less that two years old. But I have never forgotten the exact date of our departure—the day after my eighth birthday, May 10, 1923. Little did I think on that day that I would never visit Warter again until I was seventy years old and living in the U. S. A.

MARJORIE READE

Ann Arbor has been my home since I moved here in 1946 with my husband and one year old son. I grew up in the prairie state of North Dakota but the World War II years took me to Washington, D.C., as a "government girl" in the Navy Department where I was secretary to the Chief of the Bureau of Naval Personnel.

Since returning from a Sabbatical year with my husband in 1973, I have been a volunteer in a number of interesting and rewarding community projects. Most notable was to research and write, with my co-author Susan Wineberg, the book Historic Buildings. Ann Arbor *By appointment I served on the Historic District Commission for six years, as well as several years on the board of the Ann Arbor Historical Foundation.*

To recollect and put in print these stories from the past for Helen Hill's class in writing personal memoirs has been a challenge and a pleasure. It is not only the value of putting one's own life in perspective, but it is the sympathetic bonding that comes from hearing the life stories of the other class members. It is our good fortune to have lived in a century of dramatic and fundamental change.

My Childhood on
the Farm in North Dakota

I grew up in Walsh County, North Dakota, on the farm which had been homesteaded in 1885 by my mother's father and mother, Jacob and Mary Nelson. My mother and father had come to the farm in 1917 to help my Uncle John farm the land for war production, and to take care of my grandmother who had been gravely injured in a fall.

By the time I was out of diapers, I realized that my mother and my older sister Lois had a bond between them in which I would never have a part. My brother Budd was born about the time I discovered this and I latched onto him as a playmate while Lois, whom we all called Loie, took on a more responsible mothering role which we all expect of her to this day

Budd and I played all over the farm, in the dirt building roads for his trucks, or in the coulee or with the young animals. We had twenty or so pet cats and watched for new kittens which had a way of disappearing without our protection. In the winter, in our four-buckle overshoes, we slid down the snow drifts on our sled or made primitive skis to slide down the roof of the potato house, a half-buried structure covered with straw on the other side of the coulee.

On the rainy days we hung around the men who were gathered in the shop in the back of the granary. It was warm shelter with a lot going on. I don't remember a heater but there was a large forge and anvil. When the men could not be in the fields, they reshod the horses and repaired machinery, harness and other equipment. As kids we loved to watch them work at the hot forge and to marvel at the inventiveness of some of the repairs. There was always a camaraderie and an easy holiday feeling among the men on these days. And they sometimes forgot to curb their colorful language for little ears.

We soon had our jobs to do. Every summer we walked up and down the fields of grain pulling the yellow mustard plants so the fall wheat would be clean. We gathered the eggs, fed the chickens and washed dishes. My sister and I each had various ruses to leave the other with the job of dishwashing, but we had other kitchen duties which were much more pleasant. Loie was the salad specialist and I began to bake cakes. I kept a record the summer I was nine. I read *Little Women* three times and I baked a cake for the men's morning or afternoon coffee break every day. We helped take these lunches to the field and often shared in them. Nothing was ever so good as a sandwich or a piece of cake eaten under the warm sun in the fragrant air of the harvest field, and washed down with coffee, cream and sugar.

My parents were known for "setting a good table" for the hired men. Mother had a very large bread bowl from which she produced seven or so loaves of bread every other day. We took an afternoon now and then to pick fruit, crabapples and choke cherries which grew wild along the coulee banks to make jelly. Fall was a big canning time when Dad brought in crates of peaches and pears to be put up in jars for the winter. Vivid memories still are the spoiled vacation days of Thanksgiving and Christmas when we killed and canned a hundred chickens or put up an equal amount of newly killed beef into canning jars. The men butchered pigs which were turned into bacon, hams, and sausage, or frozen, as it was already deep into winter. Our Polish neighbors made blood sausage and headcheese, but Mother shuddered at the very thought and wouldn't have such coarse fare in the house.

The days we canned meats and the days we had to dry the Monday wash inside because of the below zero weather were so very dreary. Although we occasionally hitched up the horse to the big sled to spend a festive evening with neighbors, that didn't happen often and we sometimes passed six or more weeks in the dead of winter without any outside entertainment. The new Atwater Kent radio which came into the house when I was about ten, crackle as it did with heavy static, lifted our spirits with music and broadened our lives with politics and baseball as well as the "soaps."

Along with the radio which sat on a table at one end of the dining room, came a huge, deep leather chair and a magazine rack to hold the farm journals. Dad suffered severely from stomach ulcers and needed naps several times a day just to survive. He would come in suddenly and grimly from the fields to lie back in his deep cushioned chair for twenty minutes or so, and then be on his way again. The minute he was gone, if the weather was bad, it became our refuge. I read a lot of books curled up in that great chair.

Dad went to town almost every day for the mail. Town was the village of Voss with a population of 26 people, two country stores and a machine shop as well as two grain elevators. It was such a treat to be permitted to go so we could play with the "town kids" or examine the candy under the glass in the country store, hoping for a generous handout. Mother's brother Andy, who often lived with us then, was a very kind and indulgent uncle.

There was also a grange hall where there were dances on special occasions. Everyone went, from tiny infants to grandmothers. The able bodied danced and the others sat in the chairs that ringed the walls. Budd and I ran around and played games outside with the other children, often stumbling over men who had passed out dead drunk. We shuddered over the ugliness of their lying there and I wondered at their surrendering themselves so helplessly to liquor. There was never anything alcoholic in our house, but I didn't learn until much later that an alcoholic ancestor had left the whole family resolutely opposed to drink.

Monday was wash day but it began Sunday evening when a large boiler of water was put on the stove to heat and to soak the very dirty clothes until morning. The work day began early, certainly no later than five o'clock. In the early days, clothes were scrubbed on a washboard and one tub of water washed many loads of clothes, starting with white sheets and ending with the dark overalls. Water was scarce and precious as it had to be caught in the cistern or melted from the snows. The wet pieces were put through a hand turned wringer and finally given two rinses, swinging the wringer back and forth over three tubs. Then it was off with a large basket of wet clothes to hang them by clothes pins on the long rows of lines back of the granary. The winds were strong over the plains and the clothes were soon dried which was just as well as the lines were filled right up again. I remember how nice those fresh sheets smelled when in the late afternoon they were all sprinkled and rolled up for ironing the next day. Some time in the late 20's the first semi-automatic washing machines came in—one of the greatest boons to housekeepers I can think of. They were run by a generator, as electricity didn't come to the farm until much later. I won't even talk about diapers. That was such a major undertaking for an already harried farm wife. Even with a hired girl, and often there was not enough money for that luxury, there was endless work.

Automation, birth control, and disposable diapers took women out of slavery. In 1980, when my daughter-in-law came home with her second new born and was overwhelmed with the amount of work involved, I couldn't help compare the relative ease of her situation with that of my older sister when her second child was born. After several days in the hospital, she came home, probably quite refreshed actually, to a wooden farmhouse with no running water, a husband in bed with rheumatic fever, a two-year old, and no help. One of her neighbors came over to congratulate them on the new baby, bringing along a pail of fresh green beans to be canned, and I'll be darned if she did not put those beans up in jars for the following winter. Farm women were hardy and resilient.

Work started on the big basket of ironing early Tuesday, and everything was ironed—dishtowels, sheets, pillow cases, to say nothing of 20 or more shirts for the men. I started doing the flatwork as soon as I was able to lift the hot irons from the fiery hot cookstove and I think I was eight when my father undertook to show me how to do his white shirts. He was very particular and it took a while before I learned to do them to his entire satisfaction. My mother, my sister, and I took turns at the ironing board as it was an all day job. When I was about five I was leaning on the ironing board one day watching the ironing process and as my mother went to put the hot iron on the iron rest, it landed on my arm instead. That stopped the ironing for the day while we took a trip to the doctor twelve miles away. I had a scar for a long time.

My mother must have baked 20 loaves of bread every week. It was customary to take bags of wheat in to the flour mill in Grand Forks and bring back 100 pound bags of white flour. In the summer, we opened up the cotton flour bags, washed them and spread them on the grass back of the house to bleach in the sun. I sometimes saw them made up into garments, such as a child's romper, but ours were hemmed and became the best dish towels in the world. Eventually the faint coloration of the *Dakota Flour* label bleached out and they were white as snow.

Of course we had milk cows, usually ten or so at a time from the larger herd. Mother was adamant that her daughters were not going to be milkmaids, so it was a skill I never learned, but I would often be there to watch along with the cats and kittens waiting their share. There was something very appealing about the drafty barn with its warm organic odors of manure and milk and the lowing and tail switching of the very domesticated cattle. Sometimes we chanted this nonsense rhyme:

> We have a cow on our farm
> She gives us milk without alarm
> One day she fell beside the stream
> And split her tail right up the seam
> And now she's giving us ice-cream
> Golly, ain't that queer?

The men milked at daybreak and sunset. They brought the milk in open pails to the house where it was separated into skim milk and cream through the cream separator, a tall machine just inside the door which then had to be taken apart to be washed and sterilized, an onerous job to say the least. Some of the cream was kept for making butter and the rest went into large cream cans to be sold at the local dairy co-op.

Wednesday we made butter. We children took turns rotating the churn barrel until we could hear the slosh of the buttermilk and the plop of the gathering butterfat. Then mother drained the buttermilk through a spigot at the bottom, washed the butter clean, worked salt in until it was smooth, and finally scooped it into earthenware containers to place in a cool spot in the cellar.

House flies were a plague in the summer. It took constant care to keep them out of the milk and other foods. Fly swatters, sticky fly paper, and cloth covers over pitchers and platters were our only weapons in the house, but we used a kind of tar smelling fly spray in the outbuildings. The cook car, a sort of kitchen on wheels which we used during harvest, with a "girl" to do the cooking for the big crew, was always alive with buzzing flies that she would try to drive out the screen door every hour or so by whipping around a large dish towel while one of us held the door open.

We were also on the watch constantly for any sign of tuberculosis in the animals and birds. The tell-tale sign for chickens was white spots on the lungs or liver and I remember well the consternation and care when we occasionally came across a diseased one.

The chickens became my job when I was about eleven. The chicks arrived by mail and were put into a brooder house where I cleaned and put down new straw every day, filled their food dishes, added potassium permanganate to their drinking water, and kept the heater going until they were old enough to roam outside. By July we were thinning out the ranks by eating the "spring fryers." If company came for noon dinner, as buyers or the county agent sometimes did, I could catch a chicken, hold it firmly by the legs and wings while I cut off its head, dip it in boiling water to remove the feathers and have it cleaned and nicely fried in butter in little more than an hour, as I had often seen my mother do before me.

Then there was the farm garden. The hired men plowed a half acre or so in the spring and Mother put in the rows of onions, carrots, radishes, peas, beets, and beans. Later the cucumber seeds would go into little mounds of earth. The tomato plants waited until the first of June. There was no cabbage or squash in our garden—that must have been a matter of family taste. In that rich, black soil, the germination and the growth was like magic. At first I just helped with the weeding, but when I was nine I took the garden on as a 4-H project. The next year I became serious and entered the garden in a competition which was to be judged on the 4th of July. On July 1st I was smug about winning as my garden looked perfect to me. On the 2nd of July, the deep blue sky became covered over with ominous clouds and in the late afternoon that dreaded funnel cloud came tearing out of the west cutting a wide swath of destruction through the county. I ran out after the storm to look at the devastation and was about to go in and wail to my mother that my garden was just gone, when I saw my father walking back from the fields across the road with his shoulders sagging and a look on his face that said to me that all was lost on the whole farm.

Very little was said but the faces took on that closed, stoic look I learned to know so well. As I look back, my parents were undoubtedly thankful that the farm buildings suffered so little. The crop loss was fairly general in the community and at the 4th of July picnic in Minto, where farm families gathered, there was that look of worry and endurance on every face, but again very little was said.

The house I grew up in comes up in my dreams every now and then. A typical wood frame house of its time, at one end there was the summer kitchen with a tin roof, the full kitchen with a table that could seat at least ten people, a pump by the porch door that brought rainwater in to the sink from the cistern and a faucet from the artesian well. At the far wall was a large cookstove, a trap door to the cellar, and the door to the back stairs. A large pantry was off the kitchen to the south. I can remember a severe lightning and thunderstorm one summer afternoon. My mother was terrified and as she literally jerked the three of us by our arms past that pantry door, I saw a large ball of fiery light flash down toward us through the pantry window. The bolt of lightning burned out a section of the pantry and dining room walls taking the telephone as well but we were unharmed.

The dining room held the large dining table with chairs, and Mother's sewing machine on which sat a large fern when the sewing machine was not in use. At the other end of the room was the radio, the farm magazines and Dad's large leather chair. A large pot-bellied stove that warmed the house sat in one corner next to my parents' bedroom. Beyond the dining room was the front hall and the living room with a wind-up phonograph and a piano. The front porch on the end was seldom used, as the one off the kitchen caught all the traffic.

There were four bedrooms upstairs, warmed none too well by the chimneys from the two stoves. One bedroom was used by the hired men. Today, when there is so much talk of homosexual practices and men would do anything to avoid sleeping together in the same bed, I recall that two men slept in that room on a double bed. In the country in those days, one could get killed for any hint of homosexuality, so sharing the bed must have caused some tension, especially if they were strangers.

Speaking of matters sexual, I can remember that when I was perhaps four years old, before my brother was old enough to be a playmate, I often sat in a swing which hung from a box elder tree in front of the house, contemplating the world at large. It was there, watching a rooster mount a hen before the barn door one summer day that I was struck with enlightenment about the sexual act and the results thereof. When I read today about child abuse and the naiveté of children, I am baffled. At a very early age, my sister and I certainly caught the nuance of any sexual overture long before it became open and we knew very well how to get ourselves out of the way. Of course we were backed up by the knowledge of the retribution that would have come to anyone who molested us. It would have been swift and without the benefit of court action.

No one ever talked to us about sex and the very word put my mother into near hysterics as my sister and I discovered when we were in our teens. However my brother and I were curious, so one summer day when I was about eight and he was six, without any great conversation about it, we went out into a field, sat upon an abandoned tractor, carefully examined his private parts and mine and decided just how it must be done. Satisfied to understand this, and feeling a little guilty, we quickly went back to the yard and on to other things. However, even that had a powerful impact. Some years ago when I was well into my sixties, he asked me if I remembered that day—which of course I did very clearly.

Budd and I were given a pony when he was about seven. We named him Peanuts and learned to ride bareback as there was no saddle. During those very dry years Dad had a hundred or so sheep which we herded in the open fields with the help of our trusty steed. We tried to get Peanuts to rear up on his hind legs and be a real Western cowboy horse, but there was no spirit there. He was just a patient and long-enduring pony. However, there was a very bad tempered ram in the herd that we loved to catch by the horns and swing ourselves onto his woolly back, making him more furious than before. The dozen or so horses on the farm we knew by name and temperament as we might have known another person.

When I go back home for a visit now, I sometimes ask my great nieces and nephews if they ever find arrow heads as they play. We found so many in the 1920's when we were children. Perhaps there had been Indian villages and gardens along our coulee banks. There are none to be found there today except in museums. Even the ones Budd and I found and saved have disappeared who knows where.

I realized when I got out into the world that, like the English gentry, we actually dressed for dinner, not in satins and lace, it's true, but in fresh cotton house dresses. After the kitchen was cleaned up from the afternoon lunch for the men, my mother, my sister and I bathed at the kitchen sink and put on fresh clothing for the evening meal. It was quite a delicious feeling to be all cleaned up after the day's work.

On Saturday, chores were finished early, and the whole family dressed up and went to town, the big town, Grafton, twelve miles away, to shop and visit as we shopped with the other farm families of the area. Dad went off on his errands and my sister and I hung around with my mother, choosing patterns, buying fabrics, or buying shoes. We bought a lot of shoes. The evening often ended at the soda fountain where my parents sat back, relaxed and easy, chatting with friends.

My childhood ended when I went to Fargo at the age of twelve, to live with my grandmother for my freshman year in high school. I had always bossed Budd around a bit and we played by my rules, but when I returned that spring, he was some inches taller than I and I had lost my authority. We stayed friends, but began to go quite different ways.

When I go back "home" to visit, which I have done almost every year since I left North Dakota in 1941, I still get a spiritual lift from that blue bowl of a sky, and a verse comes back to me which I learned long ago in our one room school house, written, I think, by James Whitcomb Riley.

> It's so big and broad and boundless
> And its heavens are so blue.
> And the mettle of its people
> Always rings so clear and true.

Just as taking refuge for a while in Dad's big leather armchair would put me back on track when I was a teenager, a visit "home" today "restoreth my soul," or at least my energies.

From Mud to Mystery

Still a clear memory for me is the trip our family made one May, probably in 1926, from our farm home near Voss, North Dakota, to visit Grandma (my father's mother) in Fargo, where we stayed a few days. Our drive to Fargo had gone well, as the weather was sunny and mild and our touring car was able to make the trip in five or six hours, but on the way home it started to rain. As we continued driving north, we found it had already rained a great deal and the roads had become very muddy. The Red River Valley rises very slowly to the west so that the terrain appears to be absolutely flat. The fine black soil goes deep, very deep, or did in those days. The car followed ruts already made in the soggy road so we did not slip but rather became mired in the deep mud. We would have to get out of the car every few miles, all of us, and use what tools we could find to clean the heavy black muck from the wheel spokes and from up under the fenders so we could move forward again. Then, covered with the black goo our-selves, we got back in and, as we lurched from side to side, we anxiously watched as Dad coaxed the car along another stretch of the way.

We had started in the morning, but nightfall came and we were still far from home. There was not even the question of stop-ping. It was pitch dark and although the rain had stopped, we drove through wet clumps of clouds that seemed to sweep the ground. There were no places to stay. We must have been near the tiny town of Ardock by this time, but there were no visible farmhouse lights and on the flat prairie one can get lost in the dark. Dad plowed on with the car; the driving was suddenly a little easier, and we three children dozed, mud covered and chilled, under a blanket in the back seat.

We were jolted awake when the car came to a sudden halt. Dad got out from the driver's seat and walked forward into the darkness, just beyond the hazy gleam of the headlights. We could see the flicker of matches and then he came slowly back to sit in the car, silent and stunned.

Mom asked what the matter was and we heard him say that the bridge was out. After a few minutes we all ventured out of the car and walked carefully ahead about twenty feet where, by striking several matches, we could just make out the sharp-sided small chasm with the fallen bridge down in the torrent of what was usually a shallow creek.

With the help of the feeble headlights, solemnly we found our way back to the car. Mom asked quietly, "How did you know?"

"I don't know how," Dad said. "I just suddenly had this intense feeling of danger and knew that I must stop the car."

Dad was able to turn the car around and we made our way home by small country roads, arriving about dawn, sleepless and in awe, each of us rolling over in our minds the mystery of the power that had kept us from injury or death.

Christmas 1941

It was Christmas morning, 1941. I looked down from our fourth floor apartment window to the strange emptiness of Pennsylvania Avenue, usually so crowded with vehicles and pedestrians. My forlorn feeling intensified as I looked out at the cold skies and the wisps of dusty snow blowing down the empty street. Forget *Silent Night* I said to myself. "This is silent morning. It seems like there is not a living soul in this whole apartment building or even in this block."

Then I took myself firmly in hand. I had not a reason in the world to be so forlorn. Yes, there was a war on, and yes, my roommates had all gone home for Christmas, but I was warm and comfortable, and I was about to try to squeeze into the tiny apartment-sized oven a 26 pound turkey which my Dad had sent me from our farm in North Dakota.

Still, the day ahead was not exactly appealing. When that huge box containing the turkey had come two days before and I knew I must cook it, I thought the only thing I could do was to search the twelve story apartment building to find if there was anyone else at all remaining there for the holiday. I had found three other lone women and had invited them to join me for dinner. Each of them was bringing a food contribution and the four of us, all strangers to one another, would do the best we could with the day.

My thoughts went over the previous year and how I happened to be there in the first place. At the very beginning of the year I had responded to ads in the local North Dakota papers, inviting young men and women to take civil service exams for potential jobs in Washington, D.C. I was in the process of regaining my balance after a broken love affair, and very eager to leave my job in Grand Forks to see something of the rest of the world. My prayers were answered when I was immediately invited to take a position in Washington at an inviting salary of $2400 a year. At home I had worked myself up to the top secretarial pay of $80 a month. I quickly accepted the offer, borrowed $200 from my father, and caught the train east, arriving on the 8th of April. Now I was sharing this convenient apartment with three young women, all Midwesterners whom I had met the day I arrived. I was pleased that my job with the Navy Department was going well too and I already had had a promotion from clerk to a full secretarial position.

It was a real shock to me on that Sunday just two and a half weeks before when the announcement came on the radio of the Japanese attack on Pearl Harbor. In my position as a secretary in the Bureau of Naval Personnel I fully realized the severe blow the American naval forces had suffered on that fateful Sunday, and it was clear to me now that the American people might have innocently thought they would not be dragged into the war, but the powers in Washington had been well aware that it could not be avoided. That was why they had been out seeking hundreds of young women to staff the wartime offices.

No point in being gloomy. I turned back to the turkey. Fortunately I had had a lot of experience cooking for harvest crews on the farm. In fact I still had the irrational habit of peeling a full pot of potatoes for my three roommates which brought on a lot of "country girl" kidding. Today I had prepared a lot of stuffing for the bird, for it was really a huge bird, but I had dutifully peeled only four potatoes. I wasn't going to invite that kind of laughter from those three strange women.

I had had to buy a baking pan large enough for the turkey, and now, as I put it with the bird into the oven, I found the breast had only a quarter of an inch clearance from the top. Oh well, it would have to do. Perhaps basting often would help.

To cheer myself up, I put my favorite record on the phonograph. It was an English dance hall performer, Gracie Fields, singing such songs as "It's the Biggest Aspidistra in the World," "Walter, Walter, Lead me to the Altar," and "He's Dead but He Won't Lie Down." That lightened my mood while I cleaned the apartment and took a shower. Then I looked at the rest of the gifts sent by my father and mother. Chanel #5 perfume. Imagine Dad and Mom thinking of that for me! I could never have afforded that myself. The second package I might have anticipated, as my father gave all the women in the family the same gift every Christmas: two pairs of fine, silk, sheer, black hose, far nicer than anything we bought for ourselves. I decided to wear a pair of the hose. I straightened the seams in the back nicely and whisked on some of the perfume. What a divine fragrance!

I had invited my guests to come at 4 o'clock, so I was surprised when the phone rang at three. When I answered, a male voice responded. "Hey there, Marj, this is Sam Gershon. There are six of us down here in the lobby. We were able to get liberty for the rest of the day. What are you doing today? Do you know any other women around?"

Sam Gershon. Wow! The man from New York. He was an army sergeant I had danced with recently at the USO, and a really nice guy. We had gone out once after we met at the dance, just to walk around the city. I could just picture the cluster of eager young men in the lobby. Those poor guys, the day at liberty, miserable weather, and nothing to do. They must be far more unsettled and lonely than I was.

I told him all about the turkey and my prospective but unknown guests. There was a desperate urgency in his voice. "Hey, let us come up. We'll finish the turkey, make the gravy, serve the dinner. You'll see. You don't know this, but that's what I do in the army. I'm a mess sergeant, a cook. That's what I do."

"But you don't really want a bus man's holiday, do you?" I protested. "That's all right," he said. "'We are so lonely. You don't know what it will mean to us to be in a home and relax and to see some women. Besides, you know, we'll be shipped out in January and this is probably our last leave."

Who could resist that? Besides, I was really glad for the call and told him they were welcome to come up. When they stood at my door, those six young men in their rough wool khaki uniforms, I thought, "They are such babies really. And these rosy cheeked fellows will be shipped abroad in three weeks! The ache really does come in one's heart, or is it the upper part of your stomach?" I almost wept.

The soldiers piled up their overcoats on one of the beds and immediately took over in the kitchen while I phoned the other women to tell them to bring chairs and more food if they had it. It was comical to see those six big bodies acting at being efficient in that tiny 4 by 4 kitchen space.

The maple table in the small dining area was the average apartment size, seating not more than six. The other women arrived and we all milled around for an hour or so while the turkey finished cooking, getting acquainted, and having a beer which the men had brought up with them. Then they invited us to sit down at the table which they had moved into the living room while they served the dinner in the style of a first class New York restaurant. Even the stiffest of the women relaxed and enjoyed the attention.

Eventually the men took their turn at eating but they had already been stuffed with turkey at the base. After the dinner I put a stack of records on the phonograph and encouraged them to push all the furniture back and dance to Tommy Dorsey, the Ink Spots, and all that lovely wartime music. "The other women are not very young and are quite reserved," I worried to myself, as we danced in the dimmed light. From the vantage point of my 23 years, I thought, "They must be at least 30." They were pretty good sports, though, and everyone seemed to be having a good time. Truly, it was time itself that was in short supply as the soldiers had to report back at the base by 9 o'clock.

Sam called a day or two later to say they were shipping out even earlier than they had thought. In a kind of panic that I surely understood, he wanted to set up a firm relationship, but I, heartlessly honest, was not ready for anything more than friendship. He came by once more to say goodbye and then so far as I knew they were gone. I never heard from him again, not even one letter, which surprised and worried me. I thought of him often during the years that followed and hoped he had made it through the war to get back to his beloved New York City.

Forever after, the scent of Chanel #5, glamorous and seductive as it is, has never failed to bring a catch in my heart for those early wartime days when suddenly the young men were sent to battle in a war for which we were just beginning to build up our fortitude.

ELOISE SNYDER

Three childhood influences helped shape my adult years: the Edison phono-graph, the Saturday Evening Post, and my father's work as editor of a country weekly. The tall phonograph in the corner of our living room intro-duced me to the enjoyment of music; the weekly arrival of the magazine with stories to read aloud as a family taught me the pleasure of words on paper; and my father's experience was ultimately the deciding influence in my own career choice as a journalist.

All this took place in south central Nebraska, in a small town named for the Indian chief Red Cloud. My high school years were spent in Iowa, but I returned to Nebraska for college, where I met my future husband. After grad-uation in 1943 I left small-town life to live and work in Chicago. Wartime opened unanticipated opportunities for women of my generation, and I be-came one of the first women in a crew of reporters covering the city's news for the daily newspapers. Nothing in my sheltered life had prepared me for nights on the South Side police beat and days in inner-city courtrooms, so my education was considerably expanded in those years. After the war's end I returned to Nebraska, married, and began the years of raising our two boys with all the usual jobs on the side: den mother, church school teacher, PTA officer, etc. There were jobs with paychecks as well, including work on daily newspapers, in college public relations, and later on a national magazine for educators. Nearly thirty years after my B.A., I earned a master's from the University of Michigan, and my last eleven years of paid employment were with publications of the U-M Institute of Gerontology.

After my husband's sudden death in 1982 I retired from the University to become a full-time volunteer at a small college in the Blue Ridge Moun-tains. There I had the fun of directing Elderhostel programs (including the "world's first" for grandparents and their grandchildren) and developing other educational series for retirees and for women at a nearby prison.

Early in 1995 I returned from North Carolina to be a Michigander again, in order to live within commuting distance of some of my six grand-children and eleven great-grands who are now my best reason for attempt-ing to preserve on paper my own memories and the tales I was privileged to hear from earlier generations.

Those Happy
Depression Days

I was nearly nine when we moved to Broken Bow, Nebraska, and I found it a strange new kind of place. Located at the edge of the sand hills, it was wide-open cattle country with a distinctly western atmosphere. The big event in Broken Bow every year was the Custer County Rodeo, which brought eager riders and enthusiastic spectators from a wide area. There was an air of freedom in the town, and I quickly learned to like it.

It was the Depression that brought us to Broken Bow, and the Depression that shaped our experiences there. At the time, I was not aware of this. I well knew that our family had to be careful about money, but so did everyone else; it seemed normal. Now, putting together the fragments of my memories, I realize how much our life in Broken Bow typified the Depression years.

I remember, for instance, the shabby men who came one at a time to knock on our kitchen door and ask for food. We called them hoboes and out of their hearing we children parodied a familiar church song with, "Hallelujah, I'm a bum. . . . Hallelujah, give us a handout to revive us again." Yet my mother never turned any one away hungry. Sometimes these transients were welcomed in to sit at the table; those who seemed less trustworthy were invited to rest on the porch steps, and well-filled plates were taken to them there.

For the most part the hoboes were decent men, luckless victims of the times, and we were taught to treat them with respect.

New school buildings were out of the question for the community during the "hard times," so the school I attended was a venerable building with well-worn wooden stairways and high transoms that had to be opened and closed with long hooked poles. But it had a special attraction: the tubular fire escape. There were always eager volunteers to stay after school and clean the erasers, since tolerant teachers permitted us to slide down the tube to the playground with our armloads of chalky erasers. There we whacked the chalk dust out with great gusto, and climbed back up the inside of the fire escape—clean erasers, dusty clothes, and all.

Mostly, Depression memories are of events that seemed happy or exciting to me at that age. Our church had "Depression parties," to which we all wore our oldest clothes—a fine social leveler. We created multicolored crystal forms out of coal clinkers, ammonia, and bluing and called them our Depression gardens. We drove out to farms to buy corn cobs to burn in the kitchen range. One summer we marveled at the elaborate sand sculptures created along the creek bank by an itinerant artist—a hobo too, but one with a profession. We also learned to darn socks, to turn out the lights when we left a room, and to glue on new shoe soles from the dime store.

The teenagers of those Depression years had no cars and little money to take their dates to the movies, but they were resourceful. I felt that my brother Bill was leading a very glamorous life when he and his high school friends spent their Saturday nights roller skating through the town streets, ending up at some one's home for food and dancing. When they came to our house, I peeked around the kitchen door to watch. Those 17-year-old roller skaters seemed to me the ultimate sophisticates.

Equally awesome in my mind was that Bill became a member of the locally famous Cowboy Band, formed to promote the local rodeo and perform at rodeos in other parts of the state. When he prepared for a performance, he was resplendent in heavy black leather chaps, a yellow silk shirt with neckerchief, and a genuine ten-gallon Stetson hat. It was tough being a mere pre-teen female when an older brother could live such an exciting life. But other entertainment came with no gender or age requirements and carried no price tags. I felt better about it on Wednesday evenings, when the Cowboy Band played in the town square and my friends and I could romp on the fringes of the crowd.

My own career in music began and ended at Broken Bow. Finding few families able to afford private piano lessons, a local studio offered a weekly hour of "class instruction" at 25 cents. Our teacher was a well-intentioned farm wife who must have seen little hope for my musical future, but perhaps some hope for my soul. At least, my memories are mainly of her efforts to convert me to her form of religion. I must admit it was appealing in those days of scarce resources; one had only to make a poster of whatever one wanted most (in my case, a bicycle), call the poster to God's attention regularly, and presto, the wish would be granted. My parents frowned on this easy method of giving orders to God, but I tried it secretly. Alas, I never did find a bicycle on my doorstep.

Nor did I grow up to become a pianist or a member of a Saturday night skating club. Still, my Broken Bow memories—i.e., my Depression memories—are happy ones. For many people the Depression caused great suffering, and for my parents there must have been grave anxiety throughout that period. For myself, I was probably at an ideal age for the experience—too young to worry over rent and grocery bills, old enough to learn some valuable lessons about thrift and making-do with whatever is available. I always contend that you can tell those of us who lived through the Depression by the careful way we still turn out the lights when we leave a room.

Going Out for Ice Cream

As my memory measures time, it was not so long ago—well, perhaps sixty or so years—that ice cream didn't "keep" at home. Many of us in small Midwestern towns had no electric refrigerators, and even the big blocks of ice in the icebox could not protect frozen foods for long. Occasionally my father hurried home from downtown to bring a wire-bailed paper carton of vanilla ice cream, and we devoured it quickly before it could soften further. (Headaches from its coldness were accepted as part of the experience.) On very special occasions there was homemade ice cream from the hand-cranked freezer—and a dasher to be licked. For the most part, however, ice cream was a treat to be enjoyed away from home. Going out for ice cream was an event to be anticipated joyfully, savored fully, and remembered long and fondly.

I suppose there were times when we went as a family for cones, but my earliest memories are of going alone as a kindergartner. On Wednesdays Mother and my older brother worked with Dad to get his weekly paper out, and I met them downtown after school. It took only a little misbehavior on my part to show that it would be helpful to have me out from underfoot, and so Dad would give me a nickel and permission to go buy myself an ice cream treat. Our town was very small and nothing bad had ever happened to a child on the street, so like others my age I had freedoms that seem enviable today.

The ice cream parlor was also a bakery, thus always warm and fragrant. The tables were small and round, just the right size for two to share a soda, and the chairs with their looped wire backs and round seats were the originals of the replicas that shops today buy when aiming for a "quaint" decor. It was a place where a 5-year-old could sit alone with an Eskimo Pie and feel exceedingly grown-up.

Going out for ice cream did not always mean going to a shop; there were also the ice cream socials. Festive occasions, the socials were usually after dark on the grounds of a church. Big slices of made-from-scratch cakes (no box mixes in those days) were served at long tables along with generous scoops of vanilla, chocolate, and strawberry. As the women of the church served, the men were busy cranking still more freezers, rounded up from many homes for the occasion. Strung from tree to tree overhead were paper Japanese lanterns holding light bulbs. To a small child, the lights and shadows created a scene of enchantment that was even more memorable than the desserts.

By high school days, I was past begging for nickels for cones, and must carefully save up money for ice cream treats from a small allowance. Once in a while, when we felt able to splurge, my friends and I stopped after school at the soda fountain in Rice's drug store. A "Rice's Special" was a small soda offered in a great variety of flavors. One I remember trying, but only once, was a celery soda. A few years later, the place to go for cones was a tiny restaurant on the corner across from my college campus, where Myrtle the proprietor served a more limited range of flavors but dished up motherly advice for young students along with the ice cream.

Fast forward, now, to ice cream memories from the days when our children were small. We lived in Dubuque, and the best place in town for cones was on a narrow street beyond the business district. Again, the choices were many. The shop was noted for its surprising variety of flavors, and concocted new ones almost weekly. My husband coined the term "Exoticones" to embrace all the unusual flavors. So popular was this shop on warm summer evenings that cars were double parked up and down the street and it was not feasible for the whole family to go inside to make flavor choices. As the father of the family slipped from behind the wheel to make the purchase, he always called out "What flavors tonight?" and a chorus came from the back seat: "Exoticones!" That was his *carte blanche* to choose the very wildest and most far out flavors he could find —from banana peanut butter to cranberry pumpkin. The family waited in the car with great excitement to see what was new this time.

Nowadays, there are grandchildren and great-grandchildren with whom to share the pleasure of going out for ice cream. How thankful I am that packaged ice cream from the supermarket, though always conveniently ready in the home freezer, has not made obsolete all the Dairy Queens, the Baskin & Robbinses, the Washtenaw Dairies, and their kind. May my great-grandchildren someday take THEIR great-grandchildren out for Exoticones!

An Afternoon with Grandmother

Dear Grandmother Anna Maria Hewitt,

This letter brings you greetings from a place, a time, and a granddaughter you never knew. Although you died two years before I was born, I am so full of questions for you that I cannot resist creating in fantasy an afternoon of visiting together. What a wonderful heart-to-heart talk we might have if some magic wand made it possible! I imagine us sharing a pot of hot tea and chatting away eagerly, two women who have led amazingly different lives but are linked in love by the generation between us.

The only picture I have of you was taken in your last years, well after you and Grandfather left the Nebraska homestead where you lived more than thirty years, beginning in 1872. The picture shows a small woman in an ankle length black silk dress—your Sunday best, no doubt. Your hair is drawn severely back from the face into a knot at the back, and to be honest, I find your expression prim and humorless. But this wasn't really you, was it, Grandmother? I feel quite sure there was a twinkle in your eye that the photographer failed to capture.

What I'd most like to discover in our afternoon of visiting is the person you really were. What things made you laugh? What small delights were there amid the daily strains of your life as a pioneer woman? Nebraska, with its wide open spaces, is still famed for its sunsets; did Grandfather, in the midst of evening chores, sometimes call you to leave the dishes and come outside to marvel with him at the many splendored sky? Did the willow whips you carefully brought from Iowa and planted along the river warm your heart as they grew into real trees—points of beauty in a barren vista? You bore nine children, some of them without the aid of a doctor or midwife; was each tiny infant anticipated with joy or, given the austerity of frontier life, did pregnancy and child care seem just two more hardships? I hope you were happy. I want to believe you found adventure and reward in pioneer life on the Plains, arduous though it was. Yet . . . I remember, reluctantly, that my mother once told me that your words to her on her wedding day were "The duty of a wife is to bear and forbear." It has always seemed to me a dismal view of marriage. Is it possible that Grandfather Hewitt was not always the kind and affectionate man I remember from a time when I was very young and he was very old? I do know that chronic illness contracted while he was in the Civil War was a lifelong problem; perhaps there were times when misery made him less than amiable? I would feel better at the end of our afternoon visit if I felt assured that your years together were much more than just day after day of bearing and forbearing.

Perhaps my questions are too personal, considering that this is our first meeting. Let me change the subject to friendship. At first your nearest neighbors were miles away, and many of them spoke only Swedish, a language you did not know. How did you get acquainted? As more families took up their homestead claims, were there barn dances and quilting bees? Did some of those women become true friends, as dear as those you left behind you when you climbed aboard the covered wagon to head west? Of course there were at least two reasons for your neighbors to seek you out. One was your knowledge of herbal medicines, learned as a child from your father who was a Christian Church minister and committed herbalist. With doctors and drugstores many hours away by horseback, your neighbors must have depended upon you often for help in sickness. Did the responsibility weigh heavily?

In seasons of good health, women from other homesteads came to your door for a quite different reason, I've been told. As families wore out the wardrobes brought with them from the East, replacements had to be made by the wives and mothers, from Sunday suits for the men to knitted long stockings for the girls. Your prized sewing machine was the first one in that part of the country, and women from many miles around offered eagerly to come do your housework and look after your children while you sewed new garments for their families. What a lot of good visiting there must have been while you pumped the treadle and they scrubbed your floors! I look back from the year 2000 to the 1800's and think how easy our homemaking tasks are now. I can imagine your astonishment if during our afternoon together I could show you how much can be done today by merely pressing a button or turning a dial.

Was there any time in your long work days for letter-writing? How I wish your letters had been preserved, especially if they reflected your true feelings about prairie life, so different from the lives your sisters were living in the East. Did you write of the overwhelming discouragement you must have felt when grasshoppers devoured all your crop the second summer on the homestead? Or your anguish during the great blizzard of 1888, when for two long days you waited to learn the fate of your missing husband, gone out to herd in the cows, and the children, on their way home from the one-room school? Then there was the story I love most, about the Pawnee woman, wife of the Indian chief, whose seeming fixation on your small barefoot boys frightened you—

until she returned one day with the beaded moccasins she had made for each of them. How I wish I could hear these stories in your own words!

Perhaps the oldest of your grandchildren were lucky enough to sit on your lap and hear all your stories. As the youngest child of your youngest child, I can only cherish the bits of information that have been preserved, and fantasize about the rest. But please know, Grandmother, that I do it with love, respect, and everlasting awe.

Devotedly,
Eloise

Long Nights
on the Great Lakes

Perhaps it was inevitable that we would find the Great Lakes irresistible when we moved to Michigan in 1961. Both my husband and I had grown up on the plains of Nebraska, where any body of water was prized, no matter how small it might be. And now the largest lakes in the country were not just big blue swatches on the geography-book maps but real places nearby.

Perhaps it was also inevitable that the combination of excitement and inexperience would lead us into trouble when we began exploring those lakes in boats.

Our sons were grown and in homes of their own before our dream of having a sailboat came true, so there were just the two of us to try it out. We had named the boat *H. Puffin*, as in "huffin' and puffin'," aware that we were well over-age for taking up sailing.

So where to go for the maiden voyage? Lake Erie beckoned. The plan for our first sail was to find an uninhabited island to hike on, have supper beside a blazing campfire, and then sleep aboard. Arriving at what seemed a good spot along the western shore, we managed to get the boat off the trailer and into the water, the mast stepped and the sails hoisted—this we had practiced in the backyard. We had a small outboard with us, but intended not to use it.

The first hours were glorious. The breezes cooperated, the sails billowed, the boat was responsive to Dick's hand on the tiller, and the cold spray in our faces felt just the way we had imagined it. Life was good. We wanted to sail forever.

Eventually we found our island and tied up beside a concrete sea wall. The island was obviously uninhabited, and just large enough to offer a chance for exploration. We tossed out the anchor and prepared for our hike, but suddenly the land was no longer uninhabited. An enormous population of seagulls returned just then from its own excursion and took possession. With hundreds of birds flapping just above our heads, a hike on the island was definitely unwise.

But it was all right; the circling birds were interesting to watch from the security of our cabin, and we enjoyed supper aboard. The lake trip had been strenuous for a pair of novices, so it was no hardship to give up evening plans and unroll the sleeping bags as soon as dusk came. What bliss, what a dream come true to go to sleep to the sound of waves gently lapping against the hull.

Gently? Not for long. Less than an hour later we awoke to quite different sound effects. A fearsome lake storm had come up and the winds were battering *H. Puffin* against the sea wall. The anchor line had broken, leaving nothing to hold us away from the concrete when the gale forced us in that direction. Donning slickers over our pajamas, we spent all the rest of the night perched side by side on that narrow wall in a drenching rain. We took turns at the work that had to be done: one of us pushing the boat away with both feet to keep it from hammering the wall, and the other tugging desperately on the rope to keep the boat from starting off to Buffalo every time the winds shifted.

It was a very long night.

By dawn, the rain was beginning to let up and the winds had diminished. We made coffee—how good it felt going down!—and waited for signs that it would be safe to begin the trip home. By mid-morning conditions were more favorable and crossing the water under combined sail and power seemed manageable. It was not until we were within clear view of the shore that our inexperience showed again. Despite what the night had brought, the scariest part was now at hand.

We had launched from a site where currents were favorable to moving away from land, but resistant to any force trying to move from the lake in to the shore. As we struggled to make headway, *H. Puffin* rocked madly from side to side, but could make no progress forward. We were being propelled back out to sea. With enormous effort we struck the sails, and after what seemed hours of pitching and tossing the small outboard finally delivered us to dry land.

No doubt about it, our first sailing adventure was a learning experience: it taught us that there was much we didn't know about sailing. Weekends, we practiced diligently on smaller lakes, and our efforts paid off that fall when another memorable night came as we were cruising the North Channel of Lake Huron. We encountered a very similar nighttime storm, but we were better prepared this time. We had been careful to choose our overnight spot between the shore and a sandbar. Our anchor line was the sturdiest we could buy. We were able to stay dry in the cabin through the rain and wind, though dressed and ready to jump for land at any moment. We weren't real sailors yet, but we were learning.

One more long night was in store for us, this one on Lake Superior. We left *H. Puffin* behind the summer we traveled to Isle Royale for camping,, but we rented a flat bottomed boat on the island. The season had not yet officially opened, and we were the only ones in the campground. Nights were cold, and there was ice on the water pail each morning, but days were sunny. One day in particular was so beautiful that we decided it was made for a picnic—even though we were already eating three meals a day outdoors. We rowed down the coast until we found the perfect cove, and after our meal we set out on foot to see this new part of the island.

Suddenly-rising winds sent us hurrying back to the boat, but the waves were already too high for our small craft. We secured the boat and gathered driftwood in case we might need a fire, since the air was cooling rapidly. Before long it was too dark to navigate, and we knew we would be there until morning. The wind had abated somewhat, so Dick built a spectacular fire and we cheerfully recited as much Omar Khayyam as we could recall as we unpacked the picnic leftovers. Not quite the romantic "jug of wine, loaf of bread, and thou beside me in the wilderness" of which he wrote, but close. At least we had a partial loaf of sliced whole wheat, half a bottle of Mogen David, and each other. Plus wilderness aplenty. This was not going to be half bad.

Then, the howls from the darkness. For a moment we sat in stunned silence, straining to hear above the crackling of the fire, and then it came again, unmistakably. There were wolves out there, and they sounded hungry. A wolf call can be spine tingling under any circumstances. On the remote shore of a lonely island, with no shelter and no other humans for miles, it is a sound the hearer never forgets.

We were pretty sure we had read that a good fire keeps away wild animals, so we piled on more driftwood. We hoped we were right, since we had no other strategy to try. We agreed to take turns on watch, one of us sleeping as best we could while the other listened to make sure the howling came no closer. Not much sleep happened—for one thing, even in the absence of tension it's hard to relax into sleep when one side of you is being broiled by the campfire and the other side is freezing. But some time after midnight the wolf calls began to sound farther and farther away. Finally we could hear them no longer.

Daylight came eventually. The waves had subsided and we sleepily doused the embers and paddled our way back to the campground. For the first time, we wished there were other campers there. We really wanted to tell someone about our night with the wolves.

Three different big lakes. Three different all-night adventures. I wonder what new tales there might have been to tell our grandchildren had we ventured onto Lake Michigan or Lake Ontario.

LLOYD ST. ANTOINE

Writing one's memoirs is like soul food, especially if one has had the good fortune of being a member of a large and close family and the wife of a re-markable man, as I have. I was born in Flushing, New York, in 1934, the youngest of nine children. My arrival was welcomed but inopportune. My father was already squeezed by the exigencies of the depression. In 1936 a job opportunity opened in Mexico City and all of us, accompanied by a black, wooly Newfoundland dog, Barkus, sailed off from New York Harbor to Veracruz and by train from there to Mexico City. We children had a wonder-ful time in Mexico. Most of us eventually returned to the United States, but not until after absorbing in eight years the Mexican mentality that leaves room for miracles, suffers unimportant things with grace, translates "mañana" into respect for the long view, and confirms that beautiful things survive amid chaos and deprivation.

Because of World War II we younger children moved to Washington, D.C. in 1944 to join our father who had returned to the army and was serving at the Army Security Agency in Arlington, Virginia. It would take four years more before he would be permanently established in business—this time in Cleveland, Ohio—and we could put together a permanent home once more.

In Cleveland, I attended Beaumont, a private Catholic school for girls run by the Ursuline nuns. Later I followed many of my new friends to Ursu-line College, five blocks from our home, a move that altered the course of my life forever. There I met Sally and later her brilliant, wise and noble brother, Ted, my husband of over forty years.

Ted and I courted in Washington, D.C. while he began his career in labor law and I worked at the CIA. We married in 1960 and moved to Ann Arbor in 1965, where Ted joined the faculty of the University of Michigan Law School. Our two boys, Arthur and Paul, and two girls, Claire and Sara, unlike Ted and me, were able to enjoy the stability of one town and one school system until they left home.

In 1971, when Ted became the Dean of Michigan's Law School, we moved to a larger, more accommodating house and accelerated the space and scope of our lives, entertaining distinguished visitors and new faculty, sometimes cocktails for over a hundred guests, but mostly dinners of twelve, or buffets for students in Ted's case clubs or seminars. Ted's widowed mother moved in with us, and later two nieces from Washington joined us to attend Eastern Michigan University. When they graduated, three nephews took their place. To save my sanity, I enrolled in a Masters in Education program at Michigan, did my student teaching in English at Tappan Junior High School, tutored children and supervised interns at Michigan's Reading and Learning Skills Center. Later, when our children began to leave home for college, I worked as Office Manager in Edward Surovell's first real estate office. After that I began to volunteer, first for Ars Musica, Ann Arbor's original instruments orchestra, and finally, for Arbor Hospice, where for the last ten years I have helped in the Development Office.

I belong to three book groups, and travel when I can with Ted on business or sightseeing trips, or to visit our children and five grandchildren. I still occasionally play the piano—I was fortunate to have been a student of Estelle Titiev for a few years—and garden in the summer, keep up with my large family and house, and to keep serene and limber, do Yoga.

A Tale of Two Houses

The Friers' House: The Rackety Packetys

The two households I shifted between in Mexico were my own and that of my best friend, Helen. In many ways they were in sharp contrast to each other. Ours allowed for personal freedom, self regulation and a comfort level with a certain amount of confusion. Because we were a large family, individual whims often gave way to the convenience of the many. At Helen's there were only two children, with a mother who understood order and rigor and who had an impressive talent and appetite for art and music. I was not her protégé, but I have no doubt that my association with this family played a significant role in my future life style. It would be hard to say exactly how my days at Helen's influenced my future tastes and choices. There may have been other factors, but at least certain inclinations took root in those early years.

The first few months in Mexico City were extremely difficult for my mother and father. My father had to return to the United States to settle some business reverses; my mother was left in Mexico with all of us and a dwindling bank account. She had to find us housing, enroll eight of us nine children in school, and cope with the hospitalization of my sister Virginia, who needed an appendectomy. A lovely woman named Mrs. Robison ran a boarding house and took us in until we could find a permanent place to live. Soon after Christmas Mother found a house, square, yellow, stucco, a little tower at one end, and a decorative red brick wall bordering the flat roof. It was a serviceable house, not beautiful. The yard and house were protected by a brick and stucco wall, some of which was topped with glass shards to ward off intruders, an odd necessity, since one could always climb the iron gates, even if they did have spikes at the top. The back wall opposite the street abutted an open field of alfalfa and squatters often used it as a support for whatever poor hovel they could put together from pieces of cardboard and tin. They'd cook their meals on braziers and would stay until someone drove them off. A former mistress of President Cardenas was the owner and once resident of the house. She had had armed guards posted at the gate, much to the annoyance of General (and former President) Obregon's mistress, who lived in a small house across the street and had no guards of her own, probably because by then Obregon had been assassinated. It was she who was robbed and Cardenas's mistress would not allow her guards to go in pursuit, so they say. My sister, Virginia, remembers going with Mother to our landlady's to pay the rent. There was a shooting range in the back yard—with effigies of actual persons as targets.

It didn't take long for the yellow house to take on a whole new character—"The Friers" it would be called by the many friends of my parents and brothers and sisters who loved to come there just to hang out or for the spectacular parties my parents and older siblings had. I distinctly remember the "Movie Star" party. Mother and Daddy were Laurel and Hardy; Anne was Marlene Dietrich; a young man named Fred came as Sonya Heine on skates! We were always a game playing family. Charades was popular, and for us younger ones, Sardines. The front hall closet was a storage space under the stairs, filled with trunks and boxes. It was a perfect place to pile up in.

Mother always called us "The Rackety Packetys"—from Frances Hodgson Burnett's story of the two doll houses, the fine one where they had no fun, and the old worn one where everyone could be free, silly, ridiculous and all had a good laugh.

Mother was very resourceful, and with little money she augmented the few belongings shipped from the US with furniture she bought at house sales or had made. We had a long blue dining table with a matching small table and sideboard, and many blue Mexican rush seated chairs decorated with bright flowers on the back panels. A few of the beds were similarly painted. Some of the carved wooden pieces were quite lovely and my sister has them today, but mostly the couches and chairs were more for ease and comfort than for décor, and certainly we never felt inhibited about sprawling all over them. I don't ever remember any words of admonition about how to behave in the living room except not to put my feet up when I had shoes on. It was HOME, a completely unthreatening place for each of us to be secure, to have our games and projects, and to be together. I think we almost always had fun.

The first thing I remember is my goat, which I know by photos we acquired soon after moving into the house. Two of my sisters bought a little cute one from a street vendor and brought it home for me. I called her "My Sister," as if I didn't have enough. She was a very nice goat until she ate the back end off my papier-mâché hobby horse and chewed the toes off the socks on the clothes line, ate a corner of Sally's dress while she was standing nearby, and demolished everything near her in the garage where she was kept. Mother gave her to the stable where my sister Mary's horse was kept. Mother said goats kept the horses calm. I've always remembered that. Sometimes, when I'm being a peacemaker I think of myself as a kind of "goat in the stable."

There was a tower room in the house that exited onto the roof. Jimmy got that room, after some squabbling with Mary. But

Jim was the oldest, and anyway, I don't suppose anyone would have wanted him on the second floor since Barkus, the Newfoundland, slept with him and Jim has never in his life been known for neatness. Mary, Sally, Anne, Jane and Virginia shuffled between two rooms, trading around when Mary and then Sally left for college in Texas. Bill and John, known as "the little boys," got their own room, where the tracks of their electric trains took up much of the floor. Mary kept her saddle in the boys' room, hung over a rolled up mattress. We could ride it! I remember only one book in the boys' bookcase, *East of the Sun and West of the Moon*. I always wondered what that meant. I still don't know. I initially slept in an open crib in my parents' room. I think it was when I overheard Daddy say one morning that he was going to get himself a little French girl and I piped up from my bed "Why do you want a French girl, Daddy. You have Katy (his secretary)" that I was moved to the glassed-in sun porch. I loved being on the sun porch. It may have been the messiest room in the house, because it was delightfully warm, bright and sunny, and the place where Mother and Jane did their sewing. I was content with my own little corner with my green bed and my painted child's desk, my toys stored under the bed. At night I could look over the field behind our house and see off in the distance an apartment building. I once noticed a little girl being put to bed in one of the rooms. I would lie in bed making up stories about her or would imagine pictures from the irregular patterns of the stucco ceiling. Later, when my grandmother grew old and senile, she was convinced that the patterns she saw in clouds and trees were real. If I follow suit—well, there are worse things!

Dinner at our house was so lively and so much of what we expected family dinners to be that almost all of us had to adjust to the quiet of being just a couple, or a couple with babies when we first married. Daddy and Mother sat at opposite ends of the table, the rest of us probably taking favorite seats, though I remember sometimes being at Mother's right and sometimes at Daddy's, where he would play games with me—shaping an elephant with his hand, making his fingers waddle toward me, his middle finger the trunk that threatened to tickle me. Or he would slap his palm on the table and invite me to pancake mine on top of his, then his on mine, one after the other, drawing the bottommost hand on top as we got faster and faster. The dogs, Barkus, the Newfoundland, and Lorna, the Great Dane, positioned themselves where there was the greatest opportunity for a handout, sometimes daring to lay their muzzles on the edge of the table. With eleven of us at meals there was always an enlivened conversation, whether it was Daddy challenging Jim about history or politics, or Sally, with disarming innocence, telling and giggling through the latest dirty joke she heard and forgetting to stick to an innuendo, using the right words instead. I was very little when I heard of "Ike and Mike and the bull," which I liked because it had animals, costumes and sounded funny, and others were over my head but I gathered enough salacious lore to share with my friend Helen over the years. Jane was always funny and dramatic and could give us a hilarious rendition of two maids in the kitchen having a fight. In spite of being on a tight budget, we did have maids—a cook, a cleaning and serving woman and a laundress. It was part of the economy of the times, when servants were paid so little. Lupe was our cook and we still make her Brown Betty, Brownies, Green Rice. We'd met her at Mrs. Robison's. Mother took her in when Lupe, recklessly smitten with the gardener, had to leave Mrs Robison's to have a child. After we younger ones left Mexico, Sally took Lupe and kept her until retirement.

Our living room ran the depth of the house. I remember the chess games Daddy played with the girls' boy-friends and with Mother. He and I regularly played "Memory" (which I more often than not, won) and dominoes. He had an enticing set of tiles, ivory on one side, green onyx on the other. I made houses of them and used them as imaginary people. The Lindy, Swing, the Jitterbug, one or all were in style, and Sally and Anne would put on records and practice kicking their legs high. I don't remember Mary's doing this. Mary was more serene—my "Princess Sister." She was beautiful and poised. One year she was elected to be a princess at the "Black and White Ball." Her dress was black tulle with gold and silver stars. I gazed at her with rapture and I still have the photo of her all dressed up. Jim, my oldest brother, had a marvelous ability to stand on his hands and then roughhouse with the dogs without falling down. Jim was our family photographer even then. His extraordinary photos of the extended family, as it grew, are our most accurate testimonial.

It mortified me, but Mother had a few parlor tricks of her own and she'd be called upon to perform them all too often for me. She could lie on the floor, put a full glass of water on her forehead and stand up without touching it. I wanted her to be dignified and didn't like her looking foolish, but others loved her for her sense of fun! Bill, John and I would periodically litter the living room with pages of the comics our grandmother would send in huge batches from the States. "Do you have Sunday March 10th? I want to see what Orphan Annie did!" Jane read voraciously. I was so impressed when she asked for *War and Peace* and *Les Miserables,* such fat books! I picture her curled up on the couch, her hair hanging in her face, reading a book. She was also the clever one and I'd frequently seek her out to think up an activity for me or to read me one of her stories. She had one about herself coming down for Christmas and finding that there were no presents on her chair, but under it a small box with a note inside saying "Better Luck Next Year." I always got tearful, it was so pathetic, and like *The Bird's Christmas Carol,* with its Victorian morbidity, I begged for it again and again.

Sally was the older sister who became my surrogate mother when I was first born. She wanted a piano and mother let her earn it by having her care for me. I have always adored Sally and her irrepressible joy in life, her courage and spirituality. When I was around six she invited me, during Lent, to go to "the Stations." I walked hand in hand with her through the dirt path in the back field, a little perplexed as to why we were going to visit gas stations. I was quite surprised when we ended up at the church in Piedad for the "Stations of the Cross!"

Bill, next to me in age, was always a happy person—still is. One of Mother's friends thought that since she herself had no sons and Mother had so many children, Mother would sell Bill to her for twenty thousand dollars. Bill has always felt he is worth something! He loved Superman. Bill would put on his blue pyjamas, tie his dark rose bathrobe around his neck, race around the upper hall, and finally come sliding down our winding banister "to save the day." To this day he loves to perform what he calls his "Superman Poop" in Spanish—("El Superhombre!").

John and Gingie were the serious ones. Maybe that's the way with "fix-it" types. They are the only two in the family who know how things work and can make repairs. John spent long hours with the electric train, making little cotton cargo sacks he filled with sand, or laying out the track in new and interesting configurations. Once he made a small metal canon and shot it with real gun powder he probably got from a firecracker. It made enough noise that the police came! He and Bill each had wooden castles Jim built, with handfuls of toy soldiers. I was in trouble when I felt sorry for the little orphans who lived over the garage wall and threw a bunch to them! Gingie, the sister nearest to me, was the one I went to when I was hurt. If I was trying to hide something that was bothering me, she was the one who would notice. Gingie's things, her clothes, her dolls, her bric-a-brac, were always in perfect order, which attracted me considerably, especially her Shirley Temple doll with its trunk of clothes and her Oaxacan box of miniature glass animals. There is one memory of Gingie that still pains me. I wish I'd behaved more generously myself. One year she forgot to tell me about a birthday party I'd been invited to. She was miserable about it and to make amends gave me one of her favorite china dolls. I took it. How I wish I hadn't and had told her it was OK. Of course, the doll became one with my menagerie of unkempt dolls, with their hair cut and their bandaged arms and legs and appendix scars. Gingie would have kept it in perfect condition.

I would not say that the Frier home lacked order—Mother would say we had only "surface mess!" We had our predictable patterns of mealtimes, learning and culture were encouraged, my father was deeply knowledgeable about history and mathematics, and my mother had had an excellent education. She grew up surrounded by fine art and music. Both parents encouraged a thirst for learning. But there was about our family a sense that if you wanted something badly enough you'd go after it yourself. You didn't need to be pushed. Encouraged, yes, but never did I feel that someone had made plans for us. Sometimes I wished they had! There was so much to manage, Mother had to spread herself around, and she managed to do so willingly. But it was not her way to set about training us with a preconceived plan. Mother was a person to set down healthy shoots and let them grow on their own. As for Daddy, his family swirled around him. He was preoccupied with the business of keeping his company and his family afloat, and he stood on the periphery of household management.

As I look back, I have the impression that I was left to my own devices a lot when I wasn't a witness or part of the family circus. I always felt I just "came along," fitting into life as it was. Mother said later she only had to raise four children; the rest would follow suit. She practiced what she called "benign neglect." When the others were in school, I amused myself easily with my toys, or went with Mother on errands. I know I was supervised, but it seems to me that I usually put myself to bed since I never made it to the evening meal at 8 p.m., but ate a small supper around six or seven in the kitchen. I know the perspective I have of our family life in Mexico is limited because I was so young and uncritical . But if I can't remember much about our first house in Mexico in my pre-school and early elementary years, I do know that I was in a secure and loving home where there was always something happening.

A New Perspective:
Life At the Escobedos' House

I already knew Helen Escobedo a little when after I'd finished first grade Mother decided to take me out of the American School and send me to be tutored at Helen's home. At the time I went there were just the two of us, all our lessons taught by Mademoiselle Pierrota, whom we called "Zelle." The school would grow to nine children before I left. All of our lessons were in French and Spanish. English would come later with another special tutor.

At Helen's house, in contrast to ours, there was precision, a pristine simplicity, discipline and ambition—laughter and fun, too—I don't mean to suggest any austerity. Mr. and Mrs. Escobedo were generous and amusing and loved children. In fact, there was a deliberate focus on the children, Helen and Michael, three years younger than Helen. At my house, the simple fact of so many children precluded total absorption in any.

I became what was probably sometimes an annoying fixture at the Escobedos' home. Not only did I attend class daily, but the family frequently invited me to other events and I often returned to play after school. It was a good atmosphere for me, and what I learned there served me well in later years when I discovered my own love of music, education, the theatre and dance.

I was fascinated and a bit envious of the unwavering sense of order at the Escobedos' house. There was little variety to their routine, a routine that in many ways was simple but seemed so deliciously luxurious to me. There was always fresh lemonade in blue glasses by their bedsides at night, in blue, rippled Mexican glasses. Covers were turned down and dressing gowns laid out. Helen and Michael had their supper promptly at six, on trays in the kitchen. Mrs. Escobedo looked to their health and often they had yoghurt, the unflavored sour kind which I thought was disgusting, and always warm, chocolate flavored Ovaltine. Then they had baths, together, drying themselves on large white and blue towels—there were always the same towels. (Imagine the mayhem at our house where there was only one full bathroom for eleven people!) At the top of their stairs was a linen cupboard and drug cabinet. I remember that there were always chocolate or vanilla calcium wafers and if eyes were sore, there was Argyrol. I didn't envy them the Argyrol. It turned your eyes yellow! And as for pills, we only had sugar pills given us by our homeopathic doctor. I ate everyone's when I could sneak them. Mother didn't give us vitamins or calcium, much less typhoid shots in Mexico which she thought would make us more sick than the disease. Still, I appreciated the attention Helen and Michael got.

The economy and subsequent efficiency of Helen's room and wardrobe still impress me. Helen had pink furniture, bed, bureau, and cupboard, in which hung her five or so smocked dresses with Peter Pan collars and her rose taffeta party dress, her kilt in the cooler weather and the blouse/slips that buttoned to the kilt. That was all, except shoes. I was proud of having the variety of a dozen or so dresses in my closet, mostly hand-me-downs and some made for me by Mother, but what a hodgepodge to keep up! Her bureau drawers held only a half dozen underpants and vests, pyjamas and socks and a sweater. Zelle gave Helen a print of Renoir's 'Little Girl with a Watering Can", which hung over her bed, and there was a collection of blown glass ornaments on her bureau, but no more. Michael's room was even more austere, a bed and large wardrobe.

Across the front of the house was a large glass-enclosed porch where all the toys and books were kept and where we had our school. This is where we spent most of our time. School was here, at a long trestle table Mrs. Escobedo had had made for us. For recess we went outdoors, sometimes admonished to speak only in French, for practice.

Mrs. Escobedo's room had glass doors onto the enclosed porch. It was her room alone. There was a Chagall print on her wall, a large double bed where Helen and I would sleep if I spent the night, a dressing table on which there was an array of cosmetics, including the lipstick we would sometimes sample. Her closet was good for hide-and-seek, especially in the folds of her long, silk bathrobe. Mr. Escobedo had his own room, down the hall, which I suppose was very European and not a reflection of the status of their marriage. It was a distinctly masculine room, with a single bed built into a bedside cabinet that ran the length of the bed with a door where the unit ended. The cabinet was hollow and there was never anything stored in it, so we often played there or used it as another hiding place. On days when the sheets were changed we made houses of them, securing them to the desk and chairs with books from his fine library shelves. The shelves contained law books and other weighty books we had no interest in, but among his collection we discovered two favorites—a collection of Goya's paintings and *General Psychology* by Clendening. (When it was recommended to us as a reference book in college I had to chuckle!) The former had a drawing showing little boys farting—little poofs drawn in—and the latter had drawings of naked men and women. I wonder if Mr. Escobedo knew we were so devilishly attracted to that book. Did we mar the pages? Did we put it back in the same place? Did he ever even look at it? We once traced the figures to make paper dolls—well endowed paper dolls—and got into trouble!

Helen's father was a Mexican of Spanish descent, a lawyer who always drove a large, black sedan. He was never anything but charming and handsome as far as I could tell. On Sundays the Escobedos always had an outing, mostly with Mr. Escobedo. I was frequently invited to the movies, the ballet, swimming at the Chapultepec Golf Club, and almost always to Larin's candy store. I will always remember Mr. Escobedo as smelling of Yardley soap. He lathered it in a shaving dish in his bathroom. He was a wonderful man, steady, amusing, kind. His law firm became one of the foremost in Mexico City and before he died he was President of the International Bar Association.

Mrs. Escobedo was from Hampstead, England. All the English spoken in the house was "The King's." I can hear her saying, "Lloyd, dear, must you say 'wadder' like the Americans? Say 'wahter'," and I did. Once my family caught me with my "Escobedo" accent when I left the dinner table to answer a phone call from Helen. When I returned to the table they teased, "Oh, Lloyd, so you're going to a 'pahty' are you!" Mrs. Escobedo wanted me to call her Elsie when I saw her in my adult years. I couldn't. She'd been too formidable. She was a dynamic, musical, dramatic, handsome and energetic woman. Her musical friends were a circle that included the famous Roth (Rota) String Quartet. She hosted musicales, she at the piano, Mr. Roth at the violin, his wife singing, and others. A center staircase in the house was closed off nearby the parlor by a door at the bottom. Helen and I would steal down the stairs, open the door an inch, peek at the players, and then hold our sides to keep from giggling when Mrs. Roth began her arty songs. The more we tried to stop laughing the harder it became. Mr. Roth counted the rhythm with little "Pah, pah, pahs," his lips blowing out as he did. That was deliciously funny to us!

I did learn to finger my way through "Frère Jacques" on Mrs. Escobedo's piano, playing it over and over until it drove her crazy and she suggested to Mother that she give me piano lessons. It wasn't long before I was playing "On Yonder Rock Reclining" and "Carry Me Back to old Virginny" from the John Thompson piano book and annoying my family by playing them as fast as I could, over and over. I didn't have anyone who bothered to push me to practice and I suppose Mrs. Escobedo eventually gave up on me. But it was a start and I have played the piano off and on all my life.

The living room had a couch and love seat with wonderfully bouncy cushions to jump on when adults were out. We'd listen over and over to "Peter and the Wolf" and Humperdinck's "Hansel and Gretel," inventing dances and leaping from pillow to pillow.

Through Helen I met a circle of international children, Mexican, English, German, mostly. They were her social circle. I had other connections with my old schoolmates from the American School and with children of my parents' friends, but Helen was my closest comrade. We cherished our "best friend" relationship. It was probably I who once picked up a smattering of misinformation at the dining room table that friends swore permanent fealty by touching tongues! Well, Helen and I were certainly going to be true to one another and I remember how we screwed up our courage to do something so revolting. Finally, very tentatively, we leaned toward each other, squeezed our eyes shut, and touched the tips of our tongues together. We did it! We were friends forever!

I think Mrs. Escobedo was the more responsible for the conditioning of her children. Mr. Escobedo had to have concurred, but he always seemed more relaxed. She had such zest, such talent, how could she help but shower it on her children and have them enjoy the richness of life that exposure to music, art, theater, travel brought. I think she enjoyed life immensely. I thought her a little put on, and I know my mother thought of her as being too "arty." They were very different, or else they would have been friends. I am grateful now to have shared somewhat in the exposure Mrs. Escobedo provided. I was only on the periphery, however. She graciously included me in so many activities, but her children had a life beyond me, lessons in violin, cello, horseback riding, foreign languages. And when Helen was eight or nine she began to show a burgeoning artistic talent. What might have gone unperceived in my family was quickly encouraged by Mrs. Escobedo. Helen was given art lessons. By the time she was sixteen, she was admitted on trial to the Royal College of Arts in London. She did well and was the youngest graduate in a hundred years.

I have always enjoyed my association with the Escobedo family and still do. Perhaps something useful in art and music appreciation and a sense of discipline rubbed off on me from those early years. Helen has gone on to be an artist/sculptor of international repute and Michael has assumed the leadership of his father's law firm in Mexico City. Eight of us Frier children married and among us have had fifty-six children. Different legacies. Interestingly, I don't think Helen and Michael have "plans" for their children. They appear to be accomplished on their own steam. The same with ours. Helen says she wakes up in the morning eager to begin the day and her projects. She wants to live to a ripe old age as a delightful and energetic old lady. I think she will, and I hope I, in my own way, do the same.

If the Truth Can Be Told

For three years I worked at the Central Intelligence Agency in Washington. Much about its unshakeable policies at that time now gives me pause.

First of all, security clearances. Do you have any idea what it must cost for each potential employee of the CIA to be cleared for employment? Just take me as an example. Once I had sent my application into the agency I knew that at some time or other agents would begin to interview my employer and my neighbors, which they did. Of course, my neighbors hardly knew me. But they were all very loyal. One told Mother, "I don't know your daughter, but I see her walking along the street. I told them she was a nice girl!" My employer was furious because I hadn't given him any idea I was considering leaving my present position. I knew immediately, by a certain demeanor in the man who came to inquire if Mr. Izutu was available, that this was "the moment," the cloak and dagger invasion of my life.

I was hired. At least I was asked to come to Washington, where for six weeks I was holed up in what is known as "the Pool", on 16th Street off K Street, a neighborhood I knew very well. It was fun being mysterious and telling people who asked where you worked that you worked "for the Government." They all knew, of course. I enjoyed myself reading magazines, writing letters, browsing through local stores on lunch break until six of us were sent to a three week training class where the entire organizational structure of the CIA was unveiled to us. I had applied only for a clerical job, but because all of us had college degrees, someone in the hierarchy thought it might be useful if we were knowledgeable about the agency's total overt operations when we were placed in our final positions. Mind you, I was receiving pay all this time. The training staff would not have incurred a greater expense on our behalf since we were part of an assemblage of students—including, perhaps, some genuine future spies. I know we kept looking around to see if we could tell! Was it that handsome young blond man with the trench coat slung over his shoulder? I watched him anyway. He was very attractive!

What was to come once our class was over and we were ready to be placed in an office was the lie detector test. Did I need a lie detector test, fresh out of a Catholic college, I who couldn't tell the slightest lie without blushing, I who hardly knew what was going on in the world enough to relay a secret to an enemy agent? Well, we all got one nevertheless. I was terrified. Other girls who had attended the classes with me thought it was a lark. But I had spent the last seven years of schooling being inculcated with sin and guilt. There might be some indiscretion I'd committed that had never been uncovered! Would I be up to the standards of this important Government agency? My palms were sweaty as I was escorted into the small room where "my confessor" sat behind a table full of different apparatus. He explained the procedure and then attached the wires—with suction cups, I think. It wasn't so bad. The questions were really simple, like "Where was I born?" "Who were my parents?" "Where had I been to school?" "Had I lived in a foreign country?" These, I later learned, establish a pattern of "normalcy" from which an acute reaction can be measured. The first question to startle me was "Have you ever committed an undetected crime?" Committed an undetected crime? What kind of crime? Yes, I've exceeded the speed limit, I may have even crashed a stop sign. Is that what he means?" I decided I had not. Then he asked an embarrassing question, "Have you ever committed a homosexual act?" "My gosh", I thought. I hope not. What does he mean. Does he mean when my friends and I would play "You be Lawrence Olivier and I'll be in love with you and then he falls in love with me and I faint at his feet?!" Well, I decided to say no on that one too. Finally he asked one that really disturbed me, "Has any member of your family been known to commit an offense against the United States Government?" or something like that. "Does he mean when Daddy would have a few drinks and then spout off in any kind of company about how much he hated Roosevelt? Someone said he's been put on the 'black list' at the American Embassy." I did get questioned on these responses after the test, and of course my interrogator realized I was a babe in the woods and I passed with no problem. As for my father, the interrogator's wonderful comment was "I think we know more about your father than you do." If I hadn't been such a terrified nitwit I would have come to that conclusion myself, since how else could Daddy have been the Commanding Officer of the Troops at the Army Security Agency or received the Legion of Merit for interpreting the Japanese codes that enabled the US to frustrate an enormous Japanese naval engagement in the Pacific!

Then there was the work itself. I was finally assigned to the Office of Current Intelligence, and with luck eventually became the Administrative Assistant (governmentese for private secretary) in the front office. My direct boss was rather senior in the agency so I was well placed for a certain amount of overt activity. But did I do anything? Hardly. It helped that I had taken the indoctrination class and understood where the phone calls were coming from, what procedure was to be followed in the event of a crisis, but honestly, except for a few of those and for a few letters I had to type perfectly for the President, I mostly learned how to complete the New York *Times* crossword puzzle and to make a good cup of coffee for my bosses! What's true in the government is that it's the underlings that do the brunt of the scut work. I didn't have to type the eight to twelve page documents that I sent to my boss to sign. Some clerk in the typing pool did them. And there were no copiers then—well maybe one that produced a faint copy on sepia paper. We used real carbons, so if a mistake was made on seven copies, we had to start all over again if it was for a high official. Then came disposable carbons and that made all the difference.

We had a procedure we followed regularly in our own office. I think my predecessor invented it just to look busy. Every classified document that came to my desk—from "Confidential" to "Top Secret"—what ever the code name—had to be logged in and given a number. If the document wasn't filed and eventually left the office it had to be logged out. If we destroyed documents we had to log them out as well. One day, someone from "Security" came to me with a two page paper that seemed related to "men and materiel." The information didn't make much sense, but it was marked "Secret" and one couldn't just dispose of such a paper. I was asked if I had any idea from where it might have originated. I considered various possibilities, however remote, visited a number of our offices, and eventually ended up at the "Editorial Office." I was describing it to one of the employees when one of the clerk typists jumped up from her desk and came over.

"Can I see that?" she asked.

"Sure," I said as I handed it to her.

"Oh," she continued. "I'm so embarrassed. This is mine. It's my typing practice!"

I stayed at the CIA until I was six weeks shy of giving birth to my first child. I was ready to move on anyway before rigor mortis set in and would have applied for a foreign post or maybe to the Office of Scientific Intelligence, which intrigued me.

You would probably recognize some of the names of the men who came through our office for meetings; certainly, you would know the ones who phoned or who had to be alerted in an emergency. I enjoyed watching the "Old Boys Network" in operation. I'd spent enough summers in Fairfield, Connecticut, to recognize that most of the movers and shakers of the CIA were New England "preppies" who called each other by nicknames like "Red" and "White," "Andy," "Ting", etc. I wondered about the high powered secrets and began to suspect that many of these people talked rather openly at the Cosmos or Metropolitan Clubs where they gathered frequently. I have no doubt many a secret is dropped casually at a Washington cocktail party—particularly among fellow members of a certain coterie of insiders . Those were the Allen Dulles days. Perhaps the CIA has changed from that kind of camaraderie. I don't know. I also saw in action another phenomenon of strategic groups:—the particular roles generals play and their critical need for adjutants. My senior boss was a "general." He loved the dynamism trouble brought on. I once saw him jump in the air and rub his hands with glee when there was a crisis over the Russians snagging our cable lines with their fishing trawlers. "Ah! Excitement!" He'd go off and meet with the high officials and the grubby work would begin for the adjutants as they followed through on procedures. My second in command, "the adjutant," was a former Harvard dean. He came in each morning refreshed and left each day looking like a wrung out rag.

In three years I'd acquired a number of special clearances. When you depart from the CIA and other security agencies, you have to be "debriefed," which means you have to go to each office your special clearance covers, sign a document and swear you no longer know anything about what information it dealt with—like the "U-2 flights," for instance. I can understand there must be some criminal sanction involved in the knowing and telling, but for heaven's sake, how could one just "forget!" I think I had four offices to go to, and after the last, they took away my badge and escorted me to the door. That's an awful experience and I still dream about either wanting to get into the CIA or wanting to get out and not having the proper identification. I came home feeling castigated. I no longer belonged. I couldn't go in again.

I think the feeling lasted one afternoon. Six weeks later I had a baby son to care for. And I have never wanted to work at the CIA again. Maybe I was hired because they know my type are ignorant of intrigue, obedient and guilt-ridden!. We ask no questions. I'm afraid I'd have questions now!

ANTONIA TEERNSTRA

⚜

I was christened Antonia Agatha Teernstra on the 5th of April 1924, three hours after I was born in Zeist, a lovely resort town surrounded by pine woods southeast of Utrecht, the oldest city in the center of Holland. I was the third child born in a family of four siblings. While my mother was a Hollander born in Amsterdam, my father was a Frisian born in Friesland, a culturally distinct province in the northern part of the Netherlands. My parents met in Holland's internationally famous radio city Hilversum, where they married in 1919, bought a dry goods store in Zeist, and lived happily ever after? Not quite! The stock market crash of the late Twenties crashed our business, and together with mother's mental illness, the result of a severe head injury, caused a double dose of "depression" that gradually made our family dysfunctional.

From my father I inherited my levelheadedness, logical reasoning and judgment of character. His sense of humor, artistic flair for painting and pen-craft, as well as his green thumb were also passed on to me. My mother was the scholarly type, a quality that rubbed off on me. My knack for a variety of needle crafts I owe to her, as well as the inexhaustible store of proverbial metaphors she knew how to apply to many facets of life. From both my parents I learned to become a perfectionist. or better said, to be my own worst enemy. I came into this world endowed with an analytical mind, and a perpetual quest for the meaning of life. I feel very blessed by my keen sense of rhythm and ear for melody; consequently, my love for music extends from classical to ballet to ballroom dance.

The Depression, followed by World War II, prevented my further education after high school. During the aftermath of World War II, I assisted my parents in rebuilding our business and running the household. Eventually I completed a two-year course in business administration, as was legally required in Holland if I were to run our business independently, should that become a necessity.

In May 1950 I met my soul-mate, Gerhard Beisecker. When I was twenty-nine, it was a very good year! On July 14, 1953, I married my dream husband, and on the same day we emigrated to Boston, Massachusetts, America, our dream country. We both became American citizens in 1959. On June 15, 1971, I experienced the saddest day of my life when Gerhard died. During my remaining solo journey through life the axiom "God helps him who helps himself" *became a reality. In 1974, after I finished secretarial courses at a business college in Ann Arbor, Michigan, I became administrative assistant in the School of Education at the University of Michigan. In February of 1998 I retired from the University and since then I've been arranging my life's memories into a memoir. Voilà, my profile in a nutshell.*

Survival of the Fittest: From Soup To Grass

The Germans invaded the Netherlands on May 10, 1940 with the prediction that they would leave as soon as the Hollanders were down to eating grass. Incredibly, towards the winter of 1944/45, indeed, we had reached the stage when their prediction became a reality. To make matters even more unbearable was the endurance of the severest winter on record. Without heat, food, and warm clothing the entire situation hit so much harder, a taste of Siberia indeed.

Our family was fortunate enough, though, that periodically we could make a bike-trip to our family on the farm in Friesland to stock up on staples such as legumes, dried fruits, nuts, seeds, and flour, and, thanks to the bitter cold winter, we had a natural refrigerator enabling us to fetch bacon, butter, and ham as well. However, people who had to rely solely on the soup kitchen rations suffered from severe malnutrition. Many people collapsed and many dropped over dead in the streets.

Every day us kids took turns going to the soup kitchen where sometimes we had to stand for hours in line outside in the bitter cold, because if you came late and they'd run out of the slop, you were out of luck for that day and we were not allowed to use the unused coupons for double measure on the next day. Even though the stuff had hardly any nutritional value, if at all, "at least it's wet and warm," Pa would remark. Indeed, it felt good to get something warm in your stomach for at least once a day even though the nondescript stuff was merely stomach filling.

On one occasion it had taken my sixteen-year-old brother Jan over two hours to come home with the filled bucket. He looked like a ghost, death warmed over, from standing for two hours outside in below-zero weather and was unable to talk for about an hour after he'd come back in from the cold. With hardly any feelings in his hands, (fortunately he wore the thick. three-ply woolen family mittens we kept for that purpose to prevent frost-bite), he tiredly climbed the first flight of stairs to our living-quarters above our dry goods store. The pail with slop dangled off his left hand while he pulled himself up by the banister with the other hand. Almost on top of the stairs the pail slipped from his hand and bounced noisily downwards, hitting all the steps to the bottom of the stairs while emptying out and on its descent leaving the disgusting unappetizing contents on every step of the stairs while splattering multi-sizes of blobs on the side walls making it look like a road map. The repulsive mess turned quickly to ice and into the ugliest sight I'd ever seen. I couldn't believe that we were really eating that stuff every day, and I thought: "I wouldn't even feed that stuff to the animals. Come to think of it, I wonder if they would even want to eat it because animals have very delicate sniffers and know instinctively what's good for them." It seemed to me as if it didn't look and smell quite as bad in the bucket as it did from the big blobs and icicles of the greyish putty colored mess, speckled with God knows what, hanging over and blobbed on the carpeted steps of the staircase. Meanwhile, Jan cried buckets. No matter how we tried to console him by telling him that it couldn't be helped and that we surely would survive, he cried uncontrollably; I guess the extreme stress had finally got the best of him.

To clean up the icy mess was a precarious task, but we all agreed that it must be cleaned up one way or the other. Carefully, in order not to damage the stairs, we chopped, cut, and tore the frozen carpeting from the steps; it sure would have helped if soap and hot water had been available to make the job easier and better. After we had the runner in shreds, we threw the mess outside the back door to wait for Spring to thaw it out so we could burn it in the backyard.

The backyard was another very fortunate treasure we possessed in those days and very unusual, indeed, to find in a business section, in the heart of a city, business property that included a large piece of land connected to it. Because of it, during the war years, we were able to grow our own fruit and vegetables, enough to help out neighbors, friends, and family. Every year I tilled the soil with a spade; then Pa, Rients (my oldest brother) and I emptied out the cesspool to fertilize the garden. Boy! Did we smell pretty after that job! Pa did a lot of apologizing and explaining to the customers in the store and it took several days before we felt comfortable with serving the public. Of course, an old-fashioned piece of Palmolive soap and hot water would have expedited the process of de-scenting us.

Pa and Rients claimed to be experts in gardening. They put in and maintained the garden during the growing and harvest seasons, and we all watch-dogged for veggie predators. We also kept 15 chickens and one rooster. If the chickens had kept their mouths shut, the Germans would have never discovered them, but one day, upon orders of the German government, an inspector came to see what kind of business we were operating in back of the store. He made a note that we had 15 chickens and told us that we were only allowed 10. He said he would figure out for us how many eggs we were allowed to keep and how many we had to hand over to the German headquarters, unless, of course, we got rid of the extra five chickens. Pa decided to keep the 15 chickens and they behaved just beautifully when the inspector came around for the second time, when five were nowhere to be seen or heard, while exactly ten were happily picking and walking around outside the coop. Eventually, however, towards the end of the war we had to get rid of all the chickens because of lack of feed; also, Pa wasn't pleased having inspectors dropping in at any old time and snooping around. Too risky while we were active in the underground services for the Allies. It meant that taking fewer chances could mean a better chance to escape death, because as Hitler's war machine progressed, his military crew became gradually more intolerant and mean to the stubborn Hollanders who kept showing their discontent with the unwelcome visitors who had invaded, occupied, and setup housekeeping in our country.

The noisy chickens also alerted egg-thieves; at least we noticed that at nights people came to help themselves to the eggs. That's when Jan and I decided to make a trap to scare the unwelcome visitors away. We had put a pail with water on the roof above the door to the coop. In the daytime we would disconnect the rope that would pull the pail down as soon as anyone opened the door. The saying "If you set a trap for someone else you may be the one who gets his foot caught in it" became a reality when one night Pa did his last round of inspection and received the cold shower. So much for good intentions!

With reference to the shredded runner waiting outside to be burned in Spring, perhaps I should mention here that we hadn't seen trash collectors in many months. Actually, since we lived more or less like cavemen, there wasn't much of a need for trash collecting, as even newspapers and magazines had stopped a long time ago; the only news we heard was via word of mouth and from the underground services. Since we worked for the Allies, we had access to a primitive clandestine radio to keep us abreast of the news via broadcasting from London. All radios had to be turned in at German headquarters already several years ago; we had hidden our little radio literally underground in a secret tiny little cellar in the far end of our store; it took a rickety old wooden ladder, which we had painted black to make it non-conspicuous, to descend into obscurity. Every night at eleven we could hear the news from London, but at a very low volume in order to avoid suspicion.

At any rate, the now bare wooden steps of the staircase were still looking treacherous with scattered stubborn icy spots we had been unable to remove. To prevent anyone from slipping over the remaining icy spots we threw salt and sand on the steps in hopes that would save us from any mishaps.

Survival of the Fittest:
Sie Haben Die Männer
Gut Versteckt

France, Belgium, and the southern part of Holland, i.e., all the land south of the great rivers, Maas, Waal, Rijn, and IJssel, that run across Holland into the North Sea, were liberated in September of 1944, leaving the provinces north of the great rivers to take the brunt of the most dreadful winter in memory, until at last the whole of Holland was liberated on May 5th, 1945.

During the five oppressive war years only farmers, even though they worked primarily for the German Government, beyond their choice I must add, were able to maintain the essentials of life. Besides having plenty of food, they also spun their own yarn to knit and weave their own cloth. Many farmers, however, deserve great honors for their humanitarianism in serving their starving fellow men from the cities with survival rations from their hush-hush surplus, unaccounted for to the authorities, which they distributed at reasonable prices. However, not all farmers practiced such noble intents as some were afraid to take the risk of getting caught and slammed the door shut to the starving public; and then there were farmers who catered only to the wealthy who could afford high prices or to merchants who were able to trade their clandestine merchandise for farm products. The black market reigned rampant in those days, making millionaires of many businessmen and farmers who quenched their thirst for profit by taking advantage of the extremely trying times.

In that respect I have the highest praise for my family who deserve much credit for not falling into the Black Market trap. I hold my parents, as well as our farm families, in very high esteem for practicing their philosophy in caring more for the welfare of all than the wealth of a few in order to favor their own benefit. Especially my Dad, who, as a result of the depression time, was over his ears in debt, could easily have been tempted when the ship of opportunity approached to step aboard and sail along with the gold-pirates; instead, he preferred a clear conscience over sleepless nights of worrying about black money, and chose to help the needy wherever and whenever within his capacity.

Uncle Jan and Aunt Boukje followed the same principles as they tried to help the starving city people. Two days a week at specific times they accommodated the public as well as they were able to. One incident comes to mind when I saw Aunt Boukje with teary eyes sending people away because she honestly had run out of milk to spare. She felt just miserable to see these disappointed, tired and terribly undernourished, scantily dressed people leaving the farm yard after they had walked for miles, and after they had stood in line in the bitter cold only to hear the bad news.

Daily, flocks of starving people, mostly women who were less likely than men to be picked up by the Germans, could be seen walking or biking along the highways for many miles from the cities to farms where they once or twice a week could buy just a quart of milk, a pound of beans and a couple of potatoes. Considering how we had tumbled from the depression time into the equally depressing war years with little or no opportunity to recover from previous years of extreme poverty, it was no surprise to see even the most prominent classes of people walking around like hoboes, with clothes worn to bare threads and shoes beyond repair as they went on their weekly scavenger hunts to the farms.

Bike tires were already unavailable for several years and were replaced by wooden tires. Someone had invented wooden tires with a metal spring inside of the rim, and it worked, even though, on a long trip it almost caused calluses on one's derrière. In fact, if you were fortunate enough to own a bike with rubber tires, you wouldn't dare to ride around with it in fear it would be ripped off, and it usually was German soldiers who pulled you off your bike and confiscated it on the spot, upon so-called orders from German Headquarters.

From the day the Germans set up housekeeping and all during the dismal war years, food and clothing were rationed, and supply shrank gradually from scarcity into deprivation of essentials for living, into the worst form of starvation imaginable, known as Hunger-Winter '45. During those dismal years, Hitler's war machine was fed the best and foremost, draining Holland from its wealth and health into poverty, starvation, and untimely deaths. In the old days people saved gold coins, but when the Germans got wind of that, all gold coins had to be turned in to German Headquarters; if you didn't comply with their command and it would be discovered during a raid, you would be picked up without forwarding address, and it was anyone's guess when, or if at all, you would return; usually these people ended up in work camps. The same fate fell on anyone who still owned a radio after the recall; the objective was that the Germans didn't want us to hear the real true news from London. Valuable artworks disappeared mysteriously from museums. They just vanished without a trace, and everyone knew what had happened to the pieces, but nobody dared to speak their mind. Fortunately, after the war many pieces were recovered from Germany.

Houses were raided at any time of day or night; preference seemed to be early dawn in order to give people little or no chance to hide their men or possessions. However, men were trained to know exactly where to hide in the shortest amount of time and without confusion. Next to our backyard our neighbors had a dilapidated, empty old barn kept for the purpose of hiding about a hundred neighborhood men. On one of those early morning raids Pa kept guard around the barn as planned. We all thought it would be better to have someone keep an eye on the "treasured" barn by not taking the risk of the Germans kicking the door in. So, Pa puttered around and sauntered in his worn out slippers aimlessly in front and around the barn when three German soldiers on the prowl walked up to Pa and asked what was in the barn. Pa didn't say a word, shrugged his shoulders, and acted like an imbecile, clad on purpose in his old house jacket and baggy old pants. He performed his act perfectly as he played like a mute with all the questions like: "Do you have a key to the padlock so we can get in? Are you the owner? Do you know the owner? Do you know how we can get in touch with the owner?" etc. Finally one asked Pa, with a lot of sign language, as they thought that he was a mute and stupid, who he was and where he lived. Pa kept his silence upon the question who he was, but pointed his right index-finger to a dilapidated old shack across our yard as being the place where he lived. Frustrated, the two other soldiers got antsy to go on and commanded the interviewer: "Come on, let's not waste any more time here. Can't you see, the old guy is nuts?" Little did they know that Pa was far from nuts. He spoke five languages fluently, including German, and we had just discovered that he was also a great actor. A feather on his hat, he saved almost a hundred young shook up men from certain doom.

In the meanwhile two German soldiers had invaded our store. Rients had barely enough time to hide inside the roll of linoleum in the display window, and Jan dashed to lie flat on his plank which was especially installed for that purpose on the rafter under the roof-ridge of our warehouse. The fruitless scavenger hunt turned the dutiful soldiers belligerent when one of them noticed a picture of Queen Wilhelmina on the wall of the landing on top of the first stairway to our living-quarters. He tore it from the wall and with his heavy army boots he stamped the glass to splinters while giving us a sardonic look; for weeks we were still finding glass splinters. The sacred heart statue of Jesus on a shelf over the French doors to the living-room was next to be smashed into pieces, and soon followed Saint Mary's statue on top of the closet in my parents' bedroom to be thrown from her high throne through the window onto the sundeck. Finally, empty handed, on their way out, one kicked my mother against her left leg. Mumbling and grunting muffled swearwords they stumbled down the stairway to the front door. With a vibrating loud bang, they slammed the door shut behind them leaving the glass of the little window in the door resembling a spider web as a long time remembrance of the very unwelcome visitors.

It must be very frustrating if men-hunt is your job and after inspecting so many buildings and homes you must go back to your base empty handed. The soldier who killed his frustration on the holy statues, said to me *en passant* on his way out "Sie haben die Männer gut versteckt." ("You did a good job hiding your men.")

Survival of the Fittest:
A Desperate Escape

In August 1944, during their annual visit to Zeist, Aunt Boukje and Uncle Jan offered that any one of us kids could stay on the farm for as long as necessary if that would help the rest of us to have extra food stamps. "There's always plenty of work on the farm, and we can always use more help," commented my Aunt. Of course, all four of us loved to go to the farm, but Pa didn't feel right to overburden my Aunt and Uncle's generosity and decided that just one of us could go for the time being. If necessary someone else could go later on. To solve the problem of who would be the lucky one, Pa had cut strips of paper in different lengths which he held hidden in between his fingers with just the tops showing. The person who pulled the longest strip won the trip to the Farm. I was the lucky winner and anxious to go, though in the end I felt that Mieke was in a worse shape than I and offered that she could go instead of me. I cannot remember whether she went with my Aunt and Uncle to the farm or if she went by herself in September by clandestine train, as the Hollanders called those trains that were unscheduled to confuse the Germans. At that time it was still possible to make reservations on clandestine trains which ran sparingly and erratically only evenings and nights. When Mieke left it was still pleasant and balmy summer weather, a great contrast to

four months later when on Monday, January 18, 1945, on the spur of the moment, Mother and Jan left for Friesland under the worst winter weather conditions imaginable.

Earlier that same day, via our store, which in those days was open only for a couple of hours a day, even though the store was practically empty, Pa had learned by word of mouth that the last clandestine train to Friesland would leave that same night at nine o'clock. A hasty decision was made for Mother and Jan to take this final opportunity to go to the farm until the end of the war to provide Pa, Aunt Agatha, Rients, and me with extra coupons for the soup kitchen. Listening secretly to the daily London news had convinced us that the war couldn't last much longer. For it to last another four months—as it did—was almost unthinkable at that time of a most incredible state of affairs. At dawn on June 6, 1944, the great crusade of the Allied Forces waded ashore on the beaches of Normandy, France, making the greatest invasion force in history and the beginning of the end of the Third Reich. Since that day the Germans had barely hung on for dear life as slowly it became evident that winning the war was a lost cause. Their morale sank deeper and they became meaner, more hostile, and intolerable.

Perhaps I should mention here that by now any means of communication such as mail and telephone service to private citizens had already been discontinued long ago; i.e., there was no way we could let Aunt Boukje know that by tomorrow Mother and Jan would be knocking at her door. Aunt Boukje and Uncle Jan were sweethearts, though, with hearts as big as this world, and we were convinced that Mother and Jan would be very welcome.

On that blustery, frightful winter day, early in the evening at around six—we had no choice but to ignore curfew time— Mother, Jan, and I set out on foot on our six-mile hike to the train station in Driebergen, located Southwest of Zeist. There was at least one foot and a half of snow on the ground, temperature around zero Fahrenheit, and a 15–20 mile per hour blustering Northeast wind blowing piercingly against our poorly clad bodies as we plodded along through the thick snow carpet.

Actually, the northeast wind against our backs made pulling the sled with mother, and the luggage on her lap, a little easier as we traveled in exactly the opposite southerly direction. It was by a stroke of good luck that at the last moment we discovered in the shed, still hanging from the ceiling, our old sled we kids used to have so much fun with. Without the sled it would have been next to impossible for mother with her problem feet to hike six miles through the snow in the inclement weather.

The burdensome snow-carpet proved to be a blessing and a curse in disguise in our desperate escapade. It was a blessing because its light reflection helped us find our way to Driebergen more easily in the total darkness. The short winter day with no electricity also meant no street lights to guide us, because naturally, it wasn't very often—if ever—that we walked in the depth of winter six miles to a train station. On the other hand, the snow was a curse. Being too much exposed against the snow we were easy targets as trespassers of curfew regulation.

"In case you pass German soldiers"—they most often walked in pairs —"be very courteous to them," Pa advised us. "Wish them 'Einen Guten Abend,' and act as if you have a special permit to be out beyond curfew time. By all means, say no more than asked and necessary." The suggestion was specifically meant for me only because I knew how to speak German. Jan, at seventeen, was advised not to speak a word unless *absolutely* necessary. Incognito, dressed in women's clothing, we reasoned that he would have less chance to be chartered to a German work camp, perhaps never to be seen again. To do the talking was the main reason for me to tag along and see to it that they safely reached the train. Honestly, I admit I was scared to death thinking that I had to walk the whole six miles back to Zeist alone, plodding through the snow on my worn out shoes against the merciless northeast wind.

Even the train trip itself could be very risky, considering the possibilities of train raids for men-hunts. The searches for men to be shipped to German workcamps were held at the most unlikely times and places; if they caught spies or underground allies, they were often fusilladed on the spot and tossed into the fields. There was also the risk of trains to be bombed by the Germans if they suspected underground or spy activities. Like any clandestine activity, its operation always took place in obscurity and so we found our train in total darkness, inside as well as out, waiting in the station and ready to roll. These illegal trains ran only after sun-down and were never allowed to blow the whistle at any time, although this didn't seem to be too much of a concern during curfew time. Needless to say, it was a very somber "Good-bye" when Mother and Jan with sled and luggage boarded the train and felt their way around in the dark. Our mutual thoughts, "When, if at all, would we be together again?" preyed on our minds and was written all over our faces as we waved our last farewell.

On their walk from Leeuwarden to Wirdum they'd have to manage without me. Fortunately, because of the thinly populated area in Friesland, chances of being arrested by German soldiers was less of a concern than in the heavily populated province of Utrecht; anyway, it was a risk they just had to take. In that respect, the horrid weather condition worked in their favor. In the far north flat country of Friesland, where winters always seem more severe than down south, their walk through the desolate, uninhabitable winter landscape would be an even more cumbersome undertaking than our trip to Driebergen in the evening before. They would arrive in Leeuwarden around midnight and have to walk most of the trip to their destination in the dark and coldest time of day. Thank goodness for another favor of Mother Nature's benevolence as again they had the wind at their backs on their ten miles travel southeast to the farm.

The old sled had, indeed, proven to be a life-saver! Without it I cannot imagine how Mother would have been able to walk another ten miles from Leeuwarden to the farm in Wirdum.

"There's no need for you to wait until the train leaves," Mother said as she waved good-bye from the door of the train. However, in this time of uncertainty when anything unexpected can happen anytime, I felt I should wait until the train was out of sight. Furthermore, the knowledge that they were still nearby, even though we couldn't see each other, made me feel less lonely.

The train left precisely at nine o'clock and quickly vanished into oblivion, leaving me with an indescribable sense of loss and gloominess. Life had no meaning the way I saw it. The dreadful war with devastating results of pain, suffering, starvation, and death for men of all walks of life, made absolutely no sense to me; even innocent little children as well as animals were not spared the agony. What's the purpose of being in this stupid world anyway? Why am I here? I didn't ask to come into this valley of tears and strife, and for what? Perhaps I should have jumped in front of the train, I contemplated, but for that it was too late now. So, there I was all by myself, not a soul to be seen in this morbid weather of violent northeast snow squalls dumping more snow on the almost impassable roadway.

In a dazed state of indifference I left the station. The once so cheerfully decorated homes I passed were now dark, grim, lifeless, and even ghostly looking houses without light in the windows and halfway hidden in heaps of snow. Wearily I slowly pushed forward on my trashy shoes while the merciless wind gusts kept cutting through my worn-out coat. The only halfway decent coat I once owned and proudly had managed to preserve all through the first three winters of the war, had been stolen the previous winter, because of my own stupidity, I must add. After I returned from four hours ice-skating, the coat I had hung over a fence and thought was tightly secured with chain and padlock, had been snatched. I couldn't bring up the nerve to tell my parents and managed to keep it a secret until winter '44–'45 arrived with unusual severity. I lost my coat in late February, 1944, and reasoned that the end of the winter would be near and perhaps no one would notice. I was right, nobody noticed! But when winter '44–'45 arrived with a bang I had to tell Pa. On this horrid evening I was fortunate enough to wear a coat my Dad had managed to buy from the Saint Vincent de Paul organization of which he was the administrator. The navy blue wool box coat had shown its age of heavy wear and tear to the point that I had our family friend and tailor, Ferwerd Engwerda, turn the coat inside out. Tailors were quite busy those days turning coats, as it had become almost a custom to have a tailor redo a worn coat if the inside would be still worth it. He would completely rip the coat apart and re-use the pieces inside out. With good pieces to spare he would repair badly worn edges such as around the bottoms of sleeves, pockets and collar. The refurbished coat would then look as good as new with only one difference, the new look-alike coat would button in the opposite direction.

Fortunately, Mother had always kept us in heavy wool hand knit sweaters. However, nothing could withstand this frightful winter blast. With every new wind gust I had to turn around to prevent the bitter wind cutting off my air passages. As I slowly inched ahead, the familiar Volga Song from Franz Lehár's operetta *Der Czarevitch* kept whirling through my mind. The lonesome soldier standing guard in the desolate solitude of the immense snow fields on the banks of the Volga cries out in his loneliness,

> Have you forgotten me, Lord up above?
> I stand here, forsaken by all I love.
> Hear me, O hear me
> And answer my plea.
> Send an angel to earth to comfort me. . . .

and tears began trickling down my icy cheeks. A good thing tears are salty so they wouldn't decorate my face with ice pellets.

The nearer I approached home, the more I began to fantasize how wonderful it would be to be welcomed by mother with hot chocolate and one of my favorite thickly buttered slices of home made currant bread. Happy dreaming indeed! Instead, Mother and Jan sat in the cold, dark freight train wagon, not exactly an enviable place either. Hopefully, Mother will be able to sit on the sled, I contemplated.

It must have been around midnight when I finally arrived home. Numb from the cold I climbed the three flights of stairs to my bedroom, threw my coat and shoes wherever they would land and crawled into bed under a thick wool blanket and the fluffy toasty quilt my mother had made a long time ago. Suddenly, I don't know why and for no good reason, tears kept streaming onto my pillow. Meanwhile, Pa had heard the front door shut and came to find out why I hadn't come first to say "Hello" before I went to bed. He soon discovered that I was totally out of shape, unable to utter a word. He grabbed a terry cloth towel from the rack to cover my pillow, tucked me in and left without a word. After a little while he came back with a hot water bottle in a colorful wool sock my mother had knitted for that purpose, stuffed the bottle in my bed, said "Good-Night" and left quietly.

We did not learn for three weeks how Mother and Jan had fared on their final lap of the unforgettable journey to the farm. On the day of their arrival, when in the far distance slowly the farm came into sight, Aunt Boukje happened to look out of their livingroom window, when she spotted way far out in the distance some indistinguishable figures battling the strong northeast wind and blowing snow, as they trudged through the heavy snow-drifts towards the farm. Again, it was that kind of a day you wouldn't even let the dog out, a blustery day with fierce snow squalls to add more snow to the footage already on the ground. Friesland is so flat and bare that on a clear day one can practically look from one village to the other. However, on this day, with very poor visibility and the distance still too great, the intrepid strangers remained unrecognizable. My Aunt mumbled: "Oh, my God, look at those poor souls stumping along in this atrocious weather," After a while Aunt Boukje looked again. Her mind was probably spinning how she could be of any help to those poor travelers. Meanwhile the two had slowly inched forward bit by bit closer into view. At one point Aunt Boukje called Mieke and said: "Does that tall one look like your brother Jan to you?" While she went to get her binoculars, Mieke kept staring at the tall figure pulling the other one on the sled, but she still couldn't make out whether it was Jan or not. Aunt Boukje came back with her binoculars and now she could clearly see Jan pulling Mother on the sled, and she exclaimed, "Here, look! that *is* Jan pulling Cornelia on the sled," and she handed the binoculars to Mieke who now clearly recognized Mother and Jan on their way to the farm.

Survival of the Fittest: Where Have All The Roses Gone?

With our family cut in half, we would easily fit in the smallest room of the house. Our small office way in back of the store, above the little secret cellar where we hid our underground activities, fit our needs up to a tee. Under the circumstances, it looked like the small office room was the best place to conserve the little bit of heat we managed to acquire from the small emergency burner. In our "new" converted office/living-quarters we sat every night as soon as it turned dark until one or two in the morning until the end of the war and we praised ourselves lucky for at least still being together.

Our tiny emergency nest had for the size of the room, quite a large window facing west onto our big backyard. Three large roll-top desks fit against the north wall with not an inch to spare on the sides. From the desks to the south wall there was about a six foot linoleum covered floor space barely enough for three oakwood captain's chairs and room to move around.

Quite a pity though that the floor wasn't carpeted. It probably would have conserved more heat and would have been warmer to the feet. As it was, we were fortunate to have the little room to serve as our winter burrow. A rack of six bookshelves next to the window covered the south wall to the edge of the three steps stairwell in the center of the wall. Across from the steps was the office entrance. On the east side of the wall was our secret dungeon with the door concealed by a "fit-to-size poster board" which was easy to remove if you knew the trick. Opposite the secret compartment was the door to the archival closet. In the southeast corner of the office was a small anthracite burner, useless for its purpose at this time with no fuel available at any price. During the past four winters we had burned the three linden trees and the one chestnut tree from our backyard which Pa had planted at each one of our birthdays. As I mentioned earlier, we were fortunate to have the unusual treasure of a large backyard in the center of a good-sized city of approximately 65,000 population.

The longer the war lingered on, the more desperate people became, especially for heat and food. In order to keep warm, renters burned up kitchen cabinets, doors, bookcases, books, even floor boards, anything that would provide heat; needless to say, being a landlord was not exactly an enviable position during those days of lawless existence. Wealthy people, who had small lots of pine woods around their homes, had to guard their property day and night against people who kept alert to their living habits in waiting for the right time to steal the pine trees from their property. It wasn't unusual for them to come home from vacation, a weekend outing, or even just a couple of hours, to find their pine woods completely bare except for only the tree stumps. A neighborhood of men would plan the theft project to the minute details before the right moment to strike. They would cut down the trees with utmost efficiency in the minimum amount of time. Kees Aben, the fuel dealer, was usually involved because he had the perfect vehicle to haul the trees; in normal times the large cart-wagon was used for hauling coal and anthracite.

The Duiker property became target on one of those tree theft expeditions, and when the family came home late on that one particular night, they found all their pine trees disappeared; in a span of just two hours' time twelve men had cut down about 35 pine trees, and cut them in size to fit the cart-wagon. At least twelve men were needed to pull the heavy wagon because horses, which normally would do that type of work, were no longer available for lack of food and were only kept on farms. Motorized vehicles were out of the question already since the early war years as any oil products were only to be used for the Wehrmacht.

Often thieves would leave an envelope with money plus a "thank you" note for the items they had swiped away. In the same fashion, during the early war years, even iron plates and manhole covers, which people used on top of their improvised home built brick stoves, disappeared. Stealing iron plates after dark was a treacherous practice, though, especially for early morning pedestrians walking to their businesses and unaware of danger; they could easily fall into a hole. Other scavenger hunters were more considerate and covered the hole with wooden boards. On one occasion, someone had taken a manhole cover from in front of the large historical mansion named "Pavia," then occupied by the Germans; everyone rejoiced though when it was learned that a couple of Germans had stumbled into the hole.

In the later war years, when even the home built stoves became useless when fuel became unavailable, someone had invented the so-called emergency burner the size of a medium size crockpot; they sold like magic with demand greatly surpassing the supply. In the Fall of 1944, while we were on the waiting list for our emergency burner, Pa and Rients decided to burn up all old store records to manufacture our own fuel. Pa said: "After the war if, by the grace of God, we're still alive, we'll start from scratch, forget the past and wipe out the memories of bad debts." The huge mountain of 25 years of business records we soaked in water in large laundry tubs. Rients had learned from a friend how to transform the mass of paper into balls fit to burn like coal and that would last just as long in our emergency burner. Besides providing heat, we cooked and simmered the legumes we had acquired from the farm, boiled water for tea and for the hot water bottles we took to bed.

With cooking by the improvised methods all during the war years, cooking pots, not made for this type of cooking, rapidly wore out and eventually replacements were no longer available. That's when a new business of pot repair shops popped up. These repair people filled the holes with plugs until at last the pot was totally beyond repair and had to be trashed.

Like everyone else, we learned to be very conservative in using our paper balls in the little emergency burner; we waited as long as possible to light the burner, i.e., we waited until dark before we settled down for the evening, and waited for the burner to be cold before we ventured out on our trip to our bedrooms after we had used our backyard for a bathroom facility. Because of the heavy frost and no heat in the house Pa had the water shut off at the underground valve. None of us looked forward to the long nightly trip through the spooky, cold, practically empty, dark store, through the squeaky sliding doors up the three flights of stairs to our bedrooms. My bedroom was in the attic on the third floor, above our dry goods store, and a small skylight in the slanted slate roof was the only source of light. My pretty lamps were useless ever since the Fall of 1944 when electric service was discontinued to private citizens, and only available to German headquarters, some hospitals and all institutions that operated under German orders. By the way, gas supply had already been unavailable since the early war years. We all had a self-generating flashlight called "squeeze cat" (*knijpkat* in Dutch) to guide us around in the dark. People were very ingenious in those days in figuring out substitutes wherever possible to make our lives more tolerable; however, towards the end of the war even surrogates were no longer available because of lack of ingredients. The "cats" generated a dim light by a thumb rhythmically squeezing a lever. The candles we still had around we were unable to use as we needed to save the matches we still had available for the emergency burner.

In order to have some light in our little room, Rients had fabricated a light fixture from an old bicycle wheel chain and treadle. It operated like the old-fashioned treadle sewing machine before the electric sewing machine was invented. We took turns operating the treadle to generate enough light for the operator to read a book while the rest of us ate the legumes, drank linden blossom tea from our trees in memoriam, or held conversations in the faint glow of the light. Sometimes the light operator read the book aloud in order to entertain all three of us. As mentioned earlier, newspapers and magazines were just memories of better times in history. Fortunately the library was still open, although all books were closely scrutinized by German officials and banned if they contained anything against National Socialism and the new German Government. When gradually the light diminished it was a sign that the operator's leg and foot were tired and time for changing shifts. It was during that time when I learned how to play the harmonica.

Unlike the rest of my family, except for my mother who had a beautiful singing voice, I was the only one musically inclined. I loved to sing and would have loved learning to play the piano. However, unfortunate circumstances, as a result of the Depression and mother's illness, investing in a piano and piano lessons were out of the question luxuries. I also loved an accordion as well as wind instruments such as a flute and a harmonica. When one day I saw an old harmonica for trade-in, I decided to give up one of my dolls in favor of an old beat-up Hohner harmonica. It took several weeks of daily practice on my own when finally I got the drift of it. Since then I have gradually acquired a sizable repertoire of songs I know how to play and sometimes play for other people at their parties.

Most often it was well after one o'clock in the morning when we finally called it a day. We stayed in bed at least until noon to keep warm and use the least energy in our efforts for survival. Only the person designated to stand in line for the soup kitchen had to get up earlier. The soup distribution usually started at noon. The stuff had to be eaten as soon as it arrived; it was worse than taking medicine. The best way to deal with it was to gulp it down without tasting it while it was still warm. There was no way to re-heat it, and if there had been, it probably would have tasted even more repugnant. The rest of the afternoon until dark we moved around during the time the store was open for a couple of hours. Even though there wasn't much of any business to expect in the store, often people came in just to talk and discuss the daily state of affairs.

Survival of the Fittest:
Yes, Please, Squeeze Us In

It was the end of January 1945 and the food supply Aunt Agatha and I had fetched from the farm in late Fall 1944 was pretty well depleted. Although everyone was convinced that the war couldn't last much longer, the big question mark was "How long yet?" Even if the war would end soon, by now the country was so severely robbed of even the bare essentials that it would take time before life would return to the merest form of normality. And so, we decided on another bike trip to the farm in Wirdum. Pa thought it would be too risky for Aunt Agatha at age 60 to make the rugged bike trip to Friesland in the unusual severe winter weather, although the horrendous winter storms we had endured during the past two weeks had finally tapered down to pleasant winter weather with more tolerable temperatures of above twenty degrees Fahrenheit. The sun was getting stronger and had melted the ice on roadways a bit. Since traffic was almost at a standstill, except for German military vehicless, delivery trucks for institutions that worked for the German Government and the like, the roads covered with ice and snow caked onto its surfaces remained extremely treacherous, especially for bike traveling, and although we enjoyed the warmth of the sun, actually the little bit of surface thaw the sun produced made the roads even more slippery. I imagine that Aunt Agatha's soul jubilated with a sigh of relief when she was out-voted for the trip. Rients worked for the underground allied forces and was automatically out-voted which left Pa and myself as the chosen ones for the job. For me to go alone didn't appeal to any of us, especially me. And since the Germans were mainly interested in young men, Pa felt he could take the chance to go with me. Fortunately, Aunt Agatha's bicycle still had rubber tires, and since my bike had wooden tires which might be too dangerous considering the slick road conditions, she generously offered hers for my use. In our family only Pa's bicycle still had rubber tires mainly because he didn't ride his bike as often as us kids did.

On a very cold but bright sunny day in late January Pa and I set out on our food mission. We had on our bikes what were called handcaps that were lined with rabbit fur and had a sock-like tube inside that slid over the handle bars. The handcaps would keep the wind off hands and indeed, they kept gloved hands toasty warm. Any bike rider will agree that cold hands is the worst winter biking dilemma. We also made sure to have our repair kit with us in case of a flat tire. Fixing flats was usually my job; through the years I had become quite proficient at it. However in these frigid temperatures it wasn't the job I'd look foward to. We planned to start out at daybreak to have the whole day ahead of us and more daylight in case something unforeseen should happen. With smooth roads the trip would take approximately ten hours' travel time to ride the 125 miles from Zeist to the farm in Wirdum; however, with the unfavorable road conditions our pace might be much slower. The night before I had made some sandwiches from our weekly bread ration; in between the slices I had smeared the "refried" beans cooked on our emergency stove the night before. The bread was hardly edible and was sarcastically called "peatloaf", but at least the beans made the whole a bit more nutritious. The beautiful goudreinette apples from the crate we were able to buy from a farmer customer last October would at least taste wonderful to offset the "peatloaf" beanspread sandwiches.

We left in good spirits at eight o'clock in the morning after we had promised Aunt Agatha and Rients to be back home in about a week. The weather and especially the wind were in our favor the entire trip. Even though we had to travel part of the trip during curfew time, luckily we didn't meet any dangerous situations, and amazingly we made very good time as we reached our destination within twelve hours' ride. Again, the unavailability of communication meant that we were unable to contact Aunt Boukje and Uncle Jan ahead of time to ask if our visit would be convenient to them and to discuss an approximate time of arrival; instead, there we were, unannounced, knocking at their door at eight o'clock at night.

It was indeed such a wonderful treat to be with our family for a week in almost normal conditions, where the war hadn't changed life as dramatically as in the cities, except for their working under constant watch of the German Government and, of course, the fear of young men being taken away to work-camps. There was that appealing feeling of warmth we had missed for so long in our small nest in Zeist. In the fireplace were large orangey-red burning logs of wood that crackled and sparkled like music to our ears, and a lovely scent of burning wood spread through the room where we sat by lamp-light enjoying dinner from a table of plenty.

Recovered from our dismal existence in Zeist after a week of rest and plenty, we were ready for our return bike-trip home. Farmers, like mariners, depend solely on weather conditions for their successful operations and consequently, they know the weather like the back of their hands. We'd been lucky with the weather on our way up when we had relied on our intuition, but, especially with our bikes loaded to capacity, the weather was extremely important for our return trip to Zeist, and so, we trusted

Uncle Jan's expert weather advice over our own intuition when he suggested the best time for us to leave. The horrific snowstorm of three weeks ago that swept through the country during Mother and Jan's incredible journey to the farm, was forever imprinted in our memories, and to undertake a bike-trip in such weather conditions would be downright foolish.

Early morning February 2nd, 1945. Our bicycles were heavily loaded with bags filled with legumes, dried fruits, nuts, and seeds; plus large hunks of ham, bacon, and butter; anything that packed well with the most volume and the least amount of weight. It all had to fit in our canvas side bags hanging from the carriers along the back wheels of our bikes, and on top of the carriers we had tied our burlap bags, also filled to capacity, including the delicious sandwiches Aunt Boukje had prepared for us plus thermos bottles of milk to last during our trip home. Indeed, regardless of the freezing temperature, it promised to be a great day just like Uncle Jan had predicted, with the sun brightly shining in an Adriatic blue sky on a glistening winter wonderland. I checked the tires, considering the heavily loaded bikes on slippery roads made correct air pressure most crucial. I made sure that all our baggage was tightly secured on the bike carriers; then I took the short-cut through the cow stable to the house to tell Pa that we were ready for take off, to say "Goodbye" to Mother, Mieke and Jan, and the whole Hettinga family and to thank them once more for their great hospitality and all they had done for us.

Walking from the bright sunshine into the stable was blinding for a moment, but I knew enough to walk as close as possible to the left wall of the stable, because opposite on the right side of me were perhaps 75 cows, each standing in her own stall facing the wall with small windows; i.e. their derrières were facing the left wall; behind them was a foot deep trench for waste drain-off, and alongside the trench was the foot path wide enough to pull a cart.

While I walked the long cement path to the house, with my eyes not quite adjusted from the bright outside light, I suddenly felt a warm stream running over the right side of my body, even though I had walked as cautiously and as close as possible alongside the wall opposite the cows. From head to toe I was covered with cow poop; I couldn't believe cows could spout that far. I knocked at the kitchen door, but nobody paid any attention, and why should they? The inside door was never locked and I knew the way. Finally I knocked harder and yelled for help, because naturally, I wasn't about to go into the house dripping with cow poop. When at last they opened the door they couldn't believe their eyes at the sight of me and burst out laughing. My unsightly appearance was accompanied by the obnoxious smell like rotten potatoes. Almost in chorus they all commented, "Don't you know that you must hurry out of the way when you see a tail go up?" No matter how I tried to convince them that I had walked close to the wall, I even insisted to show them the spot of evidence of how far the poop had splashed down, but all my efforts to justify myself were to no avail, and I remained the laughing-stock for the next couple of days.

I never felt more embarrassed in my life as I walked for two days in a borrowed terry cloth bathrobe which was at least four sizes too big, but to remedy the problem I'd gathered the extra cloth together in the waist with a rope. The pearl-grey wool gabardine coat I had borrowed from Mieke's closet, which normally should be dry cleaned, had to be washed, and being wool and winter, it took about two days to dry. Even though we got the coat clean, eventually we had to dye the coat because of the stubborn faint beige discolored spots that wouldn't budge, and even though my underwear was spared from the poop, the smell had penetrated through all my clothes to my body, i.e. everything had to be washed. By the time it was decided how to deal with the problem may be half an hour had passed, giving more time for the stuff to cake to my body and transfer the scent onto my skin. Perhaps the speed and force of the impact made the stuff penetrate and settle into the material.

Understandably, the event had thrown a monkey wrench into our travel plan for that day and even the next two days. The hilarity wouldn't stop until it was time for Pa and me to go back home. It was a bad situation all the way around, especially for Aunt Agatha and Rients back in Zeist who would be worried about us—and there was no way to let them know of our delay for several days.

February 5th, 1945. Again, the weather angels played in our favor by treating us with another beautiful bright sun splashed morning, and the good news, Uncle Jan had predicted that the weather would be stable for a couple more days. Aunt Boukje had made a new batch of delicious sandwiches for us, our bikes were ready and so were we. Once more we expressed our last praises of "Thanks much for everything. Goodbye. So long. Have a safe trip"—waving hankies, throwing kisses, and off we were on our trip home.

Again, like in late fall when Aunt Agatha and I had taken the trip to the farm, we were strongly advised not to cross the IJssel via Kampen bridge. Instead, we were told we should try to find a farmer who was willing to row us to the other side. It was well known in the area that the Germans had become meaner than hornets, now that the war was running to its end which meant an end to their elusive dream of the Third Reich. Realizing the unpredictability of what might happen in the hands of the Germans, we heeded the advice not to take a chance on the bridge this time. Instead we took a detour to Zwolle and from there on we would start looking for a way across the IJssel.

While riding the 60 miles to Zwolle, Pa's brain kept spinning around and at one point he said: "You know what? I have an old buddy from my bachelor's days in The Hague who lives in Zwolle. Perhaps we should find out his address in a phone book and since there's no way we can call him we'll just have to stop by his house. I have a strong feeling that he may have a clue as to where we might find a farmer who'd row us to the other side of the IJssel." It was a great idea because one never knew, in those days, who could be trusted on our wild goose chase to find a farmer with a ferryboat. Not all farmers were necessarily created equal, in philosophy that is. The detour would take a lot of our precious time. In the end we'd gain time not having to search for passage across the IJssel but could ride directly to the appointed address. In the public library, with help from the librarian, we quickly located the Van Giezen family and in no time at all we were on our way to their home.

Naturally, the Van Giezens were almost thunderstruck when they opened the door in response to our timid knock; barging in unannounced ordinarily was not our style. They stared at us in disbelief. I was a total stranger to them; in fact I'd never even been in Zwolle. Pa and Meneer Van Giezen hadn't seen each other in perhaps twenty years. Both of them ran their own businesses and raised their families in different cities too far away to keep close contact in a time when the major modes of transportation were buses, trains, or bicycles, and *pedus apostolorum*. Before the war deliveries were done by bike-carts, even dog-carts; only large companies and government institutions had the luxury use of de-livery trucks.

Recovered from the initial surprise, they invited us in for tea. Meneer Van Giezen was a person of medium stature and average height, 5′7″ or 8″, with dark brown hair combed back from his high forehead. What I still vividly remember of him, even after almost fifty years, is his magnetic personality that radiated from his whole being so that should I unexpectedly meet him today, I would immediately recognize him. I remember Mevrouw Van Giezen as a very friendly lady of no pretense, matter-of-fact yet with a calm personality, more like the Barbara Bush type: "What you see is what you get." Even in stature I could easily compare her with Barbara Bush, although after so many years I doubt if I would recognize her, as I would her husband.

Meneer Van Giezen and Pa picked up their conversation as if there hadn't been a lapse of time, and I got along with Mevrouw van Giezen and their kids famously. When it came to asking the cardinal question: "Would they know of a farmer we could trust, who'd be willing to ferry us across the IJssel, we'd guessed right; they knew exactly where to go. Immediately, a road map was spread out on the table and on a piece of note paper Mevrouw Van Giezen wrote down the directions to the farm in Wijhe which Meneer Van Giezen pointed out to us. He said, "It'll be about 10 miles distance from Zwolle which amounts to approximately an hour's bike ride. This will give you plenty of time to get ready in the morning because you're going to stay here overnight," both announced in unison. "That is, if you don't mind to be squeezed in," added Mevrouw Van Giezen. The Van Giezen's had nine children which explained the squeeze method. "We'll be delighted to have you stay," emphasized Mevrouw Van Giezen as she noticed our puzzled faces. Of course, we didn't mind to be squeezed in; actually, what does one expect with a large family counting eleven heads? And above all, we'd just barged in. This hadn't been our plan and was beyond our expectation, but Meneer Van Giezen explained that since it was already late in the afternoon, it would be better to see the particular farmer he had in mind tomorrow by midmorning. And so, in this difficult time of war and deprivation, they shared with us their food and their home for our overnight lodging. Their hospitality was phenomenal. Mevrouw Van Giezen pointed out to us, as she read the uneasiness on our faces when it was time for supper, "Where there's food for eleven there's always enough for one or two more." Pa whispered to me, "Should we give them some of our food provisions?" and upon our insistence they graciously accepted some of our goodies.

The Van Giezen's were as fortunate as we to have farm family where they periodically could go for additional food supply, although their families were closer within their own vicinity. Overall, the Zwolle area was a little better, survival wise, not as congested as the overpopulated province of Utrecht and the city of Zeist where we lived. I guess with more farms around there's also more food to go around.

It turned out to be an unforgettable evening of good conversation and laughter as we talked about our families, our status of living, and of course, the war, all by candlelight and the now popular and famous emergency stove. The men had a great time rehashing the old Hague days as they rekindled the old friendship of their bachelor's days. And so, the couple of hours' detour proved to be well worth the effort all the way around, and although we'd never visited the Van Giezen's in Zwolle before, we all felt right at home with each other. We will always remember the Van Giezens as a lovely family with a heart as big as the world.

February 6th, 1945. We left the Van Giezens at about ten o'clock the next morning, filled with hopes and promises to keep in contact with future get-togethers which, sadly enough, never materialized. Uncle Jan had been right again. Another gorgeous day, moderately cold, but bright sunshine smiled on the friendly city of Zwolle we were leaving behind us, as we peddled on our way to the farmer with the ferryboat in Wijhe, Overijssel. It was a pleasant trip riding along the meandering IJssel River which was kept open with ice-breakers for through way ship traffic, and the road alongside the river was fairly good to travel. With help from the map Mevrouw van Giezen had drawn up for us we found the farmer with the ferry boat without any problem and around midday the farmer had safely landed us on the opposite riverbank of the IJssel.

There we were, landed on someone's farmland somewhere in nowhere with no paved road in sight. We managed, after twirling and twisting while walking our loaded bikes through the uneven, scrubby landscape for perhaps half an hour, until finally we reached a paved roadway. Road signs, including bicycle path directions, are very good in Holland and as soon as we'd struggled our way out of the farmland, we had no problem finding a bike path through the woods and heather fields. We noticed that those bike-paths were actually easier to ride than the paved roads we'd been riding on our way up. Because of the trees those bike paths weren't so heavily packed with snow, less traveled and consequently less slippery.

In the pine woods near Epe, at a four way bike path crossing, we had our lunch. It was an ideal spot where the sun had melted most of the snow and little appropriately called snowbells—Holland's earliest Spring flowers—popped up their pretty little heads all around us. It was, in fact, as I remember, even warm enough to shed our coats and let the warmth of the sun treat our backs instead.

I always enjoyed my outings with Pa. He was a man of few words but we could sit together for a long while in silence and yet, we both would feel the unity of our thoughts. The solitude in the woods was so peaceful, even spellbinding in the midst of the tumultuous world. The sun shining on the little flowers amid the snow patches, the sound of chirping and whistling birds, little animals playfully chasing each other, occasional breezes sweeping through the high firs, the distant barking of a dog; it was the symphony of nature at its best. For a moment it became difficult to remember the purpose—why we were sitting in these woods in the first place. On the other side of the spectrum, there was the war . . . the senseless slaughter going on by the so-called highest intelligent creature on earth—man! With his creative mind and energy, busy and industrious like the ant, man—often driven mostly by his distorted thoughts on religious convictions and philosophies—destructs his own realm of being.

"We sit here but we don't live here. Are you ready to go on?" It was Pa who called me out of my reverie into reality. We both hated to leave that beautiful peaceful part of nature. It was about three-thirty in the afternoon and already it had started to feel a bit cooler. We had about a six to seven hour ride ahead of us, depending on the road conditions, before we would reach Zeist. In two hours it would be dark and more dangerous for bike-riding, especially with our heavily loaded)bicycles, although after Nijkerk we would be in more familiar territory.

At around seven we were in Nijkerk. It was already an hour past curfew time, when Pa popped the three-point question: "Are you tired? Should we look for overnight lodging? Or should we take a chance on ignoring curfew completely and just go on home"? I opted for the final question because looking for a place after curfew time would scare the wits out of any one. Furthermore, I said: "Hey look, we're lucky, it's full moon tonight so we even have some liglit to guide us. Let's take a chance and go on home."

We had smooth sailing all the way to Zeist. We met several German bikers who were very friendly, saying "Hello," and so were we. Especially if you spoke in German to them they seemed less concerned whether you were entitled to be out after curfew time or not. It also could be military fatigue as at that time it was generally believed that the war was running to its end with the Third Reich forever to remain an illusion.

The bright moonlight was indeed a big help to guide us home safely. At about ten at night we knocked at our front door. It scared the wits out of Aunt Agatha, because she and Rients didn't expect us after curfew time. Quickly she helped Rients into his roll of linoleum, a fake roll in our display window we had kept for a hiding-place in case of a raid, and like a scared rabbit she looked through the peep-hole to see who'd be at the other side of the door. With a great sigh of relief she opened the door when she saw that it was just Pa and me, exhausted but happy to be home again and ready to settle in for the night.

Survival of the Fittest: Manna From Heaven

Our food mission had been a successful trip, and food-wise we were once again all set for the next couple of months. However, many people weren't as lucky and what people did for food in the last stages of the war ranged from the incredible to the insane.

Zeist, like any other city north of the great rivers, Rijn and Maas that run from the east to spill out into the North Sea on the west coast near Rotterdam—not yet liberated on Tuesday, September 5th, like the rest of Holland—looked like a ghost town. Businesses still operating on a semi-regular basis were service enterprises like barbers, tailors, cobblers, etc. Clothing and furniture stores were practically empty and the stuff that was available was of such inferior quality that nobody wanted to spend their money on it except in dire necessity. These stores were open for business only a few hours per day just to keep in touch with customers and mainly to discuss and update on war events. Many factories lay still because of lack of materials; dry goods were hard to come by.

Butcher shops were closed; the butchers worked for the Germans. Other businesses in the food line were open only on coupon days in order to accommodate the public with their food rations.

Once a week people were allowed to pick up their rations of small loaves of bread that scarcely deserved the name of bread. In fact, on those so-called "bread" days, instead of the delicious scents pouring out of bakeries we were so used to from before the war, the smells from these indeterminable substances coming from the bakery were repugnant. Even the bakers themselves didn't know the substance of what they were baking since the stuff came delivered from the German Government. If anyone had told us in those days that we were indeed eating peat loaf we would have believed it; at any rate, it was a far cry from manna.

However, in this time of great need, distress and starvation, heartless greedy store owners managed to take advantage of the unfortunate situation by dealing and raking in millions via the black market. Pa could have done likewise but his noble character disagreed with benefitting in self-service to accommodate the few rich in the black market at the price of the remaining suffering world in their agonizing struggle for survival. He stuck to his philosophy that a clear conscience in the knowledge of having done the right thing is easier to live with than any accumulation of black money acquired from the backs of the poor.

If there's one good thing to be said about those trying times it is the way it brought us all together. There was unity in our goals and ways of thinking. All diversity in religion and social standards from before the war were dissolved into humanism. Our goals were survival and the keeping of our identity. In unison we struggled for survival while our goal was to take back our country.

Towards the final stage of World War II, in early 1945, many people just collapsed and died in the streets; many were unable to withstand the severity of the record cold winter of 44/45 while being exhausted already from starvation. The large supply of tulip bulbs still available became wholesome food for many; that is, if one had knowledge of how to carefully avoid the highly poisonous pit deeply imbedded in the center of the bulb. Cats and dogs disappeared in large numbers to be consumed for meat.

One evening in the Fall of 1944 Pa, and the same bunch of men who on an earlier date had chopped down Mr. Duiker's pine woods next to his house, discussed this time a food mission to take place in the wee hours of the next morning. By full moon the gang would pick potatoes from a field of a German occupied farm near Odijk, about five miles west of Zeist. Even though I realized the seriousness of the time, I was still a teenager and by nature always ready for adventure. So, I begged Pa to include me in the excursion. It would be such a thrill, I thought, to write in my journal, "Today I picked potatoes with Pa in the moonlight!" However, Pa wouldn't hear of it. Under no circumstances would he let his daughter pick potatoes with a bunch of guys at three o'clock in the morning. "All I'm good for is to peel the stupid things," I grumbled. No matter how I pleaded, Pa wouldn't budge.

To solve the food shortage problem the Germans applied their own radical methods. By the end of W. W. II the mental institution in Den Dolder about ten miles north-east from Zeist was practically empty, as during the war-years its patients were gradually exterminated. During the war years it was also generally believed in Holland that the terminally ill in hospitals, the mentally ill in insane asylums, as well as prison inmates, who mysteriously had disappeared, were systematically executed.

On February the 7th, the day after Pa and I had returned from our food mission to Friesland, Aunt Agatha said suspensefully to Pa and me, "Not in your wildest imagination would you be able to guess what happened here last week on Nooitgedacht." Nooitgedacht is a street that runs three blocks south and parallel to the Voorheuvel where we lived. (By the way, Voorheuvel means "before the hill." Nooitgedacht is also the name of Holland's famous skates manufacturer—which factory, of course, lay also dormant at that time. Literally translated the name Nooitgedacht means "never thought of" and as it so happened, the incredible event Aunt Agatha told us made the name Nooitgedacht fit to a tee.)

On one bitter cold night in late January Mr. Oremus from Nooitgedacht had set the stage for his difficult operation to illegally slaughter a cow. He had prepared a heavy rope to tie around the cow's legs with the necessary knots he probably remembered to make from his marine days, and a razor sharp butcher knife lay ready on the kitchen counter. He carefully had thought out the procedure at length and breadth and felt he was ready for action. However, one thing hadn't dawned on him, that he wasn't dealing with an inanimate object but rather a creature with emotions and feelings of physical pain. Mr. Oremus had ordered his wife to take their four kids outside until his operation was completed and for this special purpose there was no other way than to take a chance and ignore the curfew ordinance.

At eight o'clock he left on foot for his mission to steal a cow at the nearby farm he had selected, approximately 3 miles west of Zeist. Another heavy rope, which was to serve as a leash, swung back and forth from the right pocket of his jacket on the rhythm of his hasty steps over the crunching snow. All went according to plan and around 10 o'clock the frightened cow filled the medium size Oremus kitchen. Next Mr. Oremus noosed the affrighted animal who squeaked in surprise. He tied the rope tightly around the cow's feet, then he pulled and jerked and struggled in order to get the terrified animal to lie down on the linoleum covered kitchen floor. Fortunately for Mr. Oremus the slippery linoleum floor helped him to make the cow slide. She lost her footing, and while crying of rage which turned to long-drawn out cries of despair, the cow smacked down on her side on the floor kicking her feet in all directions in her efforts to get up. Mr. Oremus realized that he had to act very quickly in killing the cow before the neighbors would be alarmed at the piercing noises of the anguished animal that might penetrate through the walls. So, he grabbed the knife and proceeded with brusque back and forth movements like a saw to cut into the neck of the cow who soon bled profusely, splashing and splattering blood in any direction all over the kitchen. With her tied legs the tortured creature wildly kicked the kitchen cabinets into splinters and screamed at the top of her lungs as she fought for her life and her freedom. It made Mr. Oremus's mission next to impossible to complete. He broke out in a sweat, became extremely nervous and began to swear like a trooper. In afterthought he wished he had confided in his good friend Harry who surely would have been willing to help him in this grotesque task. He'd thought of it, but decided that to keep it secret would be the safest way not to get caught and this way it would mean more meat for his own family rather than sharing it with someone else. By now the kitchen had begun to look like a war zone with blood dripping from the ceiling and pouring along the walls and the demolished kitchen cabinets.

Meanwhile, alarmed by the desperate cries from an animal in distress, neighbors had come out to investigate the matter only to find Mrs. Oremus outside with the kids, shivering from the cold while parading back and forth in front of their house. Through their tears they told them what was going on inside. Without even consulting Mr. Oremus, one of them walked straight to Mr. Haks, a butcher about a block and a half away from the Oremus residence, to ask for help. Mr. Haks came immediately to relieve the wretched cow from her misery. He finished off the cow and the meat was divided in the neighborhood. All the neighbors agreed that to report the incident to the police would result in that all the meat would end up in the hands of the Germans and Mr. Oremus would most likely be sent to a German work camp. Even though Mr. Oremus had committed a serious crime, his intentions had solely been for the survival of his family and everyone felt that his family didn't deserve to be put in jeopardy and the case was hush-hushed into oblivion.

Three months later, on Sunday April 29, 1945, it rained manna in the still occupied part of Holland! The allied bombers, under command of General Eisenhower, were dropping food packages on designated dropping zones that were marked in the center with a white cross. Green light fired from the ground would indicate safe, and red would mean danger. The week and weeks that followed were unforgettable feasts. The delicious scents that once again poured out of the bakeries caressed everyone's nostrils into memories of past times. With broad smiles on their faces people hugged their treasures of multiple loaves of real bread under their arms and nobody cared that the baker had no bags or paper to wrap around the loaves. The sight of all those smiling happy faces left an indelible imprint on my memory. Real bread with real butter and cheese . . . what a feast! Not the richest, most scrumptious cake could ever compare to that first delicious piece of bread. Rotterdam, so scandalously bombed for no good reason in May 1940 now welcomed allied bombers dropping manna from heaven.

LOUISE TIMMONS

I was born on June 29, 1926, to Catherine Chapman and Charles Malaney, the youngest of three children. I attended St. John Academy for twelve years in Jackson, graduating in 1944. I then attended Jackson Community College for a short time. Since my father was dying of cancer at the time, I quit school to go to work as my family needed the money.

When the war was over and the young men returned from service I met and married Herbert Timmons and moved to Detroit. Tim finished his business degree at the University of Detroit while I gave birth to our first child, Patrick. We had four more children over the next twelve years. When our youngest daughter was three, I returned to school.

Taking one class at a time in the evening I received my bachelor's degree in Religious Studies from Mercy College eleven years later. Following my husband's early retirement from teaching because of health conditions, I obtained a position as a religious education coordinator in a parish in Farmington, Michigan. It was during my tenure there that I worked on my master's degree in Pastoral Ministry at Marygrove College. I completed that at age 62.

After my husband died in 1990, I worked one more year before I retired. I have since remarried. I spend time writing, quilting, and enjoying my children, my nine grandchildren and my new husband. We have homes in Michigan and Florida.

A Day in the Life
of a Postulant

All signs pointed to the convent.
A strong faith,
Love of God,
The "teacher" in me.
Affirmation from Mother, Father,
 Grandma Chapman, Aunt Louise,
 teachers, friends.
I entered as a postulant.

What was it like?
Lonely, in spite of the crowd.
No privacy.
Hot and humid.
Heavy dark clothes.
Confining.
A place to escape from.

A bell rang at 5:00 a.m.
I had a corner bed in a dorm
 for twenty-four young women.

I reached for my clothes,
 black pleated skirt, black cotton shirt,
 short black cape, black cap, black stockings
 black oxfords, underwear.
I made my bed, brushed my teeth
 and left for chapel.

Now there was an unexpected sight!
I had never been around novices before
    with their blue habits, white veils—
Women who had spent a certain number
    of months preparing to be "received."
Fifty of them with their arms extended,
    praying.
For some reason it frightened me.
Except for chapel time they walked
    around with eyes cast down, hands folded.

There were professed sisters.
Hundreds of them.
Women who had taken temporary
    or permanent vows.
Poverty, chastity, obedience.
You knew them by their blue habits
    and black veils.
Besides Aunt Louise, others from my home town,
    there were former teachers,
    fifteen or twenty of them,
All at the Mother House for the summer.
But I could not visit with them.
Talking to professed sisters was discouraged.

After Mass the postulants and novices
    hurried from chapel to refectory.
We set tables and served food
    to the professed sisters.
Then we ate our meal.
A ritual repeated three times a day.
After cleaning up we met with Sister Mary David,
    mistress of postulants.
We had a brief social period
    before hearing of the day's schedule.

A ninety minute French lesson at ten,
Punctuated by a break with ice-cold milk
    and homemade cookies.
I gained six pounds in eight weeks!
Back to the refectory to set up for lunch.
Afternoon meant calligraphy lesson,
    free time to write home,
    or take a walk on the grounds,
    study time, prayer at four,
Then back to the refectory.

The postulants gathered in a circle
    outside following dinner
To do hand sewing, play a game, take a walk.
But always together.
Special relationships or pairing off
    were discouraged.
During the outdoor time mosquitoes
    buzzed around and hid under our skirts and capes.

While we were preparing for bed
    they were freed to buzz in our ears
    and bite us during the night.
Citronella-soaked rags pinned to our headboards
    were meant to discourage them.

After prayers and after a shower
    and once in our night-clothes,
    we washed out our underwear
    and hung it on drying racks on the third floor.
It was here that I looked out at the night sky and asked,
"What am I doing here?"

Two months later I went home.

Turning Point

"I loved going to school!"

That's what I said to my granddaughter, Katy, recently. And I always did. From kindergarten at Bloomfield School on Michigan Avenue, to St. John School on Cooper Street, grades one through twelve, to Junior College on Wildwood—all in Jackson, Michigan. But when I was nineteen my schooling came to an abrupt halt. My sister had graduated from Marygrove College with a teaching certificate and my brother had earned a degree in dentistry at the University of Detroit. But when my turn came, my father was dying of cancer and there was no money.

My father's death and my having to quit school were turning points in themselves, of course. But the one I wish to tell about here came many years later. After a series of office jobs—all good experiences for me—and after Tim and I met and realized we were meant to be together, we married and began our family. Our first four children were born two and a half years apart. Then there was four years before our fifth and last. I was a busy and productive person all those years, happy and content much of the time, but there was always something missing. A nagging lack of fulfillment.

When our oldest son was fifteen and our youngest child was three, we rented a cottage at Pleasant Lake near Jackson for a little vacation. As Tim and I walked along the beach one day we could hear the children arguing from the upstairs porch. I started to cry. Surprised, Tim insisted that I talk about my feelings. I am not sure what words I used, but I conveyed the message that I needed an outlet, something beyond my present state.

Tim said, "Like what?"

"I want to go back to school," came out of my mouth.

And he said, "Then you will!"

It wasn't quite that simple. I was so naive that I did not think I could pass an admissions exam for a nearby community college. So Tim brought home an SAT exam from the school where he was a counselor, and sitting at the dining room table I filled in all the blanks! I did not know how smart I was! I thought my mind had been on leave all those child-raising years. I thought I had not learned anything during that time. Was I surprised!

When I finally went to the community college for my entrance exam I remember the group's being asked to write about that old standard, "Tell about what you did last summer." I began to write and the words just poured out of me. At some point I stopped for a second and looked up and the 18-year-old young man sitting across the table was staring at me. I glanced down at his blank paper and asked him what the problem was. He said he could not think of anything to write. That was an eye-opener for me. There was not enough time or paper to write all that I had to tell. We do learn from experience!

Because we had only one car I registered for an evening English class on Tuesday night from 6:30 to 9:00. I remember the instructor, some of the students, even the classrooms. It was thrilling! My fifteen hours at Jackson Jr. College were as good as gold. I embarked on a Liberal Arts course. My problem was that each semester I had to decide what course to take. Every one offered had its appeal. I went from English to Sociology to Child Psychology to Speech (one of my favorites) to Biology to Children's Literature. After nearly every class I declared the one I had just finished was my favorite. Six years passed. By then I had accumulated 56 hours of credit. It was during this time that several people asked me what I was going to do with my education. I had never even considered this before. I remember answering matter-of-factly, "I'm going to live with it!".

By now, Kitty was in school full-time, Tim was promoted to administration in downtown Detroit and we could afford a second car. Meaning, of course, that I could now go to school days. The next step was choosing where to go. It was around this time that Sr. Mary Lou Putrow, a teacher at the parish we belonged to, offered a six session course on some aspect of faith which sounded interesting. I soon realized that the purpose of the course was to lure adults into teaching religion to the children of the parish. I went to Mary Lou and told her that I was interested in her course but that I had no intention of teaching religion, and asked if that would be a problem. She said no and I finished the course. By the time the end came I had volunteered to teach second grade the next semester! That experience pointed me in the direction I was to take.

It was soon after this episode that I enrolled at Mercy College in Detroit. Again I tended to pick and choose, always taking one course at a time, at least in the beginning of my years at Mercy. Some favorites that I recall were my psychology classes. I remember the art history course which I loved. A course in faith and human development was very special. My major was Religious Studies and I minored in both Psychology and English. Again at Mercy I just could not contain myself I was so enthusiastic! As I look back I really believe that the assigned papers I was expected to write were the highlights of many of my classes. Perhaps those papers are what led me to be interested in writing these days. Class by class my hours of credit added up. The point is that the process gave me a new focus in my life and I enjoyed every minute of those several years. I especially liked my summer courses as they were often three or four hours a day for a two week session.

By my senior year our two oldest children had graduated from college; the next two were attending college; and our youngest daughter was in high school. That year, in January of 1979, Tim had a heart attack After some time in the hospital for recuperation and tests he was encouraged to undergo aortic heart valve replacement. At the same time our oldest daughter was planning her wedding. That was one interesting spring! A blur for the most part for all of us, I would imagine. The surgery was successful with one major setback which caused a 27-day stay in the hospital. Tim was able to attend Mary's wedding, but could not go to the reception. After a time things began to settle down and Tim got the OK to return to work. But the stress was way too much. His job was one with a lot of deadlines and pressure. After carefully examining our financial situation he decided to take an early retirement.

At the age of fifty I was not in a state of mind to be a retired person. So I registered as a full time student for that year and I graduated in June of 1980 with honors. It was a thrilling accomplishment for me. Tim, my mother, and my five children all attended the ceremony. It brings back some special memories.

Over the next few years I held positions in two parishes as a religious education coordinator. In between these two jobs I taught sex education to junior high students at various parishes throughout the area where I lived. These were six-week courses which I could plan at my convenience to accommodate Tim's wish that we spend winters in Florida. It was at this time that my mother had a stroke and was confined to a nursing facility in Michigan. Our children were all in Michigan, and although we had bought a place in Florida it just did not seem right for us at the time. After a season Tim agreed that the timing was off, so we sold the place and I began a ten-year position at a parish in Farmington. As part of the package all members of the staff were encouraged to continue their education. I settled on working toward my master's degree in Religious Studies at Marygrove College in Detroit. My years at Marygrove contain some of my most wonderful educational experiences. One which stands out for me was my final project before graduation. I spent the year delving into the lifestyles and needs of older adults in the parish where I worked and in my neighborhood and among my friends. The results included a newsletter which was sent out to all the adults in the parish over age 55. I was then invited to write a weekly column for older adults. I did this in addition to my regular work for two years. At age 65 I retired from parish ministry. My pursuit of learning will continue as long as I live!